MAKING

A

NIGHT STALKER

DAVID BURNETT

Making a Night Stalker

For information on special discounts for bulk purchases please visit
www.makinganightstalker.com

For more information or to have David Burnett speak at your event please visit
www.makinganightstalker.com and submit your inquiry.

Printed in the United State of America

Editor: Kendra Middleton Williams
Book Layout & Design: Andy Grachuk - www.JingotheCat.com

CONTENTS

FOREWORD

As Rangers, we forge our brotherhood in the crucible of pain, blood, and suffering. In this crucible we form a bond with depth and strength not before seen by any of us. Not until we are a part of this brotherhood of the sacred scroll do we know its depth and strength. A bond that is invisible to the human eye. Not time, distance, or death are able to sever this bond. Our brotherhood is known for its perseverance through pain and suffering, and its unbreakable will. Though some may know of its existence, it remains a mystery. It is simply the nature of the brotherhood. Perhaps it is just a word to many, but in that name lives great power and an ability to transform the plains of reality; and push our existence into the echoes of the great beyond where it will remain for all eternity. I am fortunate to have been forged in that crucible. I have been blessed by the power of being welcomed into that brotherhood.

The price of the brotherhood, however, is high and it is a debt that lasts for all time. It will never be repaid, but it shall never cease to provide strength through honor.

I've spent most of my life running from what seems to be myself, or at least from the memories that have shaped and created who I am today. As I write these words my heart is racing and my hands are sweating with anticipation of what is to come. I've never told any of my stories of my time serving with the 2nd Battalion, 75th Ranger Regiment.

When asked to write this foreword I was truly honored. I was also terrified, because it meant I would now have to face the demons that have haunted me for years. We all have defense mechanisms that our bodies use when faced with traumatic events. As much as I try to hold on to my tough guy act, I am only a man. My storage capacity for pain, sorrow, and regret have reached the fragile limit. This privilege is a gift that couldn't have come at a better time, as I am finally ready to face my demons and live in a manner that honors the sacrifice and gift my brothers gave me.

The saying, "You never know what you have till it's gone" couldn't be any more true, and when I left my brothers I was lost. I've always tried to live with the big picture in mind. And while I was a Ranger, the mission was always first. All my choices were based on how I could be a better warrior, and how I could add more value to my unit.

I have one big regret that to this day I would take back. My choice to leave my second deployment early and attend Ranger School is it. On that deployment, America lost two of the best Rangers in the entire Regiment.

SSG Ricardo Barraza and SGT Dale Brehm were Killed in Action on March 19th 2006.

I can't get it out of my head. I can't escape the idea that if I would have stayed and finished out that deployment, maybe things would be different and they would still be with us. When I was in Ranger School after they were killed, my main mission was to get through the school as quickly as possible so I could get back to my brothers down range. Consequently, I almost failed Ranger School in the first phase, during the land nav course. I had failed day one and had to repeat it. If I failed again, that would be the end of the road for me being a Ranger. Failure just wasn't an option, neither was losing my sacred scroll and being sent back to the big Army. Failing out of the Special Operations community once you've fought and bled with your brothers is a fate worse than death. And I feared that death. I was so scared and I kept asking myself, how could I fail Ranger School and my brothers after what happened?

On the next night I had no choice but to guarantee my success, so I did exactly what I wasn't supposed to do. That thing was to use the roads, and I did it anyway. The trouble was that there were more roads than were marked on the maps, and I quickly got lost. Again. How the fuck was I going to fail!? I thought to myself, at this point in my career I had never failed anything. Yet here I was, staring failure right in the face.

In a desperate attempt I started running on the road. Attempting to make it to any way point, I was frantic. Needing to orient myself and get back on track to pass this evolution, I ran like the devil himself was chasing me. As I ran, I started to hear footsteps behind me. I quickly ran into the wood line to conceal myself. Ranger Cadre were hiding in the woods throughout the course looking for any violations of the rules. As I jumped into the brush and listened, I heard nothing. I waited for awhile since I thought the Cadre were messing with me. But no sounds of movement came at all as the minutes crept past. I decided to take off again. This time, I skirted the road to remain in the brush. Sure enough, as soon as I started again I heard the footsteps closer than before and they were gaining on me.

I once again ducked into the woods to contemplate my next move. I decided to run in a different direction, away from the intended point to throw what was surely the end of my career off my track. It seemed to work, and I heard no sounds of footsteps as I went away from my intended check point.

As soon as I changed direction to go back toward my check point, the footsteps returned and seemed to be even closer than before. I couldn't figure out how the Cadre were tracking me. I knew they had Night Vision, but even with that advantage, in the thick Georgia brush you couldn't see very far. This routine continued for a few hours and I was running out of time. As I ran toward my check point the steps returned, right on my heels. I stopped to spot the Cadre that were tracking me and saw nothing. No one was in sight! At once I was confused, exhausted, and terrified about failure.

I resumed my run and in my ears it sounded like the steps were right next to me. Suddenly it dawned on me. I realized that whenever I was heading in the right direction the steps were there, and when I was going in the wrong direction they would leave me. Not knowing if it was delirium or sleep deprivation, I decided to run with the steps because time was running out.

I made it to my next way point, stamped my card, oriented myself to the next check point, and took off as fast as my fatigued body would carry me. For the rest of the night those steps were with me in the same pattern. When I was heading in the right direction they were there, and when I would start going in the wrong direction they would stop. Those steps guided me for the rest of the night. All my points found, I made it back with about ten minutes to spare.

I was ten minutes from failing Ranger School. Ten minutes from changing the course of my life. Ten minutes from losing my sacred scroll and the brotherhood that came with it. Ten minutes from losing everything that mattered to me most on this earth. If it weren't for my brothers, I would have surely failed. Even if some people say I'm crazy, I know my brothers guided me through that course.

Perhaps it was their way of saying it's not my fault. Or maybe they were just saying good-bye one final time.

For that answer I'll have to wait until I see them again. I do know this; if I would have failed, I would not have been in Afghanistan in the winter of 2006.

To this day, I can close my eyes and be a fresh 21 year old Ranger School graduate on the deployment following the loss of our brothers in Iraq. It was a deep loss, holding a heart filled with questions, anger, sorrow, and regret. There is only one way to live as a giant forever, and that is to die as a giant with honor; knowing your sacrifice will feed the fire that burns in the heart of each and every Ranger that bears the sacred scroll.

As Rangers we are created to fight and win no matter the circumstances. And once we were trained, we were eager to find a fight. I was trained, strong, and ready to march with my brothers once again on the battlefield. I returned overseas and the brotherhood took me to one cold and bitter winter's night in Bagram.

My team that night approached the airfield and the pair of MH-47 Chinooks were already turning and roaring awaiting our arrival. The glowing blades cranking in the vast blackness, with the crew standing at the ramp waiting to guide us in to our seating positions. On this mission due to capacity requirements, I only had one of the two men assigned to me. He would fill two positions; an ammo bearer that carried ammunition for the weapon system, and assistant gunner who was responsible for taking over the gun in the event I were to fall.

As we loaded the aircraft and left the engine exhaust we were immediately reminded that it was winter in Afghanistan. The interior of the Chinook was frigid and because this was going to be a long infil from our LZ (Landing Zone) we didn't wear any snivel gear. This was to prevent us from overheating on the walk in to the target. As necessary as it is, it's truly a miserable part of the job. But when you weigh in at 335 lbs, and 150 lbs of that is gear, it is very easy to overheat on the long walk that we had before us.

The aircraft began to shake and rumble and as the chatter over the radios fell silent, we lifted off into the night sky. Being closest to the door, I had a pretty good view outside which was always secretly my favorite part. Then the cold started to really make its presence known. I looked around and couldn't tell if the aircraft was rumbling from the engines, or from all the men inside shivering violently. This was to be a long flight to the remote area where our target was located. Every second the cold penetrated our bodies down to our bones. It lit a fire inside that was burning for our lucky man and his friends that had no idea what was coming for them.

I don't know what type of snivel gear the pilots and crew chiefs had, but they seemed unaffected by the cold. Like robots just scanning their sectors as we flew toward our target area. The route we were taking required the bird to fly through a mountain pass which is where the low temperature would really get us. It was so cold we could see frost forming on each other. It was absolute misery. A crew chief took a glance back for some reason and I could see him smile. I could only imagine he was thinking, "those poor bastards." I saw him speak to the rest of the crew. Then, as we approached the pass, they started to wrap us in blankets. I could have kissed that crew chief. He didn't have to do it, but that was one of the small things that meant so much to us. In the event he gets a chance to read this, I'd like to say thank you very much for that.

Radio chatter began again, alerting us of the approaching LZ. Once the pilot set the giant black beast down, we ran off the ramp and picked up security positions. We looked on as the monstrous bird faded and disappeared into the blackness of the night sky. A silence fell over us with no radio chatter and no movement. There was just total stillness as we watched the 47's ascend and fade from sight.

We orientated ourselves and moved out toward our objective. As we marched, the only sound was the crunching of the snow beneath our feet on the white barren land before us. Even the crunching of the snow faded away after a while and silence fell upon us. Again we were left with the millions of stars in the sky. I've never seen a sky so clear with so many stars than I saw in Afghanistan. It remains one of the most beautiful skies I've ever seen.

As we entered the village it was deadly silent, like a ghost town. We continued on to the target building and surrounded it. So far we had not been detected, and I took my team to the far corner over watching a field between our location and another small village. At this point in the war we began using a call out method in hopes that the HVT (High Value Target) would just give up knowing they were surrounded and had no chance of escape. From my location I could see the front door where we would initiate the call out over a loud speaker.

For the men it was not the preferred method as it gave away the element of surprise, but the HVT's were useless to us dead. Overhead I could see our air support, just a small glow of light with my NVG's. Among our most prized assets was the AC-130 Spectre gunship. We commenced with the call out and only silence greeted us. Again we called them out and were met with more silence. After 5 to 10 mins of patience-trying, calling those clowns out, I got that uneasy feeling that bad shit was about to erupt.

Out of nowhere a hail of AK fire burst from the front door and three men on the roof popped up and opened fire on us. The man on the loud speaker was directly in the line of fire, but luckily protected behind a wall. As the fire fight continued at my back, because I was on outer security, I heard over the radio that one of us had been hit. I was called in for support as the ground force was preparing to breach the building.

I quickly relocated to a break in the wall just to the right of the target building, covering an open field just behind it. As I moved, another bad guy appeared on the roof, firing at the assault element as they prepared to breach the building. I was helpless to return rounds as I had Rangers in my line of fire.

I had to watch the fight unfold in my frustration, as I couldn't further endanger my brothers. Thankfully it didn't last long as one of the SAW (Squad Automatic Weapon) gunners put a burst into his head, ending the exchange. I could see the spray of blood and brain matter as he fell. I felt exhilaration and disappointment all in one breath. This asshole just tried to kill my brothers, and I didn't get to take him out, I was just glad he was dead.

From my position I could see a lone squirter leaving the target building from the back door right in my line of fire. He was mine and I opened up with two quick bursts, missing him when he fell into a depression as he ran toward a wall. I reset and readied for him to get up, knowing he was going for that wall. He sprinted out from the depression, running hard for the wall and safety it offered. I was patient and tracked him until he was almost to the wall. Then I opened up again. Two more bursts hit him just before he reached his objective. He was a tough sonofagun because he got up and again tried to jump over the wall! I spared him one more burst as he climbed the wall, hitting him with a tracer round as he fell over it. Of course we had troops positioned there, waiting for him in case he made it past us.

Over the radio I heard the house was cleared and our HVT was in hand. We quickly prepared for exfil due to the casualties we sustained; and time was of the essence. As we pulled out of the town our friend in the sky lit the village up with its full arsenal of weapons. It was like the Fourth of July, only way better. As we continued our evacuation and made it to our LZ, the Chinooks were already inbound. Our Air Force comrades dropped a 500 pound bomb as the grand finale. The explosion rocked us to our collective core in the most stunning way. What a beautiful sight to behold for a pack of hard hitting Rangers. Justice had been doled out by a stellar air assault and the fireworks that ensued were magnificent. After that, silence fell over our element as we waited for our exfil birds to arrive.

Our exfil went smoothly and we got our wounded on board and took off. As we left the target area another, even larger, bomb was dropped. It was a fucking spectacular ending to our mission.

Thank you, to the Chinook crews for getting us out of there and getting my brother to the hospital. He was hit when we took contact during that firefight. The evacuation was textbook thanks to the perfect standards the Night Stalkers maintained and executed on every mission. Those guys really didn't fuck anything up, ever.

It is a special thing this word we use. Brotherhood. I don't know what I would do without it. To all the 160th pilots and crew that have and continue to get our wounded back to the hospital, we truly thank you. To those that have literally saved our lives on the battlefield blazing lead with a minigun, you will have our eternal gratitude. I know I speak for all my Ranger brothers, those that are still with us and those that wait for us, we salute you brave men of the 160th for all the cover fire and evacuations. You fine men are the real life angels of our Ranger world.

George Diaz 2/75

"Strength Through Honor"

In memory of

Ricardo Barraza 19 March 2006 Attack Company 2/75 Iraq

Dale Brehm 19 March 2006 Attack Company 2/75 Iraq

AUTHOR'S NOTE

This manuscript has been submitted to the Department of Defense and has undergone the DOPSR (Department of Publication Security Review) process. The redactions ordered by the Pentagon have remained in this manuscript but have been blacked out to abide by this process and to safeguard the tactics and secrets of the Special Operations community.

This book is based on my account of my journey to become a Night Stalker in the 160th. This account does not express the opinions nor the interests of the DOD, 160th, or any other government agency. Some names, tactics, and procedures have been changed to protect the Night Stalkers and their ████████ colleagues.

Nothing I have written about in this book would have been possible without the men of Alpha Company 160th. I learned a great deal throughout my time as a Night Stalker and I will never forget the hardships that we all faced while out on mission. I hope my story informs the reader of a unique role within the Special Operations community that is rarely talked about.

I had had enough and civilian life blew. No more adrenaline pumping action, no more TDY trips, and no more brotherhood. My life officially sucked and I felt worthless. I chugged another beer as I watched Super Six One get shot down on the television. I decided in that living room that nothing was ever going to amount to the nights I had in Afghanistan under my green and black ocular vision.

I headed into the master bedroom and knelt to the floor on the side of the bed. I reached my hands underneath to feel for a hard plastic case. I grabbed a handle continuing to feel with my hands and slid out a long Army green rifle case. I unclipped the three clasps holding the case closed and opened it. On top of the soft foam insulated case a black Axis 30.06 revealed itself. I had never shot the rifle before as it was fairly new, but I knew in that moment the first shot I would take with the weapon would be directly into my mouth. I hit a new low, lower than my SERE School low while starving and sleep deprived. I felt like a miserable failure. I wasn't succeeding with my new career. I had no one around to talk to. I was lost and the brotherhood I knew was gone.

CHAPTER 1
THE DECISION

★ ★

FEBRUARY 2008

eep, beep, beep, beep, beep, beep. My deafening alarm clock began to echo in the small eight-man B-hut. The rest of the Chinook maintainer's alarm clocks began to sing throughout the shoddy shack. Our living quarters were reminiscent of a refugee camp. I honestly think the 'B' in B-hut stood for bullshit. The elongated hut was constructed from sheets of ply wood with absolutely no insulation. On either end of the hut was a door, again constructed out of what looked like left over scraps from a construction site. Above each door hung an all in one heating and air conditioning unit that worked intermittently. Unfortunately, there was only one remote between our hut and the hut behind us to control the unsatisfactory HVAC units.

The living quarters I called home, housed the day shift Chinook maintainers. The hut directly behind us housed the guys on the night shift. The night shift rooms were constructed identically to ours. Through either door ran a narrow hallway stretching the length of the building. On either side were a series of scrap plywood doors that opened into each room. When we first arrived in country the rooms were trashed from the last unit that we replaced. With no furniture or storage in the rooms, we all had to work with the same blank canvas. From constructing beds and homemade furniture to scrounging around the base for any room necessities left behind, we built our rooms to meet our needs. The cubicle-like walls didn't reach the ceiling, giving the hut a real loft type feel, the only difference was we were sharing the loft with eight other grown men. Many of us draped sheets from the ceiling down to the top of our walls to make up for the haphazard gap. One side of the hallway housed four Chinook maintainers. On the other side, were another four rooms making accommodations for eight.

The alarms kept beeping like a symphony of bad American Idol singers. It was our third month in BAF (Bagram Air Field), Afghanistan and by now we had all gotten used to the ear curdling sounds. It was 0600 local time, and it was time to dress like Ralphy leaving for school in A Christmas Story. The temperature varied in the morning during the blistering Afghanistan winter ranging from cold to colder. After I got a few inches of cold weather gear wrapped around me, I walked down the narrow wooden hallway passing room doors on either side. The floor creaked beneath my feet, and I could hear guys still tossing in their beds. The eight-man building was pitch black to be respectful of those who waited until the last minute to get out of bed. I stepped outside, and the brisk, unforgiving air pierced across my face. It must have been 10 degrees. I was already accustomed to my morning shit, shower, and shave routine, but I never could get used to the bone chilling temps. Every morning for the remaining months in Afghanistan, this is how I would start my day.

When I first landed on Afghan soil I saw what I thought to be the coolest thing ever. It was two F-18's taking off, lead followed closely by wing, the second jet in formation. The awesome phenomenon, after 3 months, began to be one of my least favorite things. Whether it was a jet blasting off the runway or a formation of helicopters, there was always something taking off or flying overhead. As I walked back to the B-hut from my morning shower I glanced up at the notorious jet engine noise to see four F-18's flying in formation followed by a banking left turn. Although the noise was annoying there was something about having an air show every morning that took me back to a place in the US.

When I was younger I remember going to several air shows. Whether with my Dad who was an accomplished A-4 Skyhawk Fighter jet pilot in the Marines, or my uncle David, a devout glider pilot. This perhaps is what struck my interest in aviation at a young age. It wasn't until I was discharged from the Army that I realized how much being around aviation at a young age led me down the path I chose.

Heading back into the warmth of the B-hut, conversations were ensuing between the thin wooden walls. It was easy to gauge what kind of day it was going to be depending on the early morning discussions. The lights were on now and everyone was getting ready to start the day at the hangar. With the poor construction of the hut, it was easy to have a conversation with a guy in the room next to you while you were getting ready. It was 0630, and by now, after heading to the shower, it was easy to gather what type of cold weather gear I needed to wear underneath my uniform for the day. After sorting through my three plastic drawers left in my 12X12 plywood room from a previous soldier, I put on my uniform, grabbed my M4 rifle, and headed out the door.

If another maintainer was dressed and ready to go, that's who I went to chow with. The time we left determined if we got our meals to-go, or ate them at the DFAC (Dining Facility). The best way to omit breakfast completely was a rocket attack. The attacks became very common throughout the deployment. When I first experienced the hellacious event, all I heard was a deafening blast followed by a redundant loud speaker chanting, "Rocket Attack, Rocket Attack," over and over again. Proper procedure was to head to the nearest bunker and wait until hearing the loud speaker again echo throughout the FOB (Forward Operating Base), "All Clear, All Clear." It was common for the DFAC to shut down and stop serving food during an event like this. I was a young private and didn't know my ass from my elbow when it came to proper procedures or technique. As a private in the Army you followed one golden rule: keep your mouth shut and do what you're told. I learned this lesson the hard way five months prior back in garrison when the unit was gearing up to deploy to Bagram, Afghanistan. The term garrison defined a military unit that was state side versus the term theater, meaning a deployed environment.

It was a cold morning during PT (Physical Training) formation in front of the big Ft. Campbell water tower. Maintenance platoon was comprised of different sections depending on what airframe we worked on. The platoon leader ordered the section leaders, normally an E-6 or higher, to take their sections and conduct PT on their own. The Chinook maintenance section broke off from the large formation and went to occupy an area of the parade field away from everyone else. We formed a smaller formation where we were told by SSG (Staff Sergeant) Chris to pull out our dog tags. Of course the one day I forget to wear them we have an inspection. Shit, up to this point I hadn't gotten into any trouble after being with the unit for only a few months. The Chinook section sergeant, SSG Chris, went down the line, one by one, checking everyone's dog tags while we stood at attention. Then he got to me, "Burnett where the fuck are your dog tags?"

Hesitant and intimidated at the demeanor of my new leader's voice, I answered, "I left them in the car, Sergeant."

"Beat your fucking face dumb ass," he ordered. I immediately dropped down and started knocking out push-ups. While continuing to do push-ups, I squinted as beads of salty sweat trickled into my eyes. Great, I have to deal with this the whole deployment, I thought while watching continuous sweat droplets roll off my nose and onto the cold dew drenched grass. After he finished inspecting the rest of the guys in formation he said, "Burnett, position of attention, move." I got up as if I had a fire under my ass. "Right face," he called out to the small 12-man section, "Forward march." Just after a few steps heading toward a road we commonly ran, he shouted, "Double time, march." Our marching pace turned into a run and it was as if the dog tag incident never happened.

After the four mile run everyone was released to go home, eat breakfast, and change into ACU's (Army Combat Uniform). No matter your after PT routine, it was always 0900 work call at the hangar, no excuses. After getting ready in my dilapidated, and what should have been condemned barracks room, I headed to the hangar. I was happily met by SSG Chris who had eagerly told me to start doing flutter kicks. A failed dog tag inspection, which I thought was resolved on the PT field, had actually just begun. For the next three hours, to put it lightly, he smoked my balls. Following the three-hour fun filled exercise event, I was told to write a 2,500-word essay on military uniform, wear, and appearance.

I quickly came to learn from the rest of the guys in the section that this type of punishment was a common occurrence from SSG Chris. It was like he was making up for a time he was bullied in high school or something. I frequently saw my new fearless leader completely lose it. When he was in a good mood and tried to joke around with the lower enlisted, everyone was hesitant. Like lighting a firecracker only to see the wick smolder and no kaboom. Much like SSG Chris, he could go off at any minute.

Back at the hangar in Bagram we arrived knowing full well the next phase was dropping that day. After a CH-47F Chinook flew 500 hours it came to us for a complete overhaul and inspection, or phase. We were part of a maintenance unit that strictly dealt with completely tearing down the helicopter. A tedious process that involved removing all the main parts and components, cleaning, inspecting, replacing, and more cleaning. We removed blades, engines, transmissions, floors, and wheels. It was our job to gut the giant helicopter and after the extensive process we reinstalled everything. Finally, the phase would finish with a detailed day long bubble bath. After we got done with a phase, the dusty, dirty, mission flown helicopter looked brand new.

The hangar wasn't anything fancy, it was a giant tent that opened wide from the bottom on either side. We referred to the hangars as clam shells by way of their shape and how they opened. The floor was constructed out of long metal planks with a tongue and groove type connection. The metal planks were coated with black grip tape. However, after several years of wear and tear, all of the coating was essentially nonexistent, making the floor very slippery. The hangar was divided in half to also house the Black Hawk maintenance team. We occupied the back half of the hangar which backed up to several rows of metal shipping containers. The Black Hawk maintainers occupied the front half of the hangar which butted up to the flight line. When there was a Black Hawk being worked on it became a chore moving the Chinook in or out of the hangar.

As the winter dragged on and a few more phases accumulated under my belt, I started to become very familiar with the 50-thousand-pound helicopter. My mechanical skills and knowledge about the aircraft started to hone in. As my knowledge for the bird enhanced, so did my understanding of who actually got to fly the giant school busses.

Prior to the bird dropping into phase, a crew chief was solely in charge of that bird. I would see these crew chiefs occasionally on the flight line. I often saw them carrying guns to the bird, taking covers off, and getting ready to go on a mission. I was fascinated by the crew chief role. I recall watching several different crew chiefs getting three birds ready. It was summer now and the heat resonating from the asphalt let you know it. The winter months were slow and there wasn't much flying going on so I didn't get to see the crew chiefs as often during the frigid lull. Not to mention if anything was taking off I wouldn't have been able to see it from our closed hangar.

A few hours passed in the hangar while the maintenance team and I managed to reinstall a forward rotor head onto the large Chinook's forward transmission. While taking a smoke break I looked out past the hangar door to monitor the progress of the three birds surely getting ready for a mission. Then I saw it. All three crew chiefs were standing next to chalks one, two, and three. Like a well-rehearsed ballet, each chief stood twenty feet away from the number one, or left, side of his aircraft facing the engine. With all three standing next to the bird they were in charge of, a loud whining emanated from all three birds at once. It was as though they followed a command spoken through the long mic cords stretched from the aircraft and clear out to their flight helmets. What they were really saying, I had no idea.

Then all three chiefs walked behind the aircraft and placed themselves in the same positions but on opposite sides, repeating the same step of their inspections. While moving from one engine to the next trying not to get their mic cords caught on anything, the blades started picking up speed, rotating faster and faster. The giant Chinooks, in orderly fashion, kicked up dust and loose debris on the airfield. The chief's uniforms were being blown about violently from the powerful gusts of heavy rotor wash. At that moment, witnessing such an amazing feat, I told myself no matter what I had to do, I was going to be a crew chief.

Next, the crew chiefs grabbed the wheel chocks, flung them on the back of the helicopter's ramps, hopped on, raised the ramp, and quickly rolled up the long ICS (Interphone Communication System) cords in their hands. One by one the birds taxied 100 feet to a portion of the runway designated for helicopters. Seconds later all three at the same time lifted off the ground kicking up more loose dust. The noise from all three Chinooks were louder than ever. I watched the three birds fly off into the distance in the direction of the majestic Hindu Kush mountain range. The loud flight noise faded into the distant Afghan villages outside the Bagram FOB perimeter. Then they crested over the notorious mountains and were gone. In the past few months I had the opportunity to work on all three of those birds I just witnessed taking off. But where was the reward in that? I wanted to fly as a crew chief and that was the bottom line.

Bam, all of a sudden I got a whiff of Bagram's most horrifying smell. As if a medic was waving sniffing salts in front of my nose and waking me up from a fantasy dream. The smell of fecal matter lingered in the air, and depending on how bad the breeze was determined how potent the air was. It came from a pond a mile down the runway where all the port-a-johns and sewage from the bathrooms ran. This is what we referred to as the poo pond or shit pond. Constantly lingering in the Afghanistan air, catching the awful smell was like a slap in the face to let you know exactly where you were. Unlike the cold weather, unbearable heat, or my demeaning boss, the smell was something I could never get used to.

After my crew chief day dream episode, the day at the hangar was nearing its end. We cleaned up the work area and gathered loose tools laying in and around the Chinook then headed to chow. My mind was still racing about the whole idea of becoming a crew chief. I had laundry to turn in and I decided to skip chow and head back to my room for the evening. The walk from the hangar back to the B-hut was half a mile. I was used to the walk, but my feet never agreed after a 12-hour day at the hangar. On the way down the rocky road way I stopped at a little wooden shack with a hand written sign that read, 'Laundry.' At the shack, behind a window stood two friendly Afghanis, always the same two. They were friendlier if you told them you wanted to buy a watch. I don't know why or how, but they always had fake Rolexes and other knock off brand watches. I finished filling out the paperwork for my laundry so I got back the same clothes I turned in. After my brief interaction at the laundry shack I continued down the road sprinkled with B-huts on either side.

The sun was beginning to set and the shit pond smell finally dissipated. On the short walk back to my room, a few AH-64 Apaches took off and my mind went back into a crew chief daze. I arrived back at the hut and it was pure silence, everyone was at chow and there was nothing like coming back to the serene home. My room was small but it was my only sanctuary to get away and let my thoughts take me back to the US. After being outside in the sun all day, having people yelling at you, and every type of aircraft flying overhead, the silence was truly surreal. I rotated the last code on my combo lock which secured my bedroom door during the day, and entered my room. Tucked away next to my wooden bed frame I had built, were two Rip-Its I acquired from the chow hall a few days prior. They weren't cold, but man after a long day a Rip-It hit the spot. They were mini energy drinks provided at the chow halls, and they always seemed to boost my morale. I sat on my bed and took a deep breath. I pondered how I was going to approach my section sergeant when he got back from the DFAC about my idea of becoming a crew chief. While waiting, I picked up my lap top from yet another ply wood made furniture piece. I blew off the layer of dust collected on the computer from the day, and opened it. I watched Anchor Man while I waited for the guys to get back. I had quite the DVD collection, and Ron Burgundy never got old.

Laughs and loud conversations echoed from just outside the thin B-hut walls. As the conversations grew closer I easily recognized the voices. The door flung open and a loud whiny voice yelled out, "Burnett! You pussy.

Wake up." My fearless leader, in an attempt to be funny, shouted through the living quarters.

Fantastic, I will never win with this guy. I found no humor in the remark, nor did any of the guys walking in behind him. I peered out of my door and gazed down the narrow hallway. I watched everyone slowly disperse to their rooms. I knew my section leader was about to head out to the porch to smoke his after meal ritual cigarette. I heard his bedroom door swing open followed by footsteps down the hallway, then out to the porch. I waited a few seconds then followed after him.

"Hey," I muttered as I exited the B-hut.

"What's up Burnett," he replied over enthusiastically, as if we had been buddies forever. In my head I'm thinking you bi-polar fuck.

I replied, "How do I become a crew chief?"

His response was what I thought, a stupid laugh followed by, "Unfortunately you can't become a crew chief in this unit because there are no flight slots for AVIM (Aviation Intermediate Maintenance) maintainers." I looked at him confused and in disbelief. He went on, "You can try and get into 160th like I did, but I doubt you would even make it through Green Platoon. If you do get in, which you won't, good luck becoming a crew chief."

Before I could respond, two F-18's launched in a left climbing maneuver overhead. The jets passed and I was intrigued that my section sergeant thought he could do something that I couldn't. I said, "Oh OK," and left him to finish his cigarette.

Back in my room, and not knowing much about 160th, I started doing research about the unit on my dusty lap top. I didn't get a wink of sleep that night. From videos, to pictures, to stories, and whatever I could find about the unit, I was amazed. There wasn't a ton of information about the unit, which made me even more intrigued. The 160th SOAR(A) (Special Operations Aviation Regiment(Airborne)) was an aviation unit comprised of the very best aviators in the world. I found out what I had to do to submit an application to the unit. If my application were accepted, I would be offered a slot to go through a five-week selection course called Green Platoon. With three months left of the thirteen-month deployment, I knew I had to take advantage of the opportunity ASAP. Not knowing what daunting and challenging tasks may lie ahead, I had to get out of the unit I was in. From the maintenance, to the leadership, and with definitely no advancement at becoming a crew chief in the near future, I had to make a change, and 160th was my answer.

The next day all I could think about was getting accepted into the advanced and highly trained Special Operations aviation unit. I never noticed any blacked out helicopters at BAF, which the unit was known for, however I was never really looking. The 160th helicopters were different than the regular Army helicopters I had been working on. Although they had the same bones, they had extras or modifications on them to cater to their secretive missions. They were always jet black unlike the tan or grey painted regular Army birds. I asked someone higher up the next day if they had a 160th unit stationed in BAF. The simple and unwanted reply I received was, "No."

A few days passed and I finally finished the extensive application. Unlike something you submit online, the lengthy application had to be turned in to my first line supervisor, then taken up the chain of command, all the way to the 1SG (First Sergeant) to review. If the chain of command approved the application, it would then be turned in to the 160th SOAR recruiters back in the states. Unfortunately, my first line supervisor happened to be the worst leader ever, whom we had all come to know and dislike very much. Later that day I turned in my finished 160th application to SSG Chris. I handed it to him on the exact same porch we discussed my future crew chief possibilities. He looked over the paper work with an appalled look on his face, as if he never thought I would go through with the tedious process. He said in a soft tone, "I'll take care of it."

I replied, "Thanks," and went back inside.

The next day we were doing unscheduled maintenance on a CH-47F Chinook, which happened to be at the farthest spot on the flight line. Out on the tarmac I started to hear the unmistakable chopping blade sound taxiing toward us. I turned around to see what Chinook it was, that I was sure I had worked on. This time was different, almost as if it were a sign from above. It was bigger than a regular Army Chinook and it was bolstered by much bigger external fuel tanks. The giant helicopter carried extra guns manned by four crew chiefs instead of the usual two. My eyes widened as the two celebrity like Chinooks continued to taxi. A long giant fuel probe jutted out several feet from the nose for aerial refueling operations. It was jet black with a matte finish, and cleaner than any other bird I had worked on or seen during the whole deployment. It was beautiful. For the first time in my career, I witnessed a 160th Chinook taxiing just 50 feet from me. All of the other maintainers I was working with paused too. In a zombie like state, I noticed what I thought to be a crew chief standing behind a Gatling gun. In a state of shock, I raised my right hand and began to wave at the mystery man behind the gun. He was in an all tan uniform, another thing I had never seen. His helmet was all black with a dark tinted visor covering his eyes, just beneath his visor was a dark mask. He was completely unrecognizable and not an inch of skin was showing.

I continued to wave like a naive kid standing in line waiting to sit on Santa's lap. The man behind the gun didn't move an inch, he didn't wave or gesture toward me. He was clearly looking at me, and all I was thinking was, this is awesome. The mystery crew chief was probably thinking; this kid is an idiot. I didn't care, I just kept waving. Then chalk two followed behind just as beautiful as the first bird. They continued to taxi past us on the flight line making their way toward the runway. I kept waving and another man behind the gun on the second bird favored the same way as the last, not a single movement. The whole stint in Afghanistan I had never seen the beautiful 160th Chinook until now. The unit rarely executed operations during the day, and that was probably why I was just now catching a glimpse of the elusive helicopters. They were all black to remain as undetectable as possible on their almost exclusively night-time executed covert operations.

A month had gone by since I turned in my application to SSG Chris, and I still hadn't heard anything from him or any 160th recruiter. I was beginning to get concerned since the deployment was about to end. I wanted a no shit answer before we left Afghanistan. I wanted to know if I was accepted to try out for the elite group or not. Getting impatient, I asked SSG Chris one hot day in the hangar if he had heard anything about my application.

His reply was one I wasn't expecting. "Oh yeah, I've been meaning to tell you, I misplaced it. Just get me another one and I'll take care of it." There was absolutely no remorse in his tone or facial expression. My insides were turning, and I slowly started to clench my fists. He continued with paper work while I looked at him in shock. He lifted his eyes from his clipboard and looked at me, "Get back to work," he ordered.

I was more furious than a mother finding out her teenage son just got arrested. This mother fucker, I thought to myself. I knew now more than ever, I had to do whatever it took to get the hell out of this unit. The day dragged on, and for some reason when I came back to my senses I realized I didn't save the application on my computer. Shit, I have to start all over, but this time I will most definitely save it.

I didn't go to chow that night. Some of my buddies caught on to what a world of shit I had been going through the past couple days, and brought me back a to-go plate of food. It may not seem like a lot, but after a year in Afghanistan it was the little stupid things that lifted you up. I was happy to talk with a few of my buddies on the porch while I ate my food. I knew them before coming to the unit since we all went to AIT (Advanced Individual Training) together. SPC (Specialist) Matt and SPC Kyle always knew when to have a good time, but they also knew how to help out a fellow brother.

The Afghan sun was slowly beginning to set. It was cool outside, and the breeze was calming. I finished my meal and headed back inside to continue the long application process all over again. I finished that night at 0200 local time. The next morning in the hangar I handed the application to SSG Chris.

Again he said, "I'll take care of it."

The hangar was quiet in the morning; no one was crawling over the Chinook, power tools weren't echoing in the air, and no one was awake enough to be yelling. With two more months left in the deployment we split our time up between working on the helicopter and packing our big tools into huge metal shipping containers. The large containers were lined up in rows behind our section of the hangar. The last two months were great because we were packing, which meant we were going home. Everyone's morale was high, but the prick of a section leader we had, always threatened to ruin our days.

Still unsure of the outcome of my special operations acceptance, I was getting impatient once again. I found SSG Chris smoking while all the lower enlisted packed the containers.

"Have you heard anything?" I asked, while standing at parade rest.

"No, I turned it in to top." He muttered, referring to the 1SG.

I said, "OK." Not being one to take rejection for an answer, I went directly to the 1SG and asked about my application. He was clueless and had no idea what I was talking about. The 1SG was impressed and happy I was taking my Army career to another level.

In a sharp tone he said, "Bring me your application tomorrow."

I kept to myself the remainder of the day instead of confronting SSG Chris. I was appalled that my supposed leader was completely blowing off my application. Maybe in some demented way he was mad because he was kicked out of the same unit just a few years ago. Maybe this was his way of being the gate keeper of the special unit. I don't know what he was thinking, but it seemed like he didn't want me to get accepted. Maybe he saw what an asset I became to the maintenance team and he didn't want to lose me. Either way I was determined now more than ever to get the fuck out of the AVIM unit.

The next morning, I went in to the 1SG's office and handed him my application. Standing in front of him at parade rest, he assured me it would be taken care of. I heard the same response in the past, but something was different this time. The conversation with him, his demeanor, and the strong leadership qualities he illustrated, were promising. I actually felt it would be taken care of this time. A week went by and we were getting closer to leaving. The guys and I started the infamous military, 'and a wake up,' count down. With just one month to go, we began at, '30 and a wake up.'

Throughout the deployment everyone in the company got a day off every 14 days. By this point, like many other things, I had a day off ritual. Well, on 30 and a wake up, it was my day off. I slept in until 0800, then made my way to a mobile trailer turned into a Burger King. Although the burgers never really tasted quite right, it would still take me back to the US. I usually got my order to go, then headed back to my room to feast while watching a DVD. I always took the first bite of the usual double whopper and would close my eyes while thinking about Colorado. While I was eating I heard a loud BOOM followed by rocks and shrapnel landing on top of the tin roof. It was another rocket attack; and I was used to them by now. The loud speaker went off, echoing through the entire FOB, and I continued to sit and enjoy my meal. The relaxing day continued in the tranquil and quiet hut.

While finishing the movie Heartbreak Ridge, I heard the door slam open. A voice angrily yelled down the hallway, "Burnett, get the fuck outside right now."

Shit, it was SSG Chris, I had no idea what I had done. I was just sitting in my room enjoying my, 'Have it your way,' meal and watching a Clint Eastwood classic. I left my room and met him on the porch. Instantly he told me to beat my face. I started doing push-ups while he went on about the chain of command and how it's supposed to work. Blah, blah, blah, stuff I already knew, get to the point already I'm thinking in my head. After 100 push-ups he told me to start doing flutter kicks.

In an angry tone he said, "Why did you go over my head and turn in your application directly to the 1SG?"

The answer was simple really, but such a simple answer may hold some serious consequences. I thought to myself, well OK you asked. I said exhaustively, "Because you weren't going to turn in my application, so I did your job for you." As the words tumbled out of my mouth I immediately regretted them. I was still doing flutter kicks looking up at him. He was furious. After another hour on the staggered 2x4 built porch, I was covered in dust and sweat. SSG Chris went inside while my team leader, who had arrived to witness the smoking, stayed outside with me.

He said in a deep country accent, "Well that's a good intro to what you're going to be getting into I guess."

My team leader was a nice guy from the south and always had a dip stuffed in his lower lip. I gave him a puzzled look while laying on my back fighting through the abdominal pain.

I responded, "What do you mean?"

He replied with a content look on his face, "Your application was accepted. You're going to Green Platoon."

The pissed off look on my face changed to ecstatic. I was elated. I guess the smoking that just ensued had several reasons. One being I went over my fearless leader's head to get something accomplished. The other was the sheer frustration from my leader that he was not only losing a key player to his team, but I was going to be afforded the opportunity to try out for the very same unit that had kicked him out. Either way I didn't care. I was leaving my unit, and I was excited to start the next chapter in my Army aviation career. The last few weeks of the deployment, SSG Chris began telling me stories, and what to expect when going through the 160th selection process. Almost as if we became best friends overnight. His front wouldn't phase me though, I just played along knowing after all the shit he put me through, it was finally over. The absolute worst person I have ever known in my life was about to be out of it. That thought combined with the excited notion I was about to try out for the big leagues made the last few weeks in Bagram a breeze.

CHAPTER 2

THE TRANSITION

★★★

he chalk leader of the C-17 started the roll call. He began calling last names beginning with A. I knew I would be called soon. "Burnett," he called.

Excited, I responded, "Moving," as in moving my ass on to the giant plane that's going to take me the hell out of here. The deployment was over and we were all packed. The metal containers were stuffed to the brim and were already shipped to the states. The hangar where I had spent the last year was passed off to the new division replacing us. My room and our hut had new occupants. It was finally time to go home. I walked up the C-17's long metal stair case just behind the nose of the plane. The seats were set up the same way they were on the flight over. The enormous cabin boasted several seats lining the interior fuselage on the left and right. Those seats were the prime seats, and were reserved for higher ups and pilots. In the center of the cargo bay was a long ten-person wide column of seats. They were attached to the airplane floor on rollers for easy removal. The worst of the rolling seats was the very middle, as I recall on the way over. If you ended up in the middle, having to pee was an absolute chore. Although, by this point I really didn't care, as long as I didn't have to sit next to SSG Chris. The flight was two hours to Manas, Kyrgyzstan. Everyone was directed to keep their Kevlar and full body armor on during the entire flight. I took my seat not completely in the middle, but not on the aisle either. Thirty minutes went by and everyone was finally seated. Another thirty minutes went by while an Air Force fork lift operator loaded several pallets containing everyone's duffle bags and tough boxes just behind us. There was a lot more room in the large aircraft behind the cluster of seats. The additional space was specifically used for the large pallets the fork lift was loading. Several minutes later I heard a hydraulic noise resonate through the cargo bay. I peered behind me as best I could with the heavy plate carrier obstructing my movement. The aft ramp slowly began to close. I saw the bright lights of the airfield begin to disappear. I thought that this was probably not the last time I would see that sight.

The load master came over the intercom to give us a safety brief, followed by the estimated departure and arrival times. I felt the giant beast slowly start to come to life, the noise grew louder. A few moments passed and the C-17 crept forward. Just a few minutes of taxiing and all I could think about were the luxuries awaiting me back in the US. The only thing my buddies and I talked about over the past week was what we were going to buy and what we were going to do once back home. Most of the guys I worked with were married so their plans were geared around family. I didn't have anything or anyone waiting for me back at Ft. Campbell, so I knew the first thing I was going to do was drink several beers. The load master came over the intercom again while I was day dreaming, "Prepare for take-off."

The words I was waiting to hear for the last 13 months finally came. The brakes disengaged and the seats slid back and hit the catches on the floor jolting our necks. At cruising altitude, the seats slowly rolled forward and caught the forward catches. Next stop was Manas and we would be that much closer to the US. No one really talked during the flight, almost as if everyone were hypnotized. We were all really thinking to ourselves, I can't believe I'm going home. I tried to sleep, but between the inside plane noise and the excitement, I couldn't.

The lights went from a dim green to a bright florescent white in the cabin. All the soldiers on board looked around at each other hoping to better understand what was going on. In that quick second I reflected back and remembered the same occurrence when we first flew into Afghanistan. I had a feeling that we were about to land. Right then, the load master came over the intercom, "If you're up using the bathroom finish up. We will be landing in 20 minutes." We were that much closer to being home.

After landing in Manas, we were going to bed down for a night and change from an Air Force operated C-17 to a Delta Airlines passenger plane.

A hot shower and a warm meal were in order. Manas transit center was run by the Air Force and set up in 2001. The base was used for this transition event for both US and international military allies.

We de-planed the C-17 and loaded an all-white bus we all easily recognized from basic training. After a short 5-minute ride to the base, we were dropped off in front of three large tents. When we got to the tent there was another unit there just getting ready to head over to the desert to start their 12-month deployment. I reflected back 13 months ago, when I was in the same position fearing the unknown. Now I was at the other end of the spectrum, heading home. I found a few of my buddies in the huge open bay tent. It was more like a warehouse sprawling with hundreds of bunk beds. After checking around the warehouse, we claimed our bunks. All the maintainers found beds relatively close to one another. We dropped our gear and made the mile-long trek to the chow hall.

We all knew what was waiting for us, as it was the same chow hall we came to love before going to the sand box. The chow wasn't like the stuff we had been eating in Bagram. This place was massive with all kinds of options, including full size candy bars and every beverage you could think of. With the next flight time not until later the next morning, it was the most relaxed and happy I had been in a long time. We all selected our different foods in the massive chow hall and gathered at a round table. We sat and ate, exchanging stories about the last 13 months. Some of us got up to get seconds, and even thirds. We sat at the table for hours just having a good time. For the first time in a long time I actually felt normal again. It was almost like I was at an Outback Steak House or a Chili's, just without the beer and good looking waitresses. We were all pretty tired by now. Stuffing our pockets with candy bars we made the journey back to the tents.

The camaraderie continued throughout the night with a game of Texas hold 'em. We used an old box someone found in the corner of the tent and set it up like a table. Setting the rudimentary table between two bunks we played cards late into the night. Several times we were told to be quiet as we continued to joke with each other. The game came to an end and we bedded down for the night.

The next morning came quicker than I expected. I was still in a dream state, as if I just spent the night out on the town with good friends. The busses came earlier than scheduled, but no one argued about that. We headed back to the Air Force run airport to be greeted by a Delta 777. We walked up the long flight of stairs and were met by several bubbly flight attendants.

"Now there is something I haven't seen in a long time," said my buddy SPC Matt from right behind me. I gave him a look and we both laughed to ourselves. A real airplane, I thought to myself. It was so odd to appreciate something like a flight attendant and a real civilian airplane. I was suddenly unsure about trying to re-acclimate myself to luxuries and nuances I had been deprived of for the last year.

The flight was long; however, it was much more comfortable than the previous flight on the crowded C-17. Everyone knew everyone on the 777 because we had all interacted or worked with one another over the last deployment. So a trip to the bathroom turned into a 20-minute excursion. Passing different people while walking down the aisle and striking up a conversation was inevitable, so we just enjoyed it. I got a couple of looks from the flight attendants, sensing they wanted to say something. They had an intimidated look. We all still had our M4 rifles and were in full uniform. Luckily on the flight we didn't have to wear our Kevlar and full battle rattle. Our next stop was Ft. Campbell, Kentucky.

I ventured back to my seat to find a hot meal waiting for me. I finished it hastily and took a Snickers out of my pocket for dessert. Sitting alone with my thoughts took me again on a reflective thought path about the astonishing things I had seen and done over the last year. The thought then dawned on me, yeah I did a lot of maintenance on a giant helicopter, but I didn't really contribute to the war. None of this had occurred to me until now. I suppose when you're doing your job nonstop for a full year you really don't have time to sit down and think about it. I would soon learn my past one-year deployment wasn't shit compared to the deployments I was about to face.

"Flight attendants prepare for landing," the pilot came over the intercom followed by a general, "Thank you," speech to everyone on board. I heard the hydraulics kick on and felt the landing gear extend beneath my feet. The happiness flooding me was nearly overwhelming as I was about to return to US soil. While looking out of my window I started to recognize roads and restaurants as we descended. The 777 hit the tarmac and the loud thrusters slowed us to taxiing speed. We came to a stop at a designated hangar I didn't recognize on Campbell Army Airfield. I noticed a crowd of people outside cheering with signs and posters. I had never seen or experienced anything like it. I guess you could relate it to a famous band or group coming out on stage for a concert. I felt like a million bucks, all these people cheering for us. In my head I thought, but why? What did I even do? All I did was work on helicopters.

In the grand scheme of things, you could say I contributed to eradicating terrorists from Afghanistan, or did I? You worked on helicopters. You didn't do shit, I thought to myself. I didn't feel I deserved the applause or grandiose welcome home ceremony. The true heroes were the ones on the front lines actually putting bullets in bad guys. I was conflicted and only hoped I could make more of a contribution to the fight in the years to follow. Would I get through the grueling five-week special operation selection process? Will I even deploy again?

As soon as I saw the crowd of people my mind started going haywire. I wasn't deployed anymore and now my responsibilities and concerns totally shifted. When do I get my phone turned on? What cable provider do I choose? Where the hell do I go when I get off this plane? After a year of being in a combat zone, I felt more uneasy than I had in the past year. In America, on one of the biggest Army bases in the US, I felt lost. Mortars were landing next to our home just a week ago. It was easier for me to deal with that than it would be dealing with this crowd of cheering families. I heard stories about the whole transition period and the toll it took on soldiers. Suicides, domestic abuse, and overdoses were all things I heard about, but never really understood. I didn't want to get off the plane. I needed to go back to do more. I sat in my cushy seat and thought, why are you clapping for me? The real heroes died on a patrol or while clearing a building. I just worked on a helicopter.

"Burnett," SPC Kyle said, "Get up, we're home mother fucker."

After seeing SPC Kyle's excited demeanor, I snapped out of it. I walked down the aisle of the plane and eventually out of the main door way. I stopped at the top of the steps for a second and took a deep breath. The air was humid but it was American air and I hadn't smelled anything that beautiful in a long time. I walked down the long airplane steps and finally onto the tarmac. Bam, US soil. Hundreds of wives and family members were still cheering, not a single one for me. It didn't bother me as I knew I would be headed back to Colorado in the next few days to be with family. After departing the plane, we made our way over to the hangar. The families began to disperse inside the building. We all stood in formation in front of the large closed hangar doors. As we stood outside in the cold Ft. Campbell air, I couldn't stop thinking about how I didn't contribute in what I believed to be a meaningful way to the war. The family members and crowd of cheering people all gathered inside the hangar now. It was quiet outside.

The hangar doors slowly began to open, and we were marched into the brightly lit enclosure. There were all kinds of flags hanging from the rafters above us. We marched in formation onto a freshly painted white concrete floor. The lights reflecting off the floor made everything look brighter than it really was. The noise was incredible. There were bleachers on either side of us. The crowd was louder than before as we marched in. I tried not to cry, but there was something about all those people cheering for the unit. We were all somewhere safe now, where the people spoke the same language, and understood what you were saying.

The post general stood in front of the formation behind a large podium. He gave a quick speech about how proud he was of the company and blah, blah, blah. Only a handful of soldiers in the hangar had ever left the wire. The majority though, never left the FOB, including myself. While deployed, leaving the wire meant you actually left the base to go on a patrol or mission to actually contribute in the war. I couldn't accept that he was proud of me. I still felt I needed to do more. While deployed I learned a term used to describe someone who never left the base, a Fobit. The term came from the word hobbit and blended with the word FOB (Forward Operating Base). It simply meant you never left the base nor engaged in real combat. Well for the last 13 months I most certainly was a Fobit, and I hated it.

The man standing behind the podium in front of the formation released us after telling all the single soldiers where the new barracks were. Tears and lots of hugs with family members commenced after that. I looked around the hangar and took it in. I loaded my stuff up in the back of my buddy's parents truck. They drove us to the new barracks that had been built while we were deployed. I walked into my room to find a little gift bag with nothing I cared much about. I just wanted a beer.

The next day I woke up and got a ride into work since I didn't have a vehicle yet. I was met by SSG Chris. He had a stack of papers in his hand and held them out in front of me, "Here you go Burnett."

I grabbed the stack out of his hands. I took a quick glimpse at the top of the papers to realize they were my new orders, with a report date for Green Platoon. It was surreal receiving the papers from the man who tried everything to keep me from going. Everyone I had worked with for the past year was happy for me, but at the same time they rather I didn't go. It was bitter sweet but I was eager for the next chapter. A chapter where I wouldn't be considered a Fobit or a soldier who really didn't get after it in the fight against the Taliban or Al Qaeda.

My new orders had my report date on them, and I realized things were about to start happening really fast. Green Platoon was in two weeks and I was ecstatic. I had just enough time to eat left-over Thanksgiving turkey from family in Memphis, and head to Colorado for a welcome home with copious amounts of liquor. I never used to drink as much before I was deployed. Some people drank to forget about certain things whereas I drank to remember Afghanistan and envision I was back there executing missions, not in the hangar.

After my short vacation home, I headed back to Ft. Campbell, KY. Luckily for me, Green Platoon took place at the very base where I was stationed. This meant I didn't have to pack up and go to another base. I was aware that there were three 160th bases located in three different states. I didn't get to choose which one I went to, but I pleaded with the recruiter that I stay at Ft. Campbell. I could end up at any of the three if I made it through the selection. There were; 4th Battalion in Ft. Lewis, Washington, 3rd battalion in Savannah, Georgia, and 1st and 2nd battalion located in Ft. Campbell, Kentucky.

I landed at Nashville International Airport after a short vacation in Colorado, and had no idea what I was about to go through. I had one day to recoup and pack all of the shit on the packing list for Green Platoon. I tried to go through the list quickly so I could get to bed at a decent hour since I had to report at 0600. I finally got done with the list and passed out on my government issued uncomfortable twin size mattress. I closed my eyes with so much emotion running through my mind knowing Green Platoon awaited me the next morning.

CHAPTER 3
DAY ZERO

★ ★

The next morning, I reported to the address specified on my orders. I pulled into a parking lot and saw what looked like an old barracks building. There were two identical buildings directly across from each other, and what appeared to be a courtyard in the middle of the them. I tried to make out the irregular shapes in the courtyard, but the silhouettes in the early morning were unrecognizable. The sun was still absent and the air felt as cold as winter in Afghanistan. I exited my vehicle and walked toward the courtyard passing underneath an interesting carved wooden arch. The intricate arch was painted red with black letters that read, 'NSDQ.' Of all the research I had done of the elite unit, I never found any mention of the four letters.

As I was looking up at the sign in the cold morning, a voice shouted over to me, "Why aren't you doing push-ups soldier?" Before I could look over to make out the distant silhouette, I got down and started doing push-ups. More soldiers arrived, and without being instructed, they started piling up around me in the push-up position. I was confused about what was going on.

While my hands were pressed against the cold concrete, a soldier next to me in an unfamiliar PT uniform looked at me and said, "You must be new?"

I heard footsteps on the paved sidewalk getting closer to the arch. "Get up," a deep and energetic voice said to the group. Still in the push-up position we all rose and stood at parade rest.

As I got up to acknowledge the voice yelling at me I said, "Hooah Sergeant." It was muscle memory for me now to respond that way. After realizing I was the only one who said it, I knew something wasn't right.

Angrily he replied, "What did you say? Get back down and do push-ups." As I got down, so did everyone else. I felt something new, like everyone was getting down because their fellow brother was on the ground. The idea and thought process of brotherhood would be burned, engrained, and etched in my mind for the rest of my life in the coming weeks.

"We don't use the H word here soldier. If you want to be in Special Operations, then start acting like it," the man finished. I learned my lesson very quickly. A common term used in the regular Army, and what I had been accustomed to for the last two years, was now unacceptable. The sun was starting to rise and the entire group was instructed to get up. The courtyard objects started becoming more clear and I could make out a stack of logs, giant tires, pull up bars, and what looked to be a river running through the middle of the courtyard. As I was making out my surroundings, the same voice that made me do all the push-ups said, "Snowbirds, get inside."

All the others bolted as if they knew what they were doing and where they were going. I followed closely behind another soldier. In my head I'm thinking what the fuck is a snowbird, sounds like a Disney character. We ran into one of the two old barracks buildings and down a long flight of stairs to a basement. An area designated for left over barracks room furniture was where we ended up. I guess this is where the snowbirds hung out. The instructor was gone and everybody looked at me like they knew I was the new guy. I didn't say anything, I just looked around at the eleven or so guys. We all had a two-quart canteen draped over our shoulders. The canteen was on the packing list and was made clear in the literature I had read prior, that the item must be on you at all times.

Before I could even ask someone about what was going on, a guy standing next to me said in a thick Boston accent, "So what's your story?" I gave him a brief description about the deployment I just completed and what my MOS (Military Occupational Skill) was. Your MOS deciphered what your job was in the Army and was decided with a recruiter well before going through basic training. After basic, your MOS determined where you went for AIT. Most of the aviation related MOS's learned how to work on their aircraft platform at Ft. Eustis, VA. My MOS was 15U. When I got done telling him my story he told me he was a 15T. Prior knowledge from my old unit helped me easily determine he worked on Black Hawks.

I couldn't get over his accent so I had to ask where he was from, and sure enough he replied, "Danvers, it's a small town near Boston."

He went on to tell me that I wasn't in the Green Platoon selection process yet, but rather in holdover platoon. I would have to report to the same place every day until the current class going through Green Platoon graduated. Once the current class was complete, then we would get our shot at becoming a part of the Special Operations community. SGT (Sergeant) Dan, the Boston native, had already been in holdover platoon for four weeks. I'm thinking if the selection process is just five weeks, then the current class should be done soon. Sweet! So I just have to come here every day, hang out, and wait for my shot.

SGT Dan went on to tell me that there was no, 'hanging out,' in holdover platoon. We were to report in the morning for PT, which was far more demanding than any other form of physical exercise I had done in the Army up to this point. After PT, during the day the snowbirds to include myself were tasked out to do manual labor on the 160th compound. I also came to find out that the river running through the court yard was referred to as the baby pit. Some days for PT in the dead of winter we low crawled in the frigid waters of the pit. This was supposedly preparing us for the bigger and longer trenched pit at OCB (Old Clarksville Barracks), where Green Platoon would take place.

A week had gone by and I was getting tired of doing bitch work. I was ready and eager to start day zero of Green Platoon. Day zero was the day that most schools in the military referred to as the first day of class. Some of the guys in holdover platoon wouldn't get to take part in the next class. This was either because they weren't able to pass a PT test, whose requirements were far more rigorous than the regular Army PT test. Or their report date was too late to prepare them to get into the next class. Another way to not be selected for the next class was simply at the instructor's discretion. If any instructor felt you weren't ready, then you weren't going. A list came out a few days before the next class start date. Just like in the movie Rudy, after the coach put the list up of everyone who made the team, we all swarmed the sheet of paper. As the crowd around the taped sheet of paper dispersed I looked over it running my finger down the A's then finally getting to the B's, Burnett. Yes, my name showed up along with SGT Dan, the thick accented

Boston. I liked Boston, he didn't give a shit about what anybody thought and he said whatever came to his mind.

To the guys who were on the list, the instructor started handing out a packing list. He was standing next to the sheet he had just hung in the hall, and after reading my name I stuck out my hand to get the thick packing instructions. I was so pumped I had made the cut to join the next Green Platoon class. The day finished after the coach handed the new varsity team their instructions. I got back to my room and read the packing list. It was precise and lengthy. I had to label everything a certain way with green tape, put certain items in Ziploc bags, and some items needed two Ziploc bags. Spare boots and running shoes, although packed and not used, the shoelaces had to be tied and tucked into the tongue. I needed to have a certain amount of socks and towels. The list was on-going, yet very important to get right. The packing process took me two days, just in time for day zero. I finished and set my stuffed bags next to my bedroom door. Eager and very excited for what was to follow the next day, I tried to get to bed.

It was 0500 and I had been watching my clock, waiting for the alarm to go off since 0400. I was nervous, excited, and eager to head to OCB, or what I would come to know as Green Platoon. My ruck sack and duffle bags were packed and ready to go. I laid my uniform neatly on the floor the night before. Fresh new patches, new boots and a brand new pair of green Army issued socks were perfectly placed next to my ACU's. The day I had been deeply anticipating, was finally here. I sat in my bed for a few seconds and recounted the first conversation I had with my old section sergeant on the porch in Afghanistan. Five months and a lot of persistence later, I was all set to embark on the most physically, mentally, and emotionally exhausting five weeks of my life. I knew there was a higher calling for me in the Army and this was it. I heard stories while in holdover platoon that soldiers who didn't make it through the selection course or decided to quit during Green Platoon were immediately sent back to their old units. What awaited me back at my old maintenance unit was my motivation to never quit or give up. I knew my only option was to fight my way through the course, or die trying.

I grabbed my gear and headed to the OCB compound. A short 5-minute drive later, I pulled into a gravel parking lot where I recognized a few vehicles from holdover platoon. Congregated by a chain link fence running the length of the lot were a handful of guys with their bags. I parked, grabbed my bags, and headed over to meet them. The early morning was brisk and the cold air bit straight to my bones. A tall well-built guy was among the group of soldiers gathered by the fence. I recognized him underneath the flickering parking lot lights as I got closer. It was SGT Morgan; I hadn't really gotten to know him in holdover platoon, but he always stuck out like a sore thumb. He was the biggest guy in the class and hard to miss.

As I got closer to the group I didn't hear anyone talking. Everyone was huddled close in an effort to share some warmth in the unforgiving cold. A few others were balling their fists and blowing on their hands in an attempt to warm them.

I got to the crowd of guys and SGT Morgan looked at me and said, "Holy shit man are you guys ready for this?" The way he said it was humorous followed by a chuckle. No one laughed. Everyone looked at him and nodded unwillingly as if confused and unsure of the weeks that we were all about to face.

It was 0530 now and our designated show time was 0600. A voice from behind the chain link fence shouted up to us sternly, "What are you doing up there? It's not story time, it's time to work." Everyone including the guys who were still grabbing bags out of their cars heard the man behind the fence. We bolted down a small gravel hill to a wide sliding chain link gated entrance. We started running through the gate, but before we could get any closer to the man wearing an all-black sweater and ACU pants, he said, "Stop, put your bags down, and read the sign."

Fastened to the chain link fence at the entrance was a white board that had the date followed by written orders reading, '50 flutter kicks, 100 push-ups, and 25 burpees.' After everyone stood looking at the sign for a few seconds the voice shouted to us again, "Well, what are you waiting for? Hurry up, and when you finish get in formation."

We all looked at him to see where exactly he wanted us to get in formation when we finished our first Green Platoon task. Everyone started doing the early morning PT exercise posted on the board. Great, I thought to myself as my feet were six inches off the ground doing flutter kicks, welcome to Green Platoon. We finished the exercises, some quicker than others, and began to get into a formation. The last few soldiers finished their exercises and joined the rest of us. We laid our bags at our feet and stood at attention. The air was freezing and looking down the row of Green Platoon candidates, I could see everyone's hot breath glisten in the few lights illuminating the area. No one said a word, just heavy panting and a few coughs here and there.

The man in black was nowhere in sight as we stood waiting for our next instructions. In front of us was a wooden post, at the top of the post hung a bell and the words on the post running vertically said, 'I QUIT.' On either side of the bell were two bunker looking structures. Vegetation and trees covered the interesting roof tops of the buildings. Each bunker had its own single door. I continued to look around the compound, but I wasn't able to make out anything else in the dark early morning hours. We stood in formation another five minutes, and our heart rates started to slow.

The door to one of the bunkers flung open and a different man than before rushed out. He was wearing the same uniform and following closely behind him were ten more men in the same uniform. They all looked intimidating, and silently walked around the formation and in between the rows. They looked everyone up and down, with wide eyes, as if we had just killed their childhood dog. It was still dark and I saw a reflection of light pierce across the two bunkers and heard the sound of gravel crunching under vehicle tires. It caught the attention of all the instructors as they peered up toward the parking lot. Though I desperately wanted to look behind me, I knew it was a bad idea. A few seconds passed and I heard footsteps running down the gravel hill behind us. An instructor shouted behind the formation, "What time is show time?" He was referring to the time we all had to be there to start class.

I faintly heard behind me a nervous raspy voice shout, "0600 Sergeant Night Stalker."

The instructor replied to the tardy soldier, "And what time is it?"

The raspy voice, who I couldn't make out by the tone, responded, "0550 Sergeant Night Stalker."

The instructor replied tersely, "You're late. Report back to holdover platoon." The unit prided itself on, and lived by the motto in training and combat; 'Plus, or minus thirty seconds.' Although the soldier was ten minutes early he was still late. With a motto like that I grasped the importance of time management early.

After the instructors finished dealing with the late soldier, they came back to the front of the formation. One instructor asked, "Do you want to be here?"

Everyone replied with a thunderous, "Roger Sergeant Night Stalker." We learned early in holdover platoon that all the instructors would be referred to as, 'Sergeant Night Stalker.'

He began to tell us, "At any time if you want to quit, please ring this bell. If you can't make it through this course and don't want to be here, then we don't want you here." He explained to us that there were 82 soldiers in the last class and only 36 graduated. Even after hearing the speech and what the graduation rate was, I knew this was exactly where I wanted to be. I was going to do whatever it took to graduate from the 160th selection course.

After the brief talk he instructed us to dump our packed ruck sacks contents out in one giant pile and our duffle bags in another. After releasing us from the formation, the frantic Green Platoon class made two huge piles of gear. Hundreds of socks, boots, towels, flashlights, and tons of filled Ziploc bags constructed two massive towers. The reason we had to label everything with our names according to the packing list was quickly understood.

After we finished dumping out our gear we were instructed to go into one of the bunkers. We all started to walk to the bunker door, then an instructor who I hadn't heard speak yet, yelled abruptly, "Why are you walking?" We picked up the pace, hustled to the door, and ran down a long linoleum floored corridor.

We arrived at a classroom at the end of the hallway and were instructed to sit down after another instructor ordered, "Take seats."

An hour passed in the bland classroom, and all the instructors had put in their two cents about why this was the best aviation unit in the world and what it took to get through the next five weeks. They also covered a few ground rules and a few things that would surely get you kicked out. One of the rules we had already had a taste of was the, 'No Walking,' rule. Anywhere we went while on the compound during the course we had to run. There was absolutely no walking allowed. The hour brief concluded and we were instructed to get back outside. Now aware of the, 'No Walking' rule everyone bolted outside. We ran in a single file out of the door, and were greeted by the rising sun.

As we hurried outside, I noticed the two giant piles of gear were strewn about the compound. There was shit everywhere; shoes, sleeping bags, canteens, uniforms, and Ziploc bags full of stuff. A few black shirts were picking through what was left of the piles and throwing gear everywhere. Before I could comprehend what was going on, I noticed another black shirt wielding a giant wrench. There was a shock and awe emotion going on. I had no idea what the wrench was for until I followed with my eyes, the direct path he was walking. He was headed for a fire hydrant positioned conveniently in front of a long winding trench. This had to be the baby pit from holdover platoon's father. The huge trench started at the base of the fire hydrant. In a serpentine fashion it wound its way under the chain link fence out of the compound. I tried to follow the small river's path, but I lost sight of it behind a grassy knoll obstructing my view. He turned the fire hydrant on with the wrench and water instantly gushed out filling the giant trench.

While I was in disbelief of the fire hydrant extravaganza, another black shirt yelled out, "You have five minutes to get your gear and put it back in the bags." All of us confused, we looked at each other thinking the same thing. This is going to be impossible. Just as I thought it couldn't get any worse, he proceeded to say, "Too slow, low crawl and get your things."

Not even ten seconds had passed with everyone trying to locate items to put back in the empty ruck sacks. We started low crawling, knowing full well we weren't going to get all the gear picked up in five minutes. The instructors knew it too. All of us were familiar with the combat technique of moving positions while under fire. A low crawl is when you make yourself as flat as you can against the ground and pull yourself using your hands and feet. We must have looked like a spilled container of night crawlers squirming to locate our gear.

I guess five minutes had passed, and the instructor yelled out again, "Too slow, go crawl in the pit and think of what you can do differently." Another instructor added, "Stop thinking as an individual and start thinking as a team."

Then another instructor chimed in yelling in the same tone just as the few before, "We didn't say think as an individual. Your gear is now your buddies gear. You guys are a team. We don't want you here if you are not going to work as a team. We said get the gear and put it in the bags." Then another instructor said in harmony, as if they had done this before. "You all need to think outside the box and work as a team, or you're never going to make it in this unit."

I was trying to take everything in as the instructors were yelling at us, but the water from the fire hydrant was freezing and the guy low crawling in front of me was kicking and splashing arctic water in my face. Ice chunks were floating in the water and I could hear the guy in front of me using his hands to smash the blanket of ice that covered the trench. While low crawling in the ice cold water, all I was trying to think about was Florida or Arizona, anywhere hot to get my mind off the freezing temperatures.

Then an instructor said, "The guy in front of you, the guy behind you and the guy to your left and right are the most important thing to you in this unit. You will go through the worst shit together, you will eat together, you will sleep together, and most of all, you will put your life on the line for that guy no matter the situation." Of all the things the instructors said, that was the one thing I will never forget. Having been in the Army for two years and a deployment under my belt, I understood the concept of brotherhood vaguely. Sure, the guys in my old unit were my brothers, but being in the freezing cold water made me realize that this was something completely different.

It was still day zero and not even 0800 yet, and I knew this was absolutely without a doubt where I wanted, and needed to be. The day continued with physically demanding exercises, building a camaraderie like no other, and learning how to think outside the box as a team.

I took a lot away from that day and will hold it close to my heart until the day I die. I began to think differently about getting things accomplished. My thought process shifted, knowing full well I had to make sure the guy to the left, right, and behind me succeeded too. We finished the day at 0200 the next morning and were told to be back at 0500. When I finally comprehended the time line I knew the remaining days were going to be no easier than the first. If I could just get through the hours, minutes, and even seconds I knew I had a good shot. The other men I was in class with had to do the same thing. We were a team now and if they helped me succeed I would surely be helping them do the same.

The time line for the next day gave me enough time to get to my room, take a hot shower, and wash my muddy wet uniform. On top of that I had to go through all my bags again and make sure everything was just as clean as the day I arrived. I went through them and cleaned everything that was either thrown in the pit or covered in mud and dirt. Of course, I was missing several items and had some Ziploc bags labeled with someone else's name. I knew I had to clean the other soldier's gear just as well as I had cleaned mine. If I had the same mentality before I started day zero, I'm not sure I would have cleaned the other guy's gear or not. I finally finished prepping for the next day. It was 0430 and I knew if I tried to take a nap I wouldn't wake up. I was certain the other guys were experiencing the same unreal fatigue.

I gave myself a mental pep talk, filled up all of my canteens, and headed out the door. The air was just as cold as the night before, if not colder. I arrived at the same parking lot and headed to the gate. Some soldiers were already taking orders from the white board and doing their exercise before entering the compound. I headed down the gravel hill and looked at the white board. I knew I was going to be doing jump squats at the very least. I saw another soldier doing them while hustling down the hill with my bags.

The board read, '50 jump squats, 50 push-ups, and 50 sit-ups.' I unwillingly set my bags off to the side in the grass to make room for myself and anyone else who showed up while I was taking orders from the white board. It was cold but I started to get warmed up after finishing the jump squats. Another soldier came down the hill and started doing his exercises behind me. About five minutes later, I was still doing the required tasks. I heard the guy behind me pick up his bags and run through the gate to join the others in formation. I thought to myself, there is no way that the guy who arrived minutes after me just did all that PT written on the board. While I was doing my white board ordered sit-ups, I heard a very recognizable voice confront the soldier.

In a very calm and collected tone I could vaguely make out the instructor ask the soldier, "Did you do all the exercises on the board?"

The soldier answered very proud and confidently, "Roger Sergeant Night Stalker."

The instructor responded, "I was in the wood line watching you and now you're going to lie?" The soldier, who I hadn't gotten to know yet, didn't say anything. The instructor ordered him to go ring the bell. I was still doing sit-ups and I glanced over toward the bell. With his head down he hesitantly rang the bell. He was instructed to get his bags and report back to holdover platoon. By now there were a few more classmates doing exercises. The ringing of the bell let everyone know that this wasn't a game. I later learned that the soldier who rang the bell was sent back to his old unit.

That morning began with a speech about integrity and how important it is to complete the mission, in this case push-ups and sit-ups. "We will not tolerate lying, that's how people get killed." All standing in formation, none of us took the instructors lesson lightly.

The remainder of the day consisted of classroom lectures illustrating what the schedule for the following weeks looked like. The current week was geared toward learning about the unit's history and how 160th was formed. I had never been a part of something that took so much pride in the history of the unit and remembrance of its fallen. I would really grasp the concept a few months later. It was a lot to take in but I knew if it was this important to the instructors who were either former or current Night Stalkers, then it was important to me. The first week sounded nice being in the classroom a lot, but there would be several demanding smoke sessions thrown in.

Our second week was going to be CLS (Combat Life Saver) week. An important part of being in the unit was knowing how to administer first aid and that's what the class taught. After graduating from the course you never knew when or where you might deploy. Clearly, understanding minor and major first aid concepts was taken seriously.

The following week was about honing our land navigation skills. We all had done it previously in basic training but nowhere near as in depth as the Green Platoon course.

Week four was comprised of learning combative skills. Every day for that week we would meet early in the morning at another separate building on the compound adjacent to the two bunkers. The building was called the Dojo where we would learn hand to hand combat and grappling techniques.

The last week was range week. It was last because I assume, they wanted to weed out the shitbags before we finally had some fun shooting weapons. Range week was a whole week consisting of shooting techniques and learning about basic weapons the enemy used.

The first week went on everyday just as bad, if not worse than the previous day. The weekend finally came and there wasn't much time for fun and games. Much like the whole class, I had to prepare, clean, and gear up for the upcoming Monday. Although we were going to begin CLS training, that didn't mean it was going to be an easy week. I knew the course was designed to teach us important skills, but the instructors made sure there was time carved out for physically demanding exercises and mental tests. As I cleaned my gear and prepared everything for the upcoming week I reflected back on the prior week. I just got through the first week, and I only had four more to go. We must have lost 10 or 15 guys the first week. They either were kicked out, or it was too demanding and they gave in to the comforting sound of the bell.

Monday morning came too fast and it was time to start week two. Everyone finished their white board exercises and lined up in formation. We looked around the formation and it was eye opening how small the class had become. The sight made everyone realize they didn't want to be that missing guy.

We were greeted by an instructor and he reiterated what all of us were thinking. "The class is getting smaller. Who is going to be next?" He went on, "Raise your hand if you want to leave." We all moved our eyes and not our heads to look around as we stood at attention. No one raised their hand. After the instructor realized the absence of cold hands, he ordered us, "Head to the first aid trailer."

The mobile trailer was tucked behind the two bunkers. We weren't yet familiar with the area, but would continue to report there for the next week. An ex-Green Beret medic was our instructor for this section of the training. He was big, but calm at the same time. By now, team work and fighting for the guy next to you was engrained in our being. The basic principle was closely related to CLS and the instructor made sure we knew it. We went over IV's the whole day mixed in with the occasional hour long smoke sessions. We were informed that the CLS week would conclude with a full day training scenario. It was explained that we would go out into the wood line and rescue a downed pilot and call for a 9-Line. A 9-Line was a radio call to an air or vehicle asset regarding a wounded soldier. It was called a 9-Line because there were nine critical pieces of information that were conveyed, which informed the assets of the wounded soldier's condition. After learning and listening to stories of actual combat 9-Line scenarios from our Green Beret medic instructor, I prayed I would never have to experience that.

The week was very informational and meaningful. The instructor always had a real life combat story to throw in with whatever it was we were learning. Our Special Forces medic brought the reality of saving someone's life into more focus. By mid-week we were getting into airway breathing procedures and techniques. We learned how to insert a Nasal Pharyngeal Airway device down someone else's nose. No one was thrilled about that part of the class. After receiving a brief instruction on how to do the procedure, we were paired up with another classmate to perform the insertion. While laying on my back I watched my partner rub medical lubricant on the long flexible tube. He tilted my head back and inserted it down my nose. My eyes watered as I started coughing violently. I could hear in the background several other Green Platoon classmates coughing. It was finally fully inserted in my nose and I could feel the rubber tube in the back of my throat. I left it in there for a minute to get the idea of what it felt like. My partner slowly pulled it out, and I could feel the tube moving in the back of my mouth and up my nasal cavity. My eyes watered worse than the insertion process. It was all the way out and I was glad it was over. It was my partners turn and I looked around the open furniture-less mobile trailer.

All of the guys who I got to know well in the past week were tearing up and coughing just like myself. I completed the insertion on my partner and was relieved that the day was nearing the end. The downed pilot and 9-Line rescue was set to take place the next day. The rest of the day was spent in the trailer being briefed on the scenario, and placing us in three and four man teams. My experience over the past week was different than anything I had ever experienced in the Army. From stories of the instructors down range to the camaraderie of all the soldiers in class, I knew without a doubt, 160th was my calling.

Throughout the five-week selection there were many requirements that needed to be completed in order to graduate. The requirements were sprinkled in over the duration of the grueling selection course. Completing three ruck marches was one of the many tasks. A four, six, and 12-mile ruck march all had to be completed in a pre-determined amount of time. If anyone failed to complete the task in the allotted time, we had a chance to try again. No one wanted to have to march around the backwoods of Ft. Campbell with a 60 lb. ruck sack for a second time. The marches started early in the morning to leave time for the rest of the day's training. While on the ruck marches, in order to know if you were keeping pace, and were on track to pass the timed march, there was a pace man. All of the black shirts did the march with us to make sure we didn't pass out and finished the testing paced march. Another way they helped us keep pace was by designating a black shirt, creatively named the rabbit. If during the march you found yourself behind the rabbit, you knew you had better start moving because this meant you were falling behind. A few soldiers didn't pass the first ruck march, and they all had a designated day to make it up. All but one didn't pass the second time during the four-mile march. There was another one down. Mental strength was a running theme throughout the course and if there was any time to use it, it was during the marches. The ability to tell yourself you could complete a task was greater than any other technique we were taught.

Another requirement to graduate was a day known as, and heavily anticipated, Black Day. We heard stories about the arduous day and were told it was going to come sooner or later. They didn't tell us the exact day it was going to take place, but it could happen at any moment. It was a day that consisted of heavy smokings, repetitive muscle failure, and constant psychological mind games. Black Day was designed to push us to our breaking points. Depending on the soldier, we would either give in to the daunting day, or push past our breaking points. Whenever the day came I knew the guys around me would have to go through the same rigorous test. Those are the kind of guys that deserved their spot and belonged in the unit. If someone gave up on Black Day, it was made clear to us that it was grounds for automatic termination. If someone wasn't able to get through the tough training day, then they weren't Night Stalker material. There was a reason the Special Operations community was special, and it was the men that made that foundation. Black Day was sure to push us, and not everyone would make the cut.

What I thought was going to be a concluded day in the mobile trailer, turned into an all-night briefing. The instructors didn't want anyone driving home that night due to fatigue and the possibility of crashing while driving home. We were instructed to get an MRE, grab our sleeping bags, and come back to the trailer to bed down.

It's a known fact in the military that everyone has their favorite MRE. If you were the guy who ended up with the breakfast omelet MRE, you would be the one trying to trade with someone else. However, everyone knows that no one in their right mind actually likes the omelet MRE. Everyone had their top choices and the meals hit the spot after a long day. I got lucky and ended up with a top five favorite. It was the rib patty which I always made into a McRib like sandwich with two pieces of wheat bread, which were included in the preserved meal kit. We needed all the calories we could get because what we were about to face couldn't compare to anything we had just endured in the past weeks. I finished my MRE McRib creation and shut my eyes. It was a long day and after I hit my T-shirt made pillow, I was out.

What felt like five minutes later the door slammed open followed by a lot of smoke and a loud speaker repeating a siren noise. I have no idea what the actual time was. Over the loud speaker an instructor yelled, "Get outside! Move, move, move."

We all rushed outside and were cordially greeted with more simulated flash bangs and all kinds of different colors of smoke. It was still dark so we must not have been asleep too long, or was it the next night? Had I slept for 12 plus hours straight? I wasn't able to decide in that moment with all the confusion. The fire hydrant was gushing at full blast and the instructors were all outside. "Get in the pit," yelled a black shirt from the mega phone.

Black Day had arrived. We all heard rumors that Black Day could last anywhere from 11 to 24 hours. In my fatigued state, I hoped this was going to be an 11-hour Black Day. Through the clouds of smoke, the entire class immersed into the icy pit. We were still in uniform as none of us had the strength to get comfy before laying down. The frigid water instantly soaked my ACU's and with the fatigue felt like my body weight was doubled as I trudged the dreaded trench. We were wet, cold, tired, mad, and confused. My mind was going a million miles a minute but my body was operating at the pace of a hobbling old man.

An instructor yelled through the mega phone again, "Sit up in the water and get nut to butt with the guy in front of you." The term was commonly used to reference how close you needed to get to the guy in front of and behind you. We were all sitting down in what now felt like Satan's trench, and I could hear the fire hydrant gushing behind me. The rushing water crashed relentlessly into my back. I noticed another instructor rolling a blue 55-gallon barrel over to one of the soldiers at the front of our long line of teammates. The first guy was given brief instructions and the rest of us had no idea what was going on. As soon as we saw the barrel being passed to the guy behind him overhead, we caught on quickly.

One of the instructors shouted over the mega phone, "Service." We all knew by now, when we heard any of the instructors shout that word we were to recite the Night Stalker Creed. We would learn to live by the creed in the subsequent demanding years in the 160th, and for the rest of our lives. The first word in the creed is, 'Service.' Still freezing in the water, and with more flash bangs exploding I managed to scream at the top of my lungs.

Once we heard the word, we sounded off. "Service in the 160th is a calling only a few will answer for the mission is constantly demanding and hard. And when the impossible has been accomplished the only reward is another mission that no one else will try. As a member of the Night Stalkers I am a tested volunteer seeking only to safeguard the honor and prestige of my country, by serving the elite Special Operations Soldiers of the United States." Something came over all of us sitting in the cold water and we began to recite the creed louder than we ever had before. The large barrel was hoisted over a guy's head and passed to the guy behind him getting closer to my position.

We went on shouting at the top of our lungs, "I pledge to maintain my body, mind and equipment in a constant state of readiness for I am a member of the fastest deployable Task Force in the world, ready to move at a moment's notice anytime, anywhere, arriving time on target plus or minus 30 seconds. I guard my unit's mission with secrecy, for my only true ally is the night and the element of surprise. My manner is that of the Special Operations Quiet Professional, secrecy is a way of life. In battle, I eagerly meet the enemy for I volunteered to be up front where the fighting is hard. I fear no foe's ability, nor underestimate his will to fight. The mission and my precious cargo are my concern. I will never surrender. I will never leave a fallen comrade to fall into the hands of the enemy and under no circumstances will I ever embarrass my country. Gallantly will I show the world and the elite forces I support that a Night Stalker is a specially selected and well trained soldier. I serve with the memory and pride of those who have gone before me for they loved to fight, fought to win and would rather die than quit. Night Stalkers Don't Quit!"

As soon as the fun ended in the pit we were told to head over to a Humvee. A long, thick, green rope was attached to the grill of the burly vehicle. We were told to start pulling the truck. Without hesitation the soaking wet class ran to the rope, and we began pulling the huge vehicle. The black shirts must have had the E-brake on because this thing was barely moveable. A two-mile-long loop surrounded the compound, and was referred to as Ranger Loop. We tugged the Humvee around the loop three times before receiving our next physically demanding mission.

A giant paved hill branched off and complemented the long loop. The hill was the only way in and out of the Old Clarksville Barracks. We were told to leave the Humvee and run down the hill. The hill was a mile or so long, and the class became used to the familiar ruck march used road. Our soaking and muddy class began to run down the hill in our soggy boots. I noticed the Humvee cautiously driving down the hill passing all of the fatigued soldiers including me. Steam was pouring off our bodies in the cold morning sun. Minutes later we made it to the bottom of the hill.

By this point I could tell who was in it for the long haul. Some students had already reached their breaking point and were just walking down the hill while we waited at the bottom for them to join. In a way I was happy they were taking their time, because we were just standing there catching our breath. I shouldn't have even thought of that, because right then an instructor told us to start low crawling back up the hill to go rescue our fellow remaining students. While crawling we were instructed to sound off with the phrase, 'Take your time buddy, take your time.' We recited the phrase repeatedly until finally making it to our severely fatigued classmates.

After crawling to our classmates we got up and carried them the rest of the way down the hill.

The day continued on no easier than the pulling of the Humvee, or enduring the frigid pit. The day taught me early on, one valuable lesson. The team is no stronger than its weakest link. We all reached our breaking points that day, some sooner than others. We learned to force our bodies and minds to push past that point. I never thought it was possible, but with the guys to the left and right of me, the impossible became possible. All together everyone was constantly yelling words of encouragement to one another. When yelling at each other to get motivated we tried to yell louder than the instructors in an attempt to block them out. Our exhausted panting voices were no match against the loudspeaker, though.

As the day dragged on, we found ourselves at an obstacle course in the wood line with more flash bangs, smoke, and that obnoxious bullhorn siren. I heard a noise louder than anything going on while crawling under a log on the obstacle course. It was a very recognizable sound, almost like a loud chopping of the sky. It grew louder chop, chop, chop, chop. I looked up through the leafless tree tops while looking through my hot breath in the cold air. I saw two black 160th Special Operation Chinooks flying in perfect formation above.

Seeing the helicopters gave me the extra push I needed, another sign telling me to keep pushing through, you're almost done. Chop, chop, chop, the noise became faint and the bullhorn and simulated machine gun fire once again overtook my hearing. I snapped back to reality and headed for a long vertical cargo net in front of me. In front of the vertical net was a large hole filled with water that had run off from the fire hydrant. I was already muddy, sweaty, and exhausted and looked at the net in frustration. A few classmates were already going through the cold chest deep water to get to the cargo net. Some of us were carrying large ammo cans filled with sand, and were instructed to work as a team to carry them up the long spider web of a net. Throughout the day different soldiers were handed different items to carry, some heavier than others. The selected soldiers had to carry their items and be accountable for them the entire day.

We concluded the fifth time through the obstacle or O course, and shuffled back to the compound. My legs had a mind of their own and I felt like I was floating. The upper half of my body and the lower half of my body weren't talking to one another. The look on everyone's faces was pure exhaustion and an unrelenting determination. Sluggishly making it back to the compound and dreading whatever was next, I slumped over and vomited. My McRib turned pulled pork sandwich spewed onto the paved road. After my puke episode, some of the other classmates and I helped the gear toting soldiers carry their water and ammo cans to give them a break. By this point we had accomplished so much, there was no way I or any other soon to be 160th soldier was going to give up now. After the mile hike from the wood line we passed the white board and entered through the compound gate. We saw the fire hydrant gushing again and I wasn't amused. We must have been 20 hours into the pain staking day and I prayed I could summon enough energy to finish. We had no idea what else the instructors would come up with.

Again a command shouted from the bullhorn, "The push-up." While down in the push-up position I heard the bell ring. No way, after all we had just accomplished, someone was going to ring the bell? It had to be one of the instructors messing with the class. Then it rang again. I tried lifting my head to see who rang the bell. I was so focused on keeping my body from touching the ground I couldn't see anything. My arms were like noodles and sweat was rolling into my eyes.

After several push-ups, we were ordered from the loud speaker, "Get up and head over to the flags." Behind the bell in between the two bunkers flew three flags, the US, 160th, and POW MIA flag. Adorned at the base of the three poles was a four tier flagstone display. We gathered around the base of the flags while the instructors stood in front of us. We waited to receive our next exhausting task as we stood around the flags.

"Sit down," a black shirt exclaimed. Relieved, I took a seat on the warm concrete ground. It was the most rest we'd had all day.

I heard the fire hydrant slowly shut off behind us. Almost as if having it on when we got back to the compound was a mental test. We would later find out that test wasn't passed by the two soldiers we heard ringing the bell. If only they had it in them to push through the pain everyone sitting there was enduring, they would have been sitting with us. Instead they gave in to the exhaustion and were defeated by the infamous Black Day. Many of the guys had the mental toughness to keep pushing through and some didn't. Black Day was implemented in the middle of the course for that very reason. By now we had gone through a lot, but Black Day would be victorious over two. As the instructors stood in front of us, each of them began to speak to us about the unit and its sacred brotherhood.

"This is what it's about men," a black shirt said. Up until now, none of the instructors had referred to us as men. We were either soldier, snowbird, or candidate. Something was different about the way they were now addressing us, some even began to cry. That day we all became bonded, forged through the excruciating training into a team. I realized what was special about the unit. It wasn't the cool name or the bad ass stories I heard or read. It wasn't the top secret missions of which we would eventually be a part. It wasn't the special rules and different regulations. It was the man to my left, and the man to my right. It was the brother who would be fighting by my side. It was the men willing to lay down their lives for mine. Like all Special Operations units, it was the brotherhood that made the unit special.

Black Day finally concluded late in the night. We had to clean the entire compound before we could be dismissed. I arrived at my room that night more exhausted than I had ever been in my life. The twin size spring built Army issued barracks mattress never felt so good. I had just enough energy to take my boots off. I left my dirty, sandy, still wet uniform on and I knocked out.

I arrived at OCB at 0600 the next morning for a 0630 show time. Approaching the fence, I saw everyone greeting each other, a lot more confidently and cordially than before. We felt like we just accomplished the impossible and were happy to have done it together. We all waited at the fence for the rest of our class to arrive, something we hadn't done in the past. Our mindset was different before Black Day. If one of our own was going to be late then we were all going to be late. Sure enough it was 0625 and we were still missing one. As we looked down to the asphalt covered compound we could see all the instructors staring at us. They continued to look up, not yelling or saying anything. It was 0628 and the last classmate showed up to the parking lot and ran over to us. We ran down the hill together to the white board. To our relief, there was nothing written on the board. Before walking through the gate we looked over at the instructors.

One of them yelled over to us, "Get in formation." We ran over and got in formation. The class was much smaller now compared to day zero, which made it easier to get into formation.

Another instructor said, "Why are you late?"

They referred to the class leader, whom we all voted for, as the penguin. The penguin replied, "We are only as strong as our weakest link Sergeant

Night Stalker."

"Who was late?" The instructor asked the penguin.

"We are all late," he replied. Everyone knew what the class leader was doing. We didn't want to throw someone under the bus. It was either all of us or none of us who were going to be punished. The moment felt a lot like my first day arriving at holdover platoon, when everyone got down and started doing push-ups with me. We all expected the worst consequences after hearing the conversation between the penguin and instructor.

The instructor simply said, "Good answer," and told us to head to the classroom.

In the classroom we were greeted by another ex-Green Beret that I had recognized from a few of the ruck marches, but I had never heard him say anything. He was bigger than the medic and spoke with a deeper voice. When he looked at you and asked a question it looked like he was seeing into your soul, and if you didn't answer in the next five seconds he would rip it out. He was going to be our combatives instructor for the next week. The day in class went over the outline of the next week, which would conclude with a day I was slightly dreading.

Clinch Day was one of the very few requirements remaining to graduate the course. If we successfully passed Clinch Day, we would receive a combatives level one certification. During the in class brief, we found out Clinch Day wouldn't be easy. To pass, we needed to clinch an instructor three times while they were whaling on us, blow after blow with boxing gloves. We would learn several different clinches over the week and could use any of them to subdue the swinging instructors. The week carried on with 12 hour days consisting of ground and pound drills, pummeling, and hand to hand combat drills. Over and over we practiced and sparred with each other, watched MMA tape, and most of all got better at fighting. It was a long week and it was coming to an end. Range week was about to start, and we were that much closer to graduating.

It was a day before Clinch Day and we were all excited. After a morning of sparring it was finally lunch time. We had been instructed to go out to the field which was enclosed inside the chain link fence adjacent to the first bunker. Instead of eating lunch that hour, the class got acquainted with our new best friend, 'the log.' The giant logs spread around the field, must have been cut from 1,000-year-old trees. They were massive in diameter, all ranging from 6 to 9 feet in length.

We ran to the field and a big, beefy Samoan instructor told us, "Four to a log. Hurry up, go meet your new friend." The classmates and I grabbed one of the logs and carried it back to the instructor's vicinity. We were side by side holding the massive chunk of wood. The instructor was in the middle of all the teams. We had formed a circle around him with our new best friend.

"Now take a seat with your new best friend," he ordered. "The sit-up," he yelled.

The whole class sounded off back to him as an acknowledgment, "The sit-up."

He began in his thunderous voice, "Up, down, up, down." While we kept doing sit-ups he said, "Repeat after me. The log is my friend."

We echoed his command, "The log is my friend."

He continued, "It will help me maintain my mind, body, and soul." Log PT continued with more intricate exercises, constantly repeating the motivational call and response speeches between instructor and students. With my team raising the log over our heads, another instructor called over to the group, "Listen up, if you're a 15U get over here." I had known by now all the 15U's in the class, and I was one of four. With no idea what he wanted from us, we all broke away from our teams and raced over to the instructor. Standing next to him were three big guys dressed in ACU's and wearing the coveted maroon beret.

The biggest of the three looked at us and asked, "Who wants to go to flight company?" When those words came out of his mouth it was like a slow motion scene in a movie. Everything I had done up to this point was exactly for this reason, and I was ecstatic. I had to play it cool and not look like I had just won the lottery. Raising my hand immediately I looked at the other three who were standing at parade rest next to me. Two of the guys were right out of basic training and wanted to go to maintenance platoon first to learn more about the helicopter. Understandable for them, but I had worked my ass off on the beast for the past year. The bones of a regular Army Chinook and a 160th Chinook were the same. Sure there were several differences, but I was confident I could learn all the nuances in a flight company. The other guy wanted to become a crew chief, but his orders were sending him to 3rd battalion in Savannah, GA. The maroon beret wearing leaders told us that they were from a company stationed at Ft. Campbell in 2nd battalion. I learned a week ago I was going to 2nd battalion. The battalion was comprised of maintainers and flight guys along with several other supporting roles.

He looked at me and said, "You want to be a crew chief?"

Without missing a beat, I said, "Roger Sergeant!"

Another one of the men said, "If you think this is hard, flight company is a lot harder. New guys don't get any slack."

Nothing could deter me now, and I knew this was my only shot. Before he could finish I said, "Yes I want to fly."

The bigger of the three told me to get through Green Platoon and they will see what they could do. "Alright, get out of here," he finished.

We ran back to our four man teams to continue log PT. I felt a rush of energy pulse over my body after the conversation and began doing everything I could to help my team conquer the humongous log. Log PT concluded and we headed back to the Dojo.

We grabbed an MRE and sat down on the wrestling mats. We ate while watching Royce Gracie's MMA fights on a large projector screen on the Dojo wall. Although watching the little Jiu-Jistsu Brazilian kick ass was cool, my mind was racing. Would I actually get in to a flight company and become a crew chief? I had no idea how the system worked in the spec ops community beyond Green Platoon. I was brand new to the special operations world and all I knew was I needed to fly. No matter what, I was going to do whatever it took to become a crew chief.

Clinch Day came sooner than I wanted, and I knew the week was almost over. We concluded our morning warm ups in the Dojo. While warming up, big burly dudes I had never seen before started trickling in the door. They were each carrying a set of boxing gloves. It seemed someone called HBO sports to get the top boxers for our test.

Concerned, I wasn't looking forward to what was to come. But no matter who was going to box my head off, I knew I just had to get through the day. All of us were instructed to line up against one wall while the MMA-looking professionals lined up on another wall. One by one, each student and pro-looking boxer were paired. The first guy went to the middle of the mat and began getting rocked, jab, cross, jab, cross. Several punches later he clinched the guy and we all began clapping for our brother who just did what we thought was impossible. The more we got into it the more we started to cheer and call out to whomever was in the ring. We wanted our brothers to lock in the ever so needed clinch. I was three guys away from going, and in the boxer line I saw a huge guy switching spots with guys in front of him. While switching he was counting the guys in our line all the while eyeing me down. He undoubtedly was attempting to get paired with me in the ring. He was like a T-Rex looking for his dinner. I was 5'11", and maybe 165 lbs. wet, but this guy was huge. What a little prick, I was thinking. The classmate in front of me finished and secured his clinch. I was up, and I paced over to the center of the mat looking up at my opponent, who only got bigger the closer I got.

Wham! First hit, he knocked me out on the mat. I woke up from my unconscious state and got back on my feet. Again, with my hands in front of my face, I began to take punch after punch. I finally worked around him to secure a lower back clinch. Phew, one down and two to go. The last two were much easier than the first. Maybe it was because after clinching the T-Rex beast I felt unstoppable.

Everyone that day ended up getting their combatives level one certification, and were able to proceed to the final week. I don't know why, but after coming so far, more soldiers rang the bell. Guys who I had developed relationships with, guys I thought would lay their lives down for mine, just quit. Guys I thought didn't just say the words, 'Night Stalkers Don't Quit,' after the creed, but actually meant it. If they had quit on the rest of the class now, then they would probably quit when we needed them the most. Those type of guys wouldn't be the ones I would come to know as my brothers.

Just like the weekends in the past over the period of the course, it gave me just enough time to reset for the following Monday. It was here, the final week. I began that age old military count down, 'four days and a wake up.' Range week, like the weeks prior, encompassed one final testing requirement. The requirement was a barrage of different shooting drills involving hitting targets from different distances like eggs, bowling pins, metal plates that move, and so on. Everyone had learned how to shoot in basic training, but nonstop 12 hour days at the range would really hone our marksmanship skills.

I pulled into the now familiar gravel parking lot. Inside the compound gate I noticed two M35 deuce and a half series vehicles, which were used for troop transportation. The class piled into the backs of the trucks, and we headed to range 2A to begin range week. Stories were exchanged on the short ride through the backwoods of Ft. Campbell. The trucks screeched to a halt on a narrow, loose gravel trail. I followed my classmates out of the back of the truck. We walked as a group to a table that was set up under a long open wooden awning. Several black shirts were standing at the table waiting for us. Making our way to them we passed several more wooden tables just behind the awning. Snowbirds from holdover platoon were hastily loading M4 and M9 magazines. Spanning 100 meters in front of the covered awning was the range. It was open with targets at the end. Behind the targets perched a large dirt berm to catch rounds from being shot into the distant woods. The posts supporting the large awning were numbered, allowing us to understand what target we were going to be shooting at down range. I recall in basic training, shooting side by side next to someone, it was easy to mistake your paper target for the one belonging to the guy next to you. There must have been 30 stations under the wooden structure. The day began with instruction and demonstration from the black shirts. After the demos, we mimicked the instructors and began to train with live rounds. I found out that the snowbirds were going to load our mags for the duration of the week. Having unlimited full magazines at our disposal that we didn't have to load for ourselves was amazing.

From upside down shooting to weak hand shooting, every day was just as important as the last. Moving drills to transitioning drills changing from our M4 rifle to our holstered pistol, we learned it all. We learned everything there was to know about shooting that week. We also learned how to take apart and shoot the enemies most commonly used weapon, the AK-47.

The last day arrived and I couldn't believe how far I made it. By now, I knew I couldn't do anything else. I set out a goal to accomplish and I didn't want to fail. The last requirement for passing the course finally arrived. In the final test we needed to sprint in full body armor a quarter mile with a partner. After the sprint, and making it to the first station, the pair would then start the shooting course. My partner and I lined up a quarter mile away from the first station under the covered awning. A black shirt, standing next to us, looked at his stop watch as we lined up and waited for his mark.

"Ready, set, go," the range instructor shouted. We sprinted like two bulls bursting out of the gate at a PBR event. Kicking up rocks behind us we calculated where we needed to set up for our first shots. The specific shot instructions would be given when we reached each station. After the long sprint and breathing heavily at the first station, my partner and I were ordered to shoot an egg with our M4's at 50 meters. The black shirt stood above us as we laid in the prone position. I looked down the range and made out two tiny eggs. By this point, I knew the shot should be a piece of cake. However, after running in heavy body armor it became difficult to control my breathing while focusing on the precise shot. The days prior we practiced steady breath control and trigger squeeze after running, so we knew what to do. My partners rifle rang out, he nailed his egg. I watched the egg explode in the distance. Seeing his accurate shot, I concentrated on my white oval target. I nailed mine first shot as well. We both stood up and ran to the next station.

We moved into a bounding or moving shooting drill. I shot a target then my partner called out, "Moving." He ran from behind then crouched in a position next to me behind a wooden wall. He made his shots while I continued to shoot my assigned targets. We moved to the next task hastily.

"Shoot off all the plates," the monitoring black shirt said.

The plates were positioned on a wheel-like target. Once we shot a plate, it sent the wheel spinning out of balance. After shooting all of the moving plates, we moved to five stationary plates at a distance of 50 meters transitioning from M4 to pistol. After my partner and I hit all five plates, we moved on.

The last station was a one-man task discussed between teams prior to starting the drill. One team member had to pick up a fully automatic AK-47 and shoot a hanging bowling pin at 50 meters. Proper stance, breath control, and trigger squeeze are critical when operating a fully automatic weapon system while standing. I unloaded the entire magazine into the pin, and the instructor at the last station yelled, "Time."

In order to pass, or get a, 'GO,' on the requirement we needed to complete it under a certain time. After the two instructors who were monitoring the last station finished a short discussion, they looked at my partner and me. The experienced marksman instructor Mr. Tony said, "You guys passed, well done."

The final AK-47 rounds into the bowling pin were the icing on the cake. I may have envisioned my old section sergeant's face on the last target. It was one last middle finger to him for thinking I couldn't make it through the course. The day finished at the range and the morale between the almost graduated Night Stalkers couldn't have been higher. Everyone in the class who started the first day of range week was going to graduate. The intensive five-week course was finally complete. We loaded the trucks and headed back to the compound.

Upon returning we were instructed to head to the classroom. Something was unusual though, all the instructors were standing at the front of the room. "Take seats," one of the black shirts ordered.

After taking our seats the instructors began to clap. It was an awkward yet rewarding moment as I looked around the room at a handful of puzzled faces. We were almost in disbelief that the selection course was finally over. Another black shirt walked in the room carrying a large cardboard box as the clapping faded. Everyone looked confused and intrigued, not knowing what was in the box. He made his way to the front of the room and said, "When I call your name come up here and grab your beret."

Holy smokes the coveted maroon beret! I felt like the voice over from A Christmas Story was narrating for the infamous Red Ryder BB gun. Only it was a more prized and a more deserving possession than a BB gun. A beret we truly earned and everyone in the room deserved.

In a few regular Army units, the maroon beret was given to soldiers upon arriving to their units. Not this beret. This beret was a rite of passage, and a direct fuck you to everyone in my old unit who said I wasn't going to make it. He was calling out names and handing out berets. He called my name and I made my way to the front of the class. As he handed me the glowing maroon beret he said, "Alpha Company 2nd Battalion."

Not really sure about the different companies in the battalion I asked him, "What's Alpha Company?"

He answered to my disbelief, "That's a Chinook flight company." Wow, I looked at him in my, I just unwrapped the Red Ryder BB gun like state. I couldn't believe it; I was going to a flight company. The only soldiers that made up a flight company in my MOS were crew chiefs. I did it. I was finally going to fly on the big beast I fell in love with on the airfield in Bagram, Afghanistan. We were given our berets before the formal graduation so we could get a flash sewn on the front of them. The flash represented which 160th battalion we were going to be assigned.

On graduation day we began the ceremony by sounding off with the Night Stalker Creed. The creed never sounded louder than any day prior, not even in the pit. We yelled at the top of our lungs to tell the whole world, we had finally done it. The graduation ceremony ended and the class was even smaller now. Green Platoon started with 86 highly motivated guys, but now on the stage stood 46 proud Night Stalkers. I had a great reunion with my family after the class was released.

While mingling after the event, I felt a tap on my shoulder. I turned around to be greeted by a First Sergeant, "Burnett?"

I immediately answered the slender and fit looking leader, "Roger First Sergeant."

He replied, "I'm your new First Sergeant. Welcome to Alpha Company." He was stern but to the point. After shaking my hand, he gave me a report time and date to meet at the Alpha Company office. He walked off in a hurry and nodded to my family.

CHAPTER 4
CRAZY HORSE

★ ★ ★

The next day was Tuesday and I was still digesting my celebratory steak from Charley's, a well-known Clarksville, TN delicacy. I left my barracks room in the morning feeling like a new man. I was still in my old unit's barracks and I eagerly headed out the door to start my new 160th career. There was never anyone walking around with a maroon beret in these parts of the base. I walked outside into the early morning air to see my entire old company in PT formation. The five weeks that I just endured was nothing like what they were about to do that morning for PT. It was silent among the ranks. I heard my old 1SG at the head of the massive formation briefing them on what they were going to do for PT. As I walked behind everyone in formation with my fresh maroon beret, thousands of eyes peered in my direction. The feeling was like that guy who pulls up next to you at a stoplight in a Ferrari. I felt like the guy driving the Ferrari. None of them knew what I had just gone through. Everyone heard stories about Green Platoon, but those who never endured or pushed through those five weeks will never know what it's really like. There was a reason all special operation units had a selection process, and I now knew why.

As I passed the last section of the massive formation I recognized several faces. They were the guys, who over the last two years, I had come to know very well. Almost like the final take in an epic Hollywood film, they all turned over to me and whispered as to not disrupt the 1SG. "Good job Burnett."

I continued to pass my old section making my way to the parking lot. At the very end of the Chinook maintenance platoon row stood SSG Chris. Our eyes crossed paths and he didn't say a word. As much as I wanted to say, 'Fuck you,' I kept walking and let my new beret do all the talking. I would never see SSG Chris again, but I would see those barracks one last night.

With in-processing papers in hand I headed to my vehicle to start the next chapter in my military career. Not knowing what to expect I took a scenic 15 minutes to get to the 160th compound. The compound was completely separate from the regular Ft. Campbell Army base and had its own guard shack. A special badge along with my military ID was required to get on the compound. The compound was comprised of several buildings, 160th personnel, and a handful of civilian contractors. All the buildings were named after fallen Night Stalkers to pay respect and never forget their sacrifices. Although I felt like I just accomplished the impossible, I knew everyone on the compound made it through the same 5-week selection process.

I flashed my newly acquired badge to the guard at the main entrance and headed into the compound. I was told by my new 1SG after the graduation, to meet at the Alpha Company building. His description was vague at the conclusion of graduation so I was a little lost. The sun was rising and I could smell and feel the spring humidity in the air. I passed a few buildings, then saw a POW MIA flag before the first curve on the compound road. It was visible yet limpidly swaying, and exactly as the 1SG had described. I parked in the full parking lot and headed for one of the two doors split evenly just behind the flag pole. As I approached the building at the base of the flag pole I noticed an arrowhead shaped rock. I was trying to piece everything together since I had barely heard or read anything about this flight company. I went in the first door and down a long hallway with several doors on either side. On the walls hung several pictures of guys flying on Chinooks, family picnics, awards, pictures with presidents, boat paddles with Navy SEAL crests engraved in them, and terrorist used machine guns. I couldn't believe my eyes; it was like walking through a super-secret museum. I slowly walked down the hall not knowing what to do or who to talk to. I had no idea what the next step was in my special operations journey. Approaching the first open door way on the left, I looked in hoping to be greeted by someone. In the middle of the room was a long, oval shaped conference table. Lining every wall of the room were cubicle desks. The shelves above each desk doubled as a bulletin board, and on them hung a sheet of paper. Written on the laminated sheets were aircraft tail numbers, and below that, a list of four to five names.

I proceeded farther into the room realizing there was no one around. I looked over at the desks and going down the list of names on each piece of paper to see if I knew anyone. As I got to the last few desks, I found myself turning around in place. The third to the last desk read, '780 (Ohanzee)' at the top, followed by four names. The fourth read, 'Burnett.' Boom, I made it. I was a crew chief, or so I thought. I would soon learn the road to becoming a crew dog was just beginning.

Feeling excited I left the room, like I found what I was looking for. I walked back into the hallway noticing more pictures of guys in uniform and in civilian clothes, again none I recognized. I walked to another door, above it a sign read, 'Platoon Sergeant.' The only thought in my head was, I hope he isn't as bad as my last boss. I walked in to be greeted by a huge guy. It was the same guy I talked to during log PT in Green Platoon. He greeted me sternly and said, "Welcome to Alpha Company, let the stress begin."

He handed me a thick stack of paperwork that I needed to fill out and began telling me what to expect, and what I was going to face in the coming year. I knew special operations wasn't going to be easy, but the list of things I had to get done before I could even start to think of flying felt impossible. He described in detail the schools I needed to complete before I would deploy with the unit. "You're going to go to Dunker School next week, followed by SERE (Survival, Evasion, Resistance, Escape) School."

He continued, informing me that the two schools alone sent potential crew chiefs packing, and even saw them kicked out of the unit. He finished, making his point very clear. Dunker School was a two-day program that took place in another building on the compound, called the Allison Aquatics Training Facility. It was named after Sergeant Thomas F. Allison, who made the ultimate sacrifice on 22 February 2002, while on board an MH-47E Chinook. He was a part of an over water training exercise when the aircraft crashed off the coast of the Philippines.

I had never been in the building but I drew a picture in my head of what I imagined it to be. The school was dedicated to water survival and over water ditching principles. SERE School, was designed and implemented for guys who had the highest probability of being captured in a combat zone. SERE was an intensive three-week program that went over interrogation techniques, wilderness survival, lock picking, hot wiring cars, and sleep and hunger deprivation. I was looking forward to both schools and figured after that I would be ready to fly.

Wrong. My new PSG (Platoon Sergeant) went on to tell me about a third school, and one that was going to teach me the ins and outs of flying. The BMQ (Basic Mission Qualification) course was a three month long, nonstop MH-47G Chinook immersion. From flying nights to days my body would endure the demanding crew member tasks while experiencing extreme fatigue. I realized after being in my new boss's office for an hour, the upcoming months would be anything but easy.

With Green Platoon completed, I had the momentum of a locomotive behind me. I reaffirmed my determination once again to do whatever it took to become a crew chief. I was committed to be the guy standing behind the mini gun I saw on the airfield in Afghanistan just half a year ago.

I was told to go to the crew dog office and bury my head in a dash ten. Not knowing what he was talking about, he must have sensed my confusion. He swiveled in his chair to a book shelf behind him and grabbed a thick manual. He looked me in the eye while handing me the chunky book, "This will be on you wherever you go. This is your bible. This is the difference between life and death. When you're not doing anything productive around here you will be reading this book."

I nodded and headed for the crew office. The place I would call home for the next four years. I sat down at the desk that had my name written above it. As I began reading my new bible, which I was told was practically my new best friend, another beefy guy walked in the door. When I say beefy, I mean this guy must have been on every steroid there was. He was wearing a dark green T-shirt tucked into his pants. I could see every muscle defined perfectly through the shirt. His only body fat was the shirt he was wearing. I continued to stare at him in shock while keeping my composure.

He kept looking at me. Then he shouted, "Who the fuck are you?"

I jumped out of my seat not knowing what rank he was. I stood at parade rest and quickly answered, "Burnett, sergeant, I'm new to Alpha Company."

He looked at me and asked, "Why were you sitting down?"

"To read the dash ten," I replied.

His face had just as many muscles as his body, and he said with conviction, "From now on you will stand. You're new and you don't deserve to sit in a chair. You need to earn that seat."

"Roger sergeant," I replied.

He kept eyeing me down, "Now stand on your head," he said. All I was thinking was, what the fuck is going on? I paused, not knowing if he was joking or serious. The stern look on his face implied the latter. "Stand on your head," he repeated.

Not one for great balance I tried standing on my head. I attempted the feat over and over again, but I was failing miserably. He sat in a chair and watched me try to do a head stand for a good ten minutes. I had no idea what I did wrong but later would come to realize it wasn't what I did wrong, it was that I was the new guy, or more commonly referred to as the FNG.

It was just me and my new personal trainer in the office. After multiple failed head stands he told me to get up. He began to ask me a series of flight related questions, not one I could answer. The incorrect answers I replied with became my homework. The -10 was a shortened name for the large MH-47G Chinook manual. The book where I could locate all the answers, would not only teach me everything about the aircraft, but would be the lifesaving hero on deployments to follow. It became clear to me that whatever was in the book, I needed to grasp immediately.

So why did I need to know everything in my new Chinook bible? Isn't a crew chief just a guy who flies around in a big helicopter and shoots a gun mounted to the helicopter window? The crew chief role is vast, elaborate, and demanding. While some have referred to crew chiefs in other books as door gunners, door gunners we are not. Many think our job is to stand behind a gun or help a team member climb into the helicopter from the ramp, also a gross falsehood. If any mechanical issues ever arise while flying on a training trip or a combat mission, it is our responsibility as a crew chief to identify the problem and fix it. Whether the problem is fixed in midair or in a random field somewhere, we are the subject matter experts on board. The pilots might have an idea of what's wrong due to what the fancy cockpit is telling them, but you will hardly ever see a pilot digging through a tool box. As a crew chief we are obligated and relied upon to correct any problems, from hydraulic to electronic, and everything in between. Proficiency on several special operations tasks are also critical in the crew chief role while supporting our ███████ colleagues.

The day dragged on, and the office chairs remained bodiless. The air of the crew dog office had a clean gym smell, and the ever so used chemical agent when completing mopping operations in the Army, Pine Sol. Pine Sol if used in excess left a piney taste in your mouth accompanied by the pungent smell. While I was standing in the quiet motionless office I wondered where everyone was. Hours passed just as slowly as the pages turned in my new helicopter manual.

My new PSG, who I met hours ago, strolled into the office. He started asking me questions about my previous unit and what I had hoped to accomplish in Alpha Company. He then began to ask and inform me about the history of 160th. The past weeks had been a physical roller coaster and now I was being fed copious amounts of knowledge to retain. He began to tell me the next weeks and years are going to be like drinking from a fire hose and I needed to retain as much information as possible. On one of the cinderblock constructed walls in the crew office was a huge painted black arrow head. Inside the massive painting were five white dots. Also inside the arrow head next to the dots, was a single red lightning bolt. My PSG pointed to it after asking me a barrage of unit history questions, he said, "Do you know what the meaning of Alpha Company's logo is?"

I replied, "Negative."

He said, "That's our company's crest, you need to know what it means."

After the questions finished and my new homework assignments were realized, I was released for the rest of the evening. I had paper work to complete for Dunker School, unit history details, and helicopter knowledge to wrap my head around. It was like Green Platoon all over again, just in the academic sense. I left the office and was puzzled as to what that arrow head meant and why it was so important.

After making a pit stop at the liquor store, I headed to my room to do some research. I found out that night the arrow head was significant to the name of my new company. Alpha Company 2nd battalion was also known as Crazy Horse Airlines. Back in the 1800's there was a Native American of the Lakota tribe who went by the name Crazy Horse. He was a courageous warrior, and before he went into battle he painted his face to intimidate his enemies. After I finished the article I looked up images, and it hit me when I saw the first image of Crazy Horse with his painted face. He painted his whole face black, on one half he painted hail stones, and on the other half he painted a red lightning bolt. The company crest arrowhead in the office was painted identically to Crazy Horse's war paint. It was slowly starting to come together. Crazy Horse was a well-known leader in battle, much like my new company. Although I was starting to piece the arrowhead together, what exactly did the hail stones and lightning bolt mean? After my tireless search I couldn't find the meaning and turned my attention to the company phone roster. After several phone calls I finally came across someone who would actually talk to the FNG. I hadn't met the guy yet but I knew he lived in the same barracks, since it showed his barracks room number next to his contact info.

After telling SPC King what my homework was before arriving at work the next morning he quickly replied, "The black in the arrow head represents the night in which we accomplish missions. The lightning bolt represents the quickness with which we strike, and the hail stones represent the unforgiving fury when we attack the enemy." Before I could say anything else he gave me the new guy welcome and abruptly hung up.

Not only was the homework demanding but forming any kind of relationship with anyone as the new guy felt impossible. I fell asleep with my head buried in the Chinook helicopter manual. Waking up the next morning in a puddle of drool, I quickly went through my daily routine and headed out for PT. I arrived at 0600 and went to the crew office where I met three more new faces. I began to notice the mentality was different. The guys in the room were calling each other by their first names, instead of rank followed by last name. I had to keep telling myself that this wasn't the big Army anymore and they did things much differently. The questions continued. I was getting used to the new guy harassment but I took it, as did everyone who came before me. I was confused about why there weren't a lot of soldiers in the office. I noticed another guy not sitting in a chair, maybe he was another new guy too. He was tall, and towered over the majority of the guys. I was excited the room focused their attention on him and not me. Almost like a school of piranhas searching for their wounded prey. They began asking him questions while everyone sat in their nice leather chairs. They continued to stare at the other new guy and me.

I came to find out the other new guy was SPC Justin. He had been in the unit for two years. He worked in another shop on the compound called ALSE (Aviation Life Support Equipment) where they worked on flight helmets and aircraft survival equipment. So in essence he knew little to nothing about the actual aircraft we would learn to crew. All of the senior guys who were asking us questions were dressed in civilian gym clothes. Nothing about their attire yelled Army or had any type of uniformity. This was one of many differences I started to notice compared to my old unit. I knew 160th was different in its cool secretive way, but strict petty rules that pertained in my old unit were cast by the wayside. I understood the unit cared more about accomplishing a mission, rather than what you wore during PT.

While the bantering continued in the office the focus shifted off us new guys and on to deployments that the senior guys had just completed. From taking RPG fire, ex-filling some of the most elite forces in the world, and fast roping guys on to rooftops, the stories were awesome. It was like listening to the plot of a blockbuster movie unfold. I couldn't wait for the day I could cut in and exchange a similar story around the office table. Just when the stories were getting good the PSG walked in and said, "Three laps around the flight line, let's go."

There were six of us, and we all walked outside. I was expecting to see a large formation, but everyone just started stretching on their own after leaving the office. The air was cool but I could feel the humidity and knew it was going to be a scorching hot Ft. Campbell day. The sun was still rising but we were shaded by the Alpha Company office, which was attached to a massive hangar. While stretching, the PSG looked at SPC Justin and I, and told us the things we needed to accomplish for the day. He also rambled on about what schools we needed to start getting ready for. SPC Justin was getting ready to leave for SERE School while I had to prepare for Dunker School. We finished stretching and began running next to the hangar, and finally out to the big inviting flight line.

As soon as we got to the end of the hangar the flight line opened up. The sun was barely illuminating the rows of helicopters. From lines of Chinooks to Black Hawks and Little Birds it was a sight to behold. It was the first time I had seen the 160th flight line, and all the lethal birds in the unit's arsenal. The sun was perfectly reflecting off each helicopter like an incandescent light on a Picasso. SPC Justin and I ran together while the other guys who I didn't know yet ran in their own pack. As I ran around the flight line I felt like a little kid in a candy store going down each aisle, but instead of candy I was looking at the special operations fleet. While running I envisioned myself in the Chinook right gun door, much like the same soldier who I caught a glimpse of in Afghanistan. The dream was getting close. I could taste my special operations crew chief goal on the gleaming airfield candy store. It was the closest I had ever been to the glorious helicopters. I was nervous about the schools I had to survive before I could even set foot in the Chinook, but running around the airfield gave me an extra motivational push to keep going. Getting this close to the bird in its parked state allowed me to notice several differences from the Chinook I was used to working on. The special operations model Chinook was the MH-47G, and had many modifications compared to the CH-47F I had come to know. The color was a clear indicator that it was a special operations bird. A flat black paint coated the entire fuselage with black lettering on either side that read, 'United States Army.' You wouldn't be able to see the letters unless you knew what you were looking for, and were standing right next to the massive helicopter. It had four huge cabin windows unlike the two I was used to. The reason for the extra windows was fire power, which included two M-134 mini guns at the front two doors on the left and right side, and two 240-H machine guns on the two aft windows.

I would come to find out each special operations flight required four crew chiefs versus the minimal two I was used to. The aerial refueling probe extended beyond the nose of the bird and was much bigger in person. It was used for refueling in midair and only utilized by the special operations Chinook. A FLIR (Forward Looking Infrared) camera was mounted underneath the cockpit for visual aid when navigating obstacles or targets. As I was looking over the new helicopter while running I had to remember to keep closing my mouth. I was in total awe. I imagine the look on my face was the same as someone seeing snow for the first time.

I finished my third lap around the vast flight line with SPC Justin, who was running next to me the whole time. We simultaneously slowed to a jog and then eventually a walk. On the walk back to the office we began to talk to each other. Talking with him he gave me some insight as to who to stay clear of and what not to do as the FNG. He specifically told me to keep as far away as I could from the office. I kind of knew what he was talking about just based on my brief encounters in the crew office. He also told me to stay away from SSG Atch. I was unsure who he was talking about until he started describing him. It was the same meat head of a beast that made me stand on my head a day ago. SPC Justin made it clear that rank didn't mean you were in charge. He gave me an example and explained that a SPC who was lower ranking than a SGT could have the final say, if the SPC had more flight experience. Specialists telling Sergeants what to do was a new concept for me but I grasped it quickly. Surprisingly it made a lot of sense, and if my old unit used the same mentality, we might have been more efficient.

We meandered our way back to the crew office. The sun was continuing to rise and it was getting hotter. We walked in the front entrance, down the hallway and into the office. All of the senior guys were half naked and the office turned into a locker room at the blink of an eye. They were carrying on a conversation that must have originated on the flight line. The discussion wouldn't be any easier to understand if they were speaking a different language. I thought I had heard all the Army acronyms by now, but their conversation took on a new level. I was well versed in maintenance but being in a flight company was like starting from scratch. I tried to listen in and understand the ongoing discussion among the senior crew chiefs. I was like Bob Ross wanting to paint a happy little deployment on the blank canvas. If only I had a 160th deployment under my belt I would know what they were talking about. I could easily gauge they were talking about a recent rotation in Afghanistan. They discussed taking on enemy fire during a mission, but beyond that I was lost. I was hoping to catch a break and retreat to one of the nice office chairs after the run but I knew it would be a bad idea. I didn't know what happened after PT since this was all new to me. SPC Justin and I must have looked like lost puppies, which made for an easy target.

One of the senior guys looked at me and said, "Hey what the fuck are you doing?"

With the helicopter manual in hand I looked at him dumbfounded and stumbled for words, "Nothing sergeant," not knowing whether or not he actually was a sergeant. With everyone still dressed in casual gym clothes or half naked it was virtually impossible to decipher who carried what rank.

Standing in the middle of the office half-dressed and still sweating, he asked me, "Do you know how to get the statuses of the aircraft?"

Somewhat familiar with aircraft statuses and operating the log book or lap top, I said, "Roger." The log book was a way to keep track of upcoming maintenance required on the helicopter, or to record any problems pilots and crew experienced while in flight. Each helicopter was assigned its own log book.

"There are the status sheets, get to work," he said pointing to a stack of papers on the conference table.

The statuses of every Alpha Company aircraft on the flight line had to be written down and provided to the PSG before the morning meeting. SPC Justin and I went to the first computer and logged on. This was when I first found out how little SPC Justin really knew about anything aircraft related. As I was writing down upcoming maintenance items he started asking questions. Knowing full well that we were both the new guys and we needed to help each other out, I didn't hesitate. I was trying to get the hang of the new status sheets, and no one informed me they needed to be ready by 0830.

"Are you almost done?" I heard from the same guy who had ordered me to get the statuses done in the first place.

Again, I fumbled for my words. I should have known they had to be done in a hurry. "Negative," I replied expecting the worst consequences.

"You better hurry," he said.

I couldn't answer any more of SPC Justin's questions, since I had to get a move on. Everyone was in their uniform for the day as I turned and glanced around the conference table. They were seated and waiting for the top dog to enter the room. I saw the clock and knew I was screwed. The PSG walked in and looked to the head of the conference table expecting to see a stack of status sheets.

"Where are the statuses?" He asked in a disappointed tone.

"Burnett what the fuck?" Said another senior guy whom I had scarcely heard speak.

"Almost done Sergeant," I replied.

"Burnett start doing push-ups," my frustrated new PSG ordered. SPC Justin dropped down next to me and started doing push-ups as well. The PSG ordered someone else to finish writing down the statuses that I couldn't complete in time. SPC Justin and I remained in the push-up position during the entire meeting. The morning meetings were to brief the crew members on what aircraft were flying that day, who was flying, and what was going on down range. The first meeting I took part in amidst my push-ups, I found out that the guys in the company who were down range had just taken enemy fire. The fire fight had completely disabled one of our aircraft. A new concept to me, but I knew the company was always deployed, and continually rotated out soldiers to complete the intense missions in Afghanistan or other foreign lands. Unlike my old unit where the whole unit deployed for a year, 160th deployed smaller groups of guys for 30 to 180 days at a time, depending on how new you were and how important you were to the mission's success. Whether deployed or on a TDY (Temporary Duty) assignment, there were only a handful of guys stateside throughout the year.

SFC (Sergeant First Class) Jayson, who was the PSG, concluded the meeting by informing us that the Alpha Company soldiers on the late night mission were all okay, and no one was hurt. "Get up Burnett," SFC Jayson said.

SPC Justin and I must have been in the push-up position for 15 minutes. After the meeting, SPC Justin was instructed by SFC Jayson to take me to a warehouse to locate and secure my newly assigned storage cage.

The company had several Polaris Razors used to transport gear to and from the aircraft on the flight line, or accomplish certain tasks around the compound. SPC Justin and I headed outside and were greeted by the scorching sun. We hopped in the Polaris and headed to a part of the compound I had never been before. About a mile away from the office we pulled up to a huge warehouse that was solely assigned to the companies in our battalion.

SPC Justin punched in a code and the secure door swung open. Inside we were met by the cool shade and a stale dusty smell. The two story warehouse was huge and lined with rows of cage looking storage compartments. The cool, concrete smelling air made the break away from the office joyous. The first floor of the warehouse was delineated for bigger aircraft components only used for certain operations, from winter equipment to over water gear. I followed SPC Justin down the wide, cage-lined center of the warehouse. We made it to the back where I continued to follow him up a single set of metal stairs that lead to the top floor. Up there, I noticed several small cages with each cage door reading a soldier's name and their company designation. Walking through the maze of cages I noticed each one was set up differently, and stored different gear depending on how each Night Stalker preferred and prepared his gear. SPC Justin began to tell me that the cages were meant for my go bags or certain sets of gear I would need to set up for different types of deployable environments. Since the unit was always on call to deploy anywhere in the world at any given time, it was important to have my gear set up and ready to go.

I had a long way to go before I could start flying, but I needed to get a locker and start setting up my go bags. Before picking out a vacant cage, SPC Justin showed me his locker and how he had it set up. He showed me all of his go bags and what type of gear he kept in each one. After going over his set up we quickly found a vacant cage and SPC Justin took a keyed lock out of his pocket and handed it to me. I locked up my cage and made a mental note that I had to get my gear ready to go and pre-positioned in my newly acquired storage unit. The warehouse was silent and acted as a nice vacation from the office, but I knew the unit was all business and I had several schools to start getting ready for. We left the warehouse and headed back to the office.

We got back to the office, and just like day one there was no one around. I imagined everyone that was there during the morning meeting was now on the flight line. Surely they were prepping aircraft or fixing mechanical issues that were addressed during the 0830 meeting. SPC Justin and I stood at the PSG's front door and informed him that I had secured a cage in the warehouse. After the brief interaction, he handed me a sheet of paper and told me to get my initial flight gear issue on my way home.

After a quick drive I ended up at another large building on the compound specifically for specialized 160th flight gear. Inside the giant building I passed the sheet of paper to an older man sitting behind the DMV like window. Without saying a word, I watched him sit up and grab one of the shopping carts stored neatly behind him. He went down several different aisles as he glanced at the sheet then grabbed items from the endless shelves. Item after item, and row after row, I continued to watch him fill up two shopping carts. After an hour, the man hoisted four large, green canvas kit bags on top of the window counter. I felt like Batman getting new gadgets for my bat suit. I was excited and I couldn't wait to sift through my new special operations treasure.

In my barracks room, while sorting through my new flight gear I thought back to my first deployment in Afghanistan and what I had gone through so far. I assembled my new flight vest and attached certain pouches to the vest trying to figure out the best set up for me. The placement of my magazine pouches was essential, since flawless mag changes could mean life or death in a firefight.

I was told to bring my kit in to the office the following morning so a more senior crew chief could inspect it. After I had all my pouches and first aid kit set up on my flight vest it was time to put in the SAPI (Small Arms Protective Inserts) plates. The two Kevlar plates tucked inside a Velcro pocket in the front and back of the vest. I was exhausted after setting up my kit and just left the remaining gear strewn on my bedroom floor, then headed to bed.

I arrived at work the next morning and the office was quiet and awkward. There were no stories from deployments being exchanged across the glorious conference table. No one was yelling at me or the other new guy. Dunker School was the next big hurdle to complete and the stillness of the room gave me a minute to reflect. I had no clue what demanding situations I would have to face at the aquatics center.

While I was standing in the office dreaming about how close yet far away

I was from my dream, a tall black man walked in the door. The unfamiliar guy was decked out in all black Under Armour gear. He paused in the office as soon as he saw me, looking me up and down staying as silent as the room. Standing in front of my desk, he walked toward me as if I weren't even there and I quickly moved out of the way. He got to the desk and unslung his Under Armour duffle bag, still not saying a word.

Looking at me, he stuck out his hand, and in what I thought to be a thick Jamaican accent he said, "I'm Kareem, nice to meet you."

Unsure if this was another plot to mess with the new guy I stuck out my hand and said, "I'm David nice to meet you." Not only was this the first real type of general respect I received as the new guy, but he introduced himself by his first name and not his rank followed by his last name. Through the following years of my special operations journey I would look up to SSG Kareem as a teacher, mentor, and friend. I would soon learn he treated me and others the way he wanted to be treated. Sure the occasional smokings would ensue through my growth as a special operations crew chief, but the respect was always mutual. Throughout the rest of my journey, SSG Kareem would refer to me as rookie or Padawan.

Each crew chief was assigned to a specific aircraft, and each aircraft was assigned to a flight engineer. The FE (Flight Engineer) was responsible for the crew, pilots, maintenance, and overall safety of the aircraft. The FE had full authority of the crew chiefs and any mechanical issues that may arise. I learned that the position on the aircraft the FE maintained was right gun, the position of the guy I anxiously waved to in Afghanistan just a year ago. SSG Kareem was the FE of our bird, and who knows, may even have been the guy I was excitingly waving to. He had the most responsibility on the bird and by our brief interaction in the office I knew I would be in good hands. After our cordial handshake he went on to tell me what he expected from me, and how his crew and his bird will always be maintained above the standard. I found out that his accent was not Jamaican but Trinidadian. He assured me he would take care of me and so long as I was in the right, he would always have my back. This depth of mentoring was new to me and almost felt foreign. I was glad that through the chain of command my newest boss was nothing like my last. Men trickled into the office for morning PT and SSG Kareem greeted each with equal respect. SSG Kareem's presence seemed to halt any FNG hazing, which was awesome. But knowing how much I had yet to prove before commanding any real respect was constantly lodged in the front of my mind. SSG Kareem had asked what my schedule looked like as far as schools. I brought him up to speed and told him that I would start Dunker school on Monday after the weekend.

Without hesitation he said, "We need to get you out of here so you can get ready for school."

That was the first time I felt like someone was on my side, and truly had my back. He made sure I had the packing list, which I did. He also gave me his own brief about the school and what to expect. Just a two-day school, I knew I would see him later in the week after completion. Without even checking with the PSG, which was common in my old unit, he told me to leave.

Before I could get out of the office door he muttered, "Don't fail rookie or you're done." I wasn't going to let him down nor my new company. If all the guys who came before me got through the school, I knew I could too.

CHAPTER 5
DUNKER SCHOOL

onday dawned and I felt rested after the weekend. Grabbing the gear that I laid out over the weekend, I headed out the door. A light fog was hovering over the wet grass just outside the building. With my new aviation kit bag slung over my shoulder I got into my truck and headed toward the compound. I flashed my badge at the guard shack and took an immediate right. A long paved driveway led me to a huge facility that was more secluded than the other buildings on the compound. I arrived 15 minutes early and noticed a few guys in gym clothes smoking outside. Much like day zero of Green Platoon, that reticence of the unknown came right back to me. I knew I just had to get this done. I grabbed my kit bag and walked through the glass double door entrance. In the facility I was cordially greeted by a man in khakis and a black polo shirt. His immediate friendliness quickly suggested that he was a civilian. He handed me a packet of papers and instructed me to put my gear in a locker, pointing to a door down the hallway behind him. The distinct pool smell hit me when I entered the locker room. I dropped my gear next to a few other bags laying on the floor, then left for the classroom. In it there were five tables with two chairs behind each. A giant image was projected on the screen at the front of the class, showing an MH-47G Chinook conducting an over water training exercise. Above the image read, 'Welcome to Dunker School.'

The three others who were smoking outside trickled into the room as

I kept quiet. After a few more stragglers made their way in, the instructor walked to the front of the class and said, "Gentlemen, welcome to Dunker School." He gave a quick introduction about himself and how long he had been working at the facility. "Before we start we will take a quick tour of the facility and then get to work in the classroom," he finished.

I followed the instructor and class down the hallway. Passing the lockers, we made it to the end and entered through a single doorway. We were standing on the side of a giant pool, and I couldn't believe my eyes. The pool was split in half delineating the shallow end from the deep end. I could see the shallow end clearly through the water and a quick 90 degree drop off that went straight down into the deep. It was almost like a giant shelf. It wasn't just any nine-foot-deep end at your local neighborhood pool, this pool was extraordinarily deep for the purpose it served. It had to be at least twenty feet deep at the far half of the pool. On the opposite side of the pool were two giant black airframes attached to a large hydraulic crane. One of the airframes looked like a modified Chinook. The other was easily recognizable as a Little Bird.

As I was looking around the vast space I noticed four giant industrial fans secured to the ceiling. Also mounted to the ceiling were a maze of hoses with various sprinkler heads sporadically placed around the fans. I was trying to pay attention to our tour guide, but the facility was something only Hollywood could dream up.

I took my eyes off the elaborate ceiling and stared back down at the pool. In the corner of the pool was a huge 5-foot diameter rubber ball floating in the still water. A long cord attached to the ball ran to the floor of the pool. Unsure of what the ball was I focused my attention back to the teacher, as he was still speaking about the facility. Right then he motioned over to the ball and said, "This ball has the capability to produce four foot waves in the pool, and when your final test comes, it will be turned up to the max."

I left the ball and my eyes followed an intricate scaffolding structure with stairs leading up to the ceiling. I continued to look up at the two-story stair case. The stairs led to a black metal platform. Edging off the platform were two breaks in the railings, and at each break were two hoists. The hoists looked similar to the ones attached above the Chinook's right gun door. I was still in amazement and the instructors voice turned into a muted Charlie Brown like cartoon.

After the quick tour of the aquatics center we headed back into the classroom and the teacher began outlining the requirements to complete the course. First, everyone in the class had to pass a swim test before we could even begin the real Dunker training. The swim test included an underwater 50-meter swim in full uniform, including flight vest, boots, and helmet. The instructor continued, "If you surface for air during the underwater swim you will have one more chance to complete the test. If you can't complete the test on the second attempt, you will be sent home."

No, I wouldn't just be sent home; I would be kicked out of flight company. I was hungry to pass Dunker School, and I was determined to become a crew chief. The instructor continued with the testing requirements. We had to tread water for two minutes immediately following the underwater swim. An instructor would time the two-minute tread and tap the student on the helmet to indicate time to then execute a dead man's float for another two minutes. Following the dead man's float was a 50-meter breast stroke starting and finishing in the deep end. After the breast stroke, the last task of the swim test was to manually inflate an LPF (Life Preserving Flotation) using the blow tubes.

The teacher continued on about what would follow if we passed the swim test. Upon completing the test, we would then have more in class work, followed by training in the SWET (Shallow Water Egress Training) chair. The SWET chair was a tubular cage design with a replica helicopter seat mounted in the center. On each edge of the tubular cage were four floating buoys. We were going to be well trained in egressing from the chair on our own breath.

After passing the SWET chair training it was on to the METS (Modular Egress Training Simulator) trainer. The METS was the giant Chinook I saw earlier on the side of the pool.

The teacher finished off the overall guidance of the class with a video of a smaller version of the Chinook, the CH-46 Sea Knight. The video depicted a crash landing on the edge of a Naval vessel with the helicopter and crew finally plummeting into the ocean. As much fun as I thought the class was going to be, seeing that video made me realize how serious the concept of over water training was. The teacher told us to change into our uniforms so we could get ready for the swim test. He motioned over to the door and said, "See you in the pool."

The handful of crew chiefs in the class walked out of the classroom, down the hall, and into the locker room. No one was talking to each other.

I think as we were changing everyone knew what was about to take place, myself included. I knew everyone was just a little bit nervous about passing the swim test. We all knew the consequences of failure and were justified in our anxiousness.

I recalled the last thing SSG Kareem told me, and knew I couldn't go back and tell him or any of the guys in my company that I failed Dunker School. Another civilian instructor popped his head into the locker room, "Let's go," his order echoed in the tile floored locker room.

We started moving faster as if we had been moving slowly to delay what we were about to face. When we entered the pool area, a voice yelled across from the deck, "Grab an LPF and flight helmet and jump in the pool."

Behind all of us was a door. One of the guys opened it to reveal a big collection of hanging LPF's, flight vests, and helmets in different sizes. Some of the equipment was still dripping water from what was likely a class that took place a few days before us. We grabbed the right size gear and jumped into the first half of the pool. I put on my flight vest, LPF, and helmet while standing in the four-foot shallow end. A few instructors were already swimming in the deep end with fins and snorkel masks. A few more were on the edge of the pool about to get in. An instructor shouted over to us again, "Swim over here. Hurry up."

We all left the comfort of the shallow end and stepped off the ledge and headed to the deep end of the pool. The combination of the water and the uniform with combat boots really weighed me down. Swimming the short distance from one end to the other, I quickly realized the test was going to be more demanding than I thought. Once to the deep end we were told to get out and line up at the edge of the pool. My heart started to beat rapidly because I knew the test that would make or break my crew chief career was about to go down. Another instructor lined up next to the rest of the class and me. He demonstrated how we were supposed to jump into the water to begin our under water portion of the test. Everyone got the gist after watching the demonstration. The instructors in the pool were lined up to what looked like unmarked swim lanes. The instructor to student ratio was 1:1, I surmised this was to prevent anyone from drowning. The instructor in my sector pointed to me and said, "Are you ready?"

I gave him a nod. I heard my classmates plunging into the water to the left and right of me. I took my right hand and wrapped it around my body to grab my left shoulder. I took my left hand and put it on the top of the flight helmet I was wearing. I looked down into the water and shouted, "Deep water entry, entering the pool." Before jumping in I saw a few more guys make the plunge.

I stepped off the three-foot-high ledge and sunk into the menacing water. My helmet immediately floated my whole body right back to the surface. Knowing I wasn't allowed to surface and take a breath, I made sure to get as close to the wall as I could. I kicked off the wall and began swimming, knowing I needed to get to the other end on a single breath. My uniform was weighing me down and my helmet was fighting me the whole way. I became flustered and I was worried I didn't have enough air in my lungs to make it to the other side. I opened my eyes under the water to see how close I was. The wall I had to touch was so far away and I could barely make it out through my cloudy vision. I felt my breath slowly depleting. I wanted to surface for a quick gulp of air but I knew I just had to keep going. Even if it meant passing out, I was hell-bent to touch the wall in one breath. I was almost there but I was out of air. I kicked and kicked, swimming frantically with nothing left in my lungs. I swam hard reaching my fingertips as far out in front of me as I could stretch. I felt the tips of my fingers hit the concrete wall and burst through the surface like a breaching orca. The only difference was, unlike the graceful orca, I was coughing and gasping for air. But I finished.

The instructor who was monitoring my swim instructed, "Swim back to the deep end now." While swimming back I noticed two other guys surfacing from their underwater lap before they reached the wall. I felt a sense of accomplishment knowing that not everyone managed to complete the demanding underwater swim.

I made it to the deep end. I wanted to pause and catch my breath. I went to grab the side of the pool, and right before my hand could hit the concrete ledge the instructor swatted my arm away. "Are you giving up?" he said.

I didn't reply I just shook my head.

He yelled back to me, "Tread water, two minutes, ready go."

Even though I had already been treading water he started the time when he felt was right. Fucking dick. I heard another instructor behind me shout the same thing my instructor just yelled. As I was treading I was reflecting back on how easy I thought the test was going to be and now realizing how hard it actually was. I must have been thinking for a while, because the instructor tapped me on my head and yelled, "Dead man's float, two minutes, ready go."

With what breath I had left I took one gasp and went face down in the water. I floated in the turbulent waters coming up every so often to catch my breath. After gasping for more air I went face down back in the water. While floating there I tried to stay at the top of the water but with little body fat my helmet was the only thing keeping me at the surface, only making the task more difficult. The instructor tapped me on the helmet, I surfaced and took a breath and found myself treading water again. The instructor looked at me and said, "LPF failure ready go."

Exhausted and both physically and mentally drained, I managed to pull the tabs on either side of my LPF, knowing full well they weren't going to inflate. I unbuttoned the inflation tubes on either side and tried to blow air into the LPF. I knew as soon as I blew just enough air into the life saver I could stop treading water. I was trying to blow in the tubes but the LPF wasn't inflating. The deflated device around my neck was pissing me off. In my fatigue, I'd made a critical mistake. While I was treading water and losing motivation, strength, and my breath, the instructor said, "What's wrong?"

Struggling to stay above the water, I looked at him and said, "My LPF won't inflate."

He responded in the same casual tone, "Think about why the LPF won't inflate."

Continuing to tread water, it hit me and I started unscrewing the tip on one of the inflation tubes. I started to blow into the tube and the LPF began to inflate. As it began inflating I slowly started treading less water and began to let the flotation device hold me above the surface. I finally inflated it enough and the instructor tapped me on the helmet and said, "Good job. Head to the shallow end." I was the last guy left to complete the test and all the other guys in the class were already standing on the shallow ledge waiting for me to finish.

"If you passed the test go change and head to the classroom. If you failed, go change, get your stuff out of the classroom, and head out," one of the instructors announced.

Exiting the pool, I wasn't sure who made it and who didn't. Back in the locker room it was easy to figure out who didn't make it. With all the guys exchanging their stories about the test, the ones who weren't saying anything and keeping to themselves were the ones whom I wouldn't be seeing anymore.

Excited and eager that we were moving on, we sat in the classroom waiting for the teacher. The teacher entered and said, "Good job gents, you got the easy part out of the way." I immediately thought to myself, what was easy about that and how hard was the craziness to follow? The classroom went on with a death by power point presentation going over critical things I would have never thought about when performing over water operations in the helicopter. From air embolisms to open water survival at sea, the instructor covered it all. The class wrapped up before lunch time. We were advised to eat something light because after lunch we were going to head out to the pool again for training in the SWET chair.

The short break concluded and it was back to work. We heard the instructor, "You know the drill. Head out to the pool in your PT uniform."

Once back at the pool, instructors were already standing in the shallow end with two caged floating SWET chairs. This portion of the training was critical and was going to prepare us for what lie ahead. The class was split in half and each half went to one of the chairs to meet with an instructor.

After a quick instruction from the teacher, he said, "Who is going first?"

The three students and I looked at each other not saying anything.

I reluctantly said, "I'll go."

With the instructor holding the floating seat on one side and a student holding the backside, they tipped it over. I swam under one of the bars and hopped on the seat. The floating chair sunk into the water and the training device felt more unstable than I imagined. I finally untangled the seat belt and got strapped in. I was facing the instructor now and he said, "Are you ready?"

Again I reluctantly nodded and he told me to get in the bracing position. I crossed my arms over each other and grabbed my left and right seat belt straps. Before I could even get ready I heard the words come out of the instructor's mouth, "Ditching, ditching, ditching."

The student and instructor flipped the caged seat over in the water and suddenly I was completely upside down. While strapped in and upside down I felt the pool water rush through my nose. During the classroom portion we were taught to keep our heads pinned back to the seat so we could prevent water rushing up our noses. I leaned my head back and immediately, although uncomfortable, the water stopped rushing through my nostrils. On one side of the cage they had fastened a mock up plastic door that was easily removed by pushing on it. Discombobulated, I pushed the door off the cage and began fumbling to detach my seat belt. I unhooked the buckle and just as fast as the rollover started it was over. I exhaled to the surface and caught my breath while coughing. I finished the first of many SWET chair roll overs.

We continued to cycle through the class until everyone had flipped three times. And just like that, we were done.

While everyone was getting out of the pool the METS and I were having a stare down. I was nervous about the last day, but once again my only option was passing. I snapped out of it and waded to the ladder at the edge of the pool. I followed all the guys back into the locker room. We finished up the day with some more classroom training and a brief on what to expect the following day. We were released at 1800 and I was spent.

At 0540 the final morning I arrived at the Allison Aquatics Center. We were instructed to be in the pool, in full uniform, and ready to go no later than 0600. I was nervous and eager to get the day over with. A few guys were in the locker room and I assumed everyone else was already in the pool. I put my gear away and went out to the pool area. Just like we had left it the day prior, there were two SWET chairs in the shallow end accompanied by a handful of instructors. The only thing that was different, was the giant Chinook METS trainer was half submerged in the deep end of the pool. The hydraulic crane arm clutched and suspended the large model aircraft. Five instructors began to pop up from around the submerged beast all wearing scuba gear.

It was the last day of the course and the final test was surely going to challenge me in every way possible. I headed to the drying room at the front edge of the pool, grabbed a helmet, vest, and LPF, then jumped in the shallow end. While the class and I waded in the water, we were told what the morning was going to look like. The day prior we learned how to egress from the flipped trainer on our own oxygen, but today we were going to learn something new. The instructor briefed us that we would learn how to egress from the SWET chair using the HEED (Helicopter Emergency Egress Device) bottle. It was just one more thing we had to remember while being upside down under water.

The demanding course started with more roll overs in the SWET chair. After a few hours in the shallow end being flipped over in the chair numerous times, the class was confident. Having the ability to use the compressed oxygen bottle under water made the ditching procedure less terrifying. Finally, it was on to the moment everyone was anxiously awaiting. The replicated front half of the Chinook, referred to as the METS trainer was huge. It had a full blown cockpit with two pilot seats. The back half of the trainer had two crew member seats that were attached side by side with three feet of space separating them. The floor of the trainer was made out of a metal grate. Once submerged the floor allowed the METS to sink and eventually roll over. The METS was half way submerged and we swam out to it after completing the training in the shallow end. We made it to the back entrance of the trainer and stood up inside to get acquainted with it. After a quick brief of the trainer, we were all told to swim back to the shallow end and decide between the class who was going first. Much like the first time in the SWET chair no one wanted to go first. I was glad when two other crew chiefs said they would do it.

Standing in the shallow end we watched our fellow classmates buckle into the two crew member seats. As the mechanical arm lifted the trainer slowly out of the pool we shouted out words of encouragement. The trainer was suspended five feet out of the pool and the left over water from the Chinook dripped like a wet sponge. Scuba divers were below the water getting ready to make sure none of our classmates drowned during the nerve wracking roll over scenario. The first round of the simulator had to be done on our own breath. The trainer was suspended for a minute while the instructors gave the students a few last minute pointers. Then the instructors inside the trainer called out just like they did while in the SWET chair, "Ditching, ditching, ditching."

All of a sudden the trainer dropped into the pool making a giant splash. The giant helicopter started to sink. While the helicopter was sinking in the deep end it slowly started to roll over. As the trainer became engulfed in water, bubbles rose furiously from the depths all around the Chinook. We were taught that once the violent motion stopped that was when we needed to start our egress. The last edge of the helicopter dunked under the water. I looked down below while standing on the shallow end ledge to catch a glimpse of the sinking aircraft. I monitored scuba divers swarming on either side of the trainer to monitor the progress. I looked on, anxiously waiting to see our fellow brothers emerge from the sunken Chinook. The trainer was under water for 20 seconds and no one had surfaced. Finally, I saw one of the guy's helmets pop out of the depths. Then as soon as he popped out, the second guy surfaced. They swam over to the shallow end, and not knowing what to expect we bombarded them with questions. While in the shallow end, having a friendly conversation about the task ahead, the trainer started appearing out of the water and flipping right side up. As the METS reset to get ready for the next two crew chiefs, I realized I was next. I swam over to the trainer just like the guys before me, and strapped into my seat. After buckling in I felt the trainer start to rise and my heart started thumping out of my chest. I hadn't been this nervous in a long time. I heard a thud sound and we had reached the top of the ride. I couldn't see the guys in the shallow end anymore while staring out the back. The window I needed to exit from was on my right side. To replicate a Chinook, the window had a mock gun mounted to the window frame.

The instructor looked at me in his snorkel mask and in the same tone while I was learning the ditching procedure in the SWET chair said, "Are you ready?"

I looked at him and muttered, "Yes." My instructor looked at the other instructor in the trainer and they gave each other a nod.

As soon as the silent nod finished he yelled out, "Ditching, ditching, ditching."

On the last ditching call the trainer dropped. I looked down at my feet and watched the water rush in, like a scene from Titanic. The water poured into the ankles of my boots then started filling up my pants. I felt like everything was in slow motion. The water slowly made it up to my chest and the trainer started to roll over. The water ran up to my neck and I began to panic. My heart started racing faster and I tried to control my breathing but I couldn't. I took one last deep breath and went under. I flipped under water and I felt the uncomfortable water up the nose sensation. I waited for the violent motion to stop while holding my breath. Finally, the trainer was completely submerged and we were upside down. It felt like I was holding my breath forever and now and I had to get out. Frantically, I unbuckled my seat belt and located the window next to me. Upside down and underwater everything became very disorienting. I grabbed the edge of the window and started my egress. I tried to swim out of the window but I couldn't get free. I was stuck. My flight vest was caught on the replicated mini gun. I pulled and pressed as hard as I could, trying to free myself from the sunken trainer. I was struggling to get free. I was running out of breath and I started to panic. The thought of drowning and dying inside the pool blanketed my train of thought. I felt a hand behind me trying to push me free, but nothing was happening. I felt another hand grab my wrist and put something in my hand. One of the scuba divers handed me a mouth piece so I could fill my lungs with air and calm down. Once I got a shot of air into my body, I freed myself and swam to the surface. Well that didn't work out as I had planned. To complete the course, I had to complete the METS simulation six times. Each egress in the trainer was different, but regardless I had to do it six times. One egress on my own breath, one on compressed air, and one cross cabin egress on my own breath. After the three were completed we had to do three more in the dark, with all the man made weather elements incorporated. So for me what would have been six attempts, now had to be seven, since I received help when I got stuck. No one else in the class had any issues trying to egress. One of the instructors told me they would wait for the first three daylight simulations before I could try again on my own breath. The next simulation was a cross cabin egress. Once submerged I had to exit out of the opposite window next to me. I had to wait for the other crew member next to me to egress out of his window before I could follow behind him.

I strapped in and got set. Crash! The trainer hit the water and began to roll over. I took another deep breath knowing and thinking the other guy next to me better get a move on so I could get out. Fully submerged and upside down again, I unbuckled myself and headed across the cabin and over to my training brothers exit window. I felt his boots in front of me and began swimming right behind him. Pow, while swimming up to the surface he kicked me right in the face. I surfaced and was glad I only had to do the cross cabin one more time because my face was not happy. After surfacing I yelled out to the other crew member, "You mother fucker."

"I thought that was the fuselage I kicked," he said.

"No asshole that was my face," I replied, both of us still laughing and trying to make the best of the situation.

The rest of the class finished the daytime iterations, and we started getting ready for the night portion of the simulator. All the lights in the aquatics building started to shut off, and the huge fans mounted to the ceiling turned on. The wind force from the fans was unreal. The plethora of sprinklers on the roof turned on and all of a sudden the calm pool turned into a raging death storm. The ball that had been so innocently sitting in the corner of the pool started violently moving up and down. Speakers in the building mimicked the booming of thunder. The relaxing pool was now a tsunami-like storm.

The first two guys swam over to the trainer just like they did during the day time portion, except it took them a lot longer to get there with the waves fighting their every stroke. The rest of us watched as the simulated rain pounded down on us. I felt like I was in the middle of an ocean and I had just been thrown off a crab boat in the Pacific.

The first guys surfaced after the Chinook plummeted into the water. They fought through the elements returning to the shallow end. We stood at the very edge of the shallow end holding our arms out to grab the guys swimming toward us. Once they were back to the small group we waited for the trainer to reset. Another classmate and I then headed out to the trainer. Every breath I took while swimming was rendered useless by a wave to the face. I finished the egress, much like the last few, without any hiccups. When I got to the surface to catch my breath I was rudely welcomed by a tyrant of a wave. I swam as hard as I could to the shallow end that seemed so close yet so far away. I finally made it to the shallow end after surfacing. The day went on and I regained some confidence after making up for my failed egress attempt earlier in the day. In the pitch dark I finished the next iteration on compressed air just fine too.

It was the last part of Dunker School and I knew once I completed the course I would be that much closer to becoming a crew chief. The last portion of the school consisted of a few extra steps once surfaced from the submerged trainer. With the weather still pumping at 100% we had to swim to a section of the pool directly beneath the hoist. Out of the powerful pool we would be extracted from the depths of the angry simulated seas.

I was willing to go first because I knew the sooner I got it done, the sooner I could start getting ready for the next school. With the increasing hope that one day I could fly on a Chinook, instead of egressing from a submerged practice one. I'm sure everyone else was thinking the same thing. I wanted to get it over with, but two guys swam out to the trainer before I was able to make my move. The two surfaced from the sunken helicopter and swam beneath the hoist. While treading water in the barreling waves they waited for the hoist to make it down to them. The first guy clipped the device to his vest and was quickly hauled up. The second crew chief was still beneath the hoist treading water. After recovering the first guy, the hoist finally made it down to him. I definitely didn't want to be the second guy, having to tread water while waiting to be rescued. I swam out to the reset trainer alongside another guy with whom I had been doing most of the iterations.

It was dark and for some reason the instructor wanted me to pull the tinted visor down on my helmet over my eyes, only making it darker. I could barely see and before I could run through the things I had to do, I heard the familiar words, "Ditching, ditching, ditching."

The trainer splashed in the water and just like before I egressed to the surface and started swimming to the hoist extraction area. I figured the hoist would just be there waiting for me to hook up. The hoist was nowhere in sight as I tread in the barreling waves. I looked up squinting while the rain poured into my eyes. I was treading water while the hoist slowly lowered down to me. I locked the hook into my vest and started to rise out of the treacherous water. With the faux rain beating on my face it was the most relieved I felt all day. Exhausted and battered from the pool and all the training, it was a relief to finally be done. While being hoisted it was hard to process my joyous emotions, knowing that I had completed Dunker School. After going through the course I prayed I would never have to use Dunker training in real life. My egress partner made it to the top of the 20-foot hoist and the wind shut off, followed by the rain, the waves, and the loud speaker. The water in the pool started to calm and all the lights flickered on. The building was quiet. All the instructors were out of the pool and stripping off their scuba gear.

We made our way down the metal stairs that lead up to the hoist, and as we were walking down all the instructors on the pool deck started clapping. The applause echoed through the big building. We all felt proud, but yet another small victory that so many before us had already accomplished. I headed to the locker room and took a long hot shower, got changed, and headed back into the classroom. A few of my classmate's gear was already gone just leaving vacant seats and desks. I must have been the last Dunker student in the building. I gathered my things in the classroom and headed out the door. On a table just outside the room was a single sheet of paper with my name on it. I looked down and realized it was my completion certificate for the course. I knew I had done something that some had failed at, yet I still knew that a tougher school was next. I snatched my certificate after being congratulated by a few instructors at the door. I left the building and I was greeted by a crimson Kentucky sunset. It was Tuesday, and I knew I had to report back to Alpha Company in the morning to tell SSG Kareem and the rest of my command the good news.

CHAPTER 6
SERE

I was glad to be done with Dunker School but I knew I had to start getting in a different mindset. One of the toughest Army schools was next on my journey. It was 0630 the day after I had completed the intense over water training at the Allison Aquatics Training Facility. As I drove through the main entrance on the compound I glanced over at the aquatics center knowing there was probably another class about to start the same thing I just endured. I made my way to the office and was greeted by SSG Kareem. "Did you pass rookie?" SSG Kareem asked.

Proudly I responded, "Roger."

"Good job. Now let the real fun begin," he concluded. Unaware what he was talking about I gave him a confused look. "SERE School rookie. It will make or break you, and a lot of guys before you have quit while at the school and lost their chance at becoming a crew chief in the company." He said in a boastful way, and was almost trying to scare me.

He went on to tell me that I was going to leave on Friday. Another crew member was tasked to drive me to the three-week long school located in Ft. Bragg, North Carolina. There were a few different variations of the school, some easier and not as in depth as others. The one I was about to embark on was the toughest and most demanding of the variations. SERE (Survival, Evasion, Resistance, Escape) School level C, was designed to train the most superior forces in the Army. Only those who had the highest risk of getting captured while deployed attended the school. A school created to teach interrogation techniques, advanced survival tactics, how not to get caught by the enemy, and how to escape from captivity. Sleep and hunger deprivation were also key elements to the school. When I found out I was leaving Friday for a Monday class start date, I found SGT Matt immediately. He was also a new guy, but had already been to the school. From getting the shit beaten out of you to being beyond starving, he pretty much described the school to me in the worst way possible. I was nervous and excited to get this one out of the way. The notion that a handful of almost Alpha Company guys failed out of SERE was incredibly nerve wracking.

It was Friday morning and a white shuttle van honked outside of the barracks waiting for me. With bags slung over my shoulder, much like the first day of Green Platoon, I left my barracks room behind. I opened the two back swinging doors of the government vehicle, threw my bags in, and jumped in the passenger seat. I told myself, the next time I come back I would be one more school complete on my path. The other Alpha Company crew member who was giving me a ride to the school was in the process of getting out of the Army. The command tasked him with jobs like taking new guys to schools and other random shit around the office. He was nice and gave me a few motivational pointers about the school. He told me to remember that although the school was hard, people have done it and passed before. We drove through the night and neither of us said much. I ran through different scenarios in my head of how difficult the school was going to be while staring out the window. The cross country road trip was over and we arrived at an on post lodge early Saturday morning. I stayed in my room and kept to myself occasionally walking around the exterior of the mundane military lodge.

Monday morning came quicker than I wanted and I didn't get much sleep the night before. My gear was packed and ready to go. I exited the lobby and met the same van at the front of the hotel. I loaded my gear and we headed to a different part of the base where I was supposed to report. After a short five-minute drive through Ft. Bragg we entered through a gate with a wooden welcome sign that read, 'John F. Kennedy Special Warfare Center and School (SWCS).' Past the sign was a large gravel parking lot full of soldiers emptying their gear onto the rocks. Several instructors were sifting through the piles of gear. I grabbed my bags and ran over to the formation.

As I ran past the driver side door of the government van, the guy who drove me said, "Hey Burnett." I skidded on the rocks to a halt and looked at him. He continued, "Good luck. I'll see you in three weeks."

I nodded and ran over to the formation. One of the instructors who was yelling out different items on the packing list was huge, and on the left shoulder of his uniform he had a Special Forces tab, a Ranger tab, and an Airborne tab. The tabs or Velcro patches were identifiers that indicated accomplishments and affiliations. The Special Forces tab meant this guy didn't fuck around and went through a year plus training program to achieve the tab. The instructor was a Special Forces Green Beret. The Ranger tab meant he successfully completed one of the hardest schools the Army had to offer. The Airborne tab meant he was airborne qualified and had been to jump school. I quickly came to find out that the SERE course and the entire compound that the training would take place is where all Green Beret or Special Forces candidates came to try and complete the requirements to join the Special Forces ranks. All of the guys in the formation emptying their gear were Special Forces candidates in the next phase of their training. Looking around I noticed I was the only guy from 160th in the entire class. While dumping out my gear and watching huge Green Beret instructors walking around going through everyone's stuff, I looked around to get an idea of the new compound I would call home for the next three weeks. There were several structures just past the gravel parking lot. Rows of five tents were directly behind me. At the end of the row of large tents was a solid building about the size of a double wide trailer, and just next to that, a metal constructed men's locker room and bathroom. Across from the bathrooms and over the paved road was a bigger building now just about 100 meters at my eleven-o-clock from where I was standing. It was a chow hall, and next to that, several other smaller mobile trailers, about five in a line. The small trailer buildings were directly in front of me just past the end of the gravel patch of a parking lot.

The instructor called out the last piece of gear on the packing list, "Bungee cords." I sifted through my items littered on the gravel surface and found the plastic tube of bungee cords I purchased from Walmart a few days ago. I lifted up my variety pack of cords, all different colors and sizes. While holding up the roll back priced variety pack, I looked around and noticed everyone else was holding up six green, what appeared to be Army issued bungees. The group focused their attention on my color coordinated Walmart bundle and everyone began to laugh.

The instructor finally made his way over to me and said, "What the fuck is this?"

Not knowing the Special Forces instructor, I replied, "Bungee cords

Sergeant."

He eyed my left shoulder to catch a glimpse of my 160th unit patch. "Well that explains it." I had never been issued bungee cords in my entire Army career, but I got the hint that the SF (Special Forces) candidates had a special set they used throughout their training.

He continued down the line inspecting the rest of the formation. I looked around and saw all the SF candidates shaking their heads at me as I started to put my gear away. The instructors finished and followed with instructions for everyone to secure a cot in the tents directly behind us. I gathered up my jumbled gear on the rocks at my feet and shoved it in my bags. I hadn't worked with or been taught by Green Berets before. If it were anything like Green Platoon, I knew that there was no time to waste and I made a gallant effort to move with a sense of urgency. I followed behind a few of the other soldiers that were just in the formation and made my way into the closest tent. I found a cot toward the back of the tent, threw my stuff down, and headed back out to the gravel parking lot. The rest of the guys started to trickle out of the tents to join the formation.

The instructor began to give a brief, mainly to the SF candidates. He went on about how far they had come and this part of training was just one more box to check on their long road to becoming Green Berets. Although I was on a different path, it was similar to the brief I was given by SSG Kareem and a few other guys back at Alpha Company. I looked around the formation during the speech, trying to validate that I was the only one wearing a 160th unit patch. Sure enough I was. I must have stuck out like a sore thumb. Although, I didn't let being the minority of the group hinder my determination to completing the course.

After the basic guidelines to follow while going through the course were complete, we were instructed to head up to a building just past the chow hall. Once we were released, everyone began running up the paved road to a building that I wasn't able to see from the parking lot. I picked up pretty quickly that these Green Beret candidates adhered to the same, 'No Walking,' rule that I became familiar with in Green Platoon. Through the door of the massive building was an auditorium set up with a giant projector screen at the front. We filed in through the stadium style seats and sat down. There wasn't much delay and the brief began quickly with several different teachers speaking. One by one they explained the different portions of the course. From civilians, to military personnel dressed in civilian clothes, and retired SF guys, there was quite the spectrum of cadre. What I gathered in the hour long brief was that the school was tough but doable, and many had gone through it before us. The outline looked something like this; the first week was dedicated to RTL (Resistance Training Labs) where we would learn interrogation techniques. Those lessons would be put to the test in the final week. Week two was going to take place in the back woods of North Carolina where we would learn advanced survival skills. From wilderness situations to surviving in an urban scenario while behind enemy lines, it was going to be covered. The final week was sure to put us to the ultimate test, and we had to use our newly acquired skills to accomplish the task. Week three, my five-man team would find ourselves in the middle of nowhere to simulate a downed aircraft scenario. We would then have to navigate through the wilderness, all the while being chased and tracked by an opposing enemy force trying to capture and kill us.

The brief in the auditorium concluded and we all headed to the chow hall. I found a seat after being served some bland Army food. While I took it for granted, I would soon miss the very food I was about to eat. A few SF candidates sat down next to me and as the minority, I began getting hit with a number of questions. Every question asked was sincere and more so about my job in 160th as a crew chief. I could only relay so much information without having earned the title yet. We wrapped up and headed to the tents to conclude the day. I spent the night interacting with a few other guys around my cot, and learned a lot about the SF selection process. Everyone was exchanging stories about the school we were about to take part in and what they had heard.

The next day would start in one of the mobile trailers shortly following breakfast. Unlike any other military school, the dress code for week one was business casual. I'm sure there was some hidden meaning behind the attire. Breakfast took place in the chow hall and the SERE class was split up and assigned to different mobile trailers. I entered the muggy trailer behind a few of my new classmates. At the front of the room was a tall blonde woman dressed in business attire. The room was long and narrow with just four seats and two tables per row. Above what I assumed to be our teacher at the front of the room was a TV. To the left of the room was a door, and the entire mobile trailer was dimly lit with fluorescent office lights above. The instructor introduced herself as Sergeant First Class something. She went on to tell us that she was going to be teaching us interrogation techniques for the next week.

The day went on with a lot of discussion on interrogation techniques and how to avoid questions if captured. She went on to tell us about the soldiers who had been to the same school and had to use what they learned in real world scenarios. One of the most notable was a 160th Black Hawk pilot, who you may know from his book, or even movie, Black Hawk Down. Although excited for the next day, I wasn't looking forward to having to put my new skills to the test. While in class, the instructor revealed what was behind the side door in the trailer classroom. It was an interrogation room and the TV at the front of the class was for us to monitor the interrogation taking place. The next day started just like the last, except the classroom experience was about to be intensified by a thousand. The instructor had a strong perfume on that morning and it covered the smell of old furniture and dingy carpet. The distracting perfume was all part of the training. It was amazing to learn what smells the mind associated with memories, and that was one way the enemy could get into our heads. She called on an SF candidate in front of me, and told him to go into the interrogation room. She closed the door behind him and left the classroom. Seconds later a big dude in a black T-shirt and a ski mask rushed in the room and swung the interrogation door open with a purpose. As the interrogation door slammed shut everyone in the room shifted their eyes to the TV at the front of the room. We looked on eagerly to monitor what was happening inside the interrogation cell. The mysterious man yanked the candidate from his chair ███████████████

██

███

███████ The entire team of instructors must have done their homework prior to the class beginning. One by one everyone had their turn in the room. The scenario was constantly changing and we were constantly learning more from each interrogation. ███████████████████████████████████
██████████████████████████████████████ While being questioned, I was able to use a psychological distraction technique we had all learned, and the punishment finally ceased. Much of the week went on like this only to prepare and teach us. Everything we learned in the classroom would come into play during week three, and we were told it wasn't going to be as easy.

Week two started just like any other except it was time to get back in uniform and head out into the woods. We all woke up at 0330 and began the five-mile ruck march to Little Muddy. A five-mile ruck was a cakewalk to everyone in the course. We all met outside on the same gravel lot we started out on just a week ago and we rolled out. I was seeing a new side of the training compound I had never seen before. You could sum it up as a field trip on steroids. We stepped off and began the trek to the mysterious training site. The sun was starting to come out now and we were a mile or two into the ruck march. The humid air was present from the beginning. I could feel the cold sweat from my cap trickle down the back of my ears. My pits were pouring like water faucets and the sun hadn't even fully started peeking through the tall canopy of pines. The trees lined the hardball road we were marching on. There were soldiers in line one after the other on either side of the road, each about 3-5 meters apart from one another. I looked ahead to see the road curving and the two lines of sweat soaked SERE School classmates. There was a dense fog rising from the black road and it looked like a scene in a movie. All you had during a ruck march was your mind and your thoughts. I thought about home, the sweat on my back, and how wet my T-shirt was getting. I wondered what was going to happen in the weeks to follow. A few more winding turns and we reached our destination. As I walked up to where everyone was congregating and dropping their packs, I noticed a large hangar looking building. We were all drinking water and waiting for someone to appear to tell us what to do next.

The sound of a metal door swinging open echoed through the calm quiet forest and a short plump bearded man appeared and said, "Get in here."

The entire class headed into the hangar structure leaving our bags behind. As we entered the structure I noticed a large set of stadium style seats lining the back of the metal building. Three other instructors stood at the front of the room, all wearing black shirts and sporting infamous operator beards. One of the walls of the interior was lined with several terrariums holding snakes, spiders, and several other critters. The rest of the walls were lined with educational survival posters including edible plants, poisonous plants, animal trap diagrams, and all kinds of different shelter building diagrams. The instructors laid out the ground rules and the essential tasks needed to pass during the week in order to move on. The list was long and sounded like something Jason Bourne had to endure.

Lock picking, hot wiring cars, fire starting techniques, raft building, river crossings, snare construction, shelter building, and food survival were just some of the things we were going to cover during the week. The brief concluded, and the instructor let us know that everything we would learn was going to be put to the test in the final week. The E and E or escape and evasion scenarios that everyone was starting to get excited about were getting closer. The entire class piled out of the classroom and we were told to meet an instructor in the wooded pines. After we navigated to another instructor waiting for us in the middle of the forest, the class was split up into two groups. Each group was assigned to one instructor and as we walked through the forest we stopped at several different shelters. Each shelter showed a different example of construction. From lean-to's, A-frames, and hammocks, the shelter tour was fascinating. The shelter class lasted into the evening, and after an MRE break we were told to scout out a location and each individual had an hour to build their own shelter. We would call these shelters home for the next few days. After building our shelters, the instructors walked around to each one giving us pointers on our newly built digs. Constructing my lean-to was enjoyable and I took pride in expanding my wilderness survival knowledge base.

The next topic leading into the night was snare traps. We learned how to make all kinds of traps to hunt and kill our own food. The instructors stressed that we would need to be able to find, kill, and eat any kind of protein we could get our hands on during the survival scenario.

Over the next days we learned how to kill and skin rabbits and chickens. I found this portion of the class very interesting and I gained a higher appreciation for the animal I was consuming. The final day of the class I woke up in my lean-to shelter and took a deep breath. The pungent smell of the small lake in the distance was strong. However, it wasn't nearly as strong as the shit pond I remembered so fondly in Bagram. The air smelled like an expired fish at the local market. Everyone woke up at the same time and the sun was once again barely cresting the tree tops. We were only instructed to bring two MRE's for the trip. So on a three-day trip I think it was safe to say we had started conditioning our minds and bodies for the effects of food deprivation. The whole class was instructed to head down to the lake where we learned how to make homemade lures and fishing traps. Everyone got creative with bobber inventions from left over MRE trash, little twigs, and used dip cans. It was important to learn in a survival situation that everything became valuable.

While we were testing our new fishing devices on the shore of the foggy lake, the instructor called us to an opening. He began digging on the shore line in the muddy water pulling out handfuls of worms. He handed some worms to the curious class and said, "If you can't find any fish start looking for other sources of protein."

After his comment he held the worm in the palm of his hand and without hesitation tossed it in his mouth. After a quick swallow he said, "Boom you just gotta DX that shit."

The term DX in the Army was used to describe the process of turning in an old piece of equipment that was no longer usable. So in this case he was sending the worm home and getting rid of it via his mouth. He pointed to one of the soldiers, handed him a worm, and said, "You, DX that shit."

Without hesitation, the SF candidate gulped the worm. The instructor pointed to the next guy then the next, and so on. From worms to washed up guppies, every one of us got to DX some form of protein for breakfast.

We finished up at the lake learning how to build rafts out of whatever nature had to offer, then swam to a spot in the middle of the lake and back. After a successful water crossing and still wet, the class formed up in a large sand pit next to the metal built classroom structure. In the sand pit we were taught how to build a Dakota fire hole. I dug a hole beneath my canteen and placed kindling under the cup. After using flint to strike up a fire it produced enough heat to bring water to a rolling boil in a matter of minutes. The day ended in the same sand pit learning pressure points and ground combat techniques. The final day of the survival portion was here. It was the day everyone was anticipating. The morning began with a brief in the classroom after we deconstructed our shelters and we were all packed up.

The time had come to put all our skills we had learned over the past weeks to the test. After being split up into groups, my small team met after the instructions in the classroom concluded. Our chosen team leader, SFC Tony, was the highest ranking guy in our group, and he was an easy choice for team leader. Each team, one by one, left from a starting point next to the metal classroom building. SFC Tony was given a map from one of the instructors so we knew where our objective was. It would take long days and nights to get there but after everything we just learned I knew we were going to get the mission complete without getting caught. It was our teams turn to leave the starting point and the instructors began searching each one of us making sure we weren't bringing anything that wasn't allowed on this portion of the course. We couldn't bring any fire starting materials, food, and the most notable was no tobacco products. A couple guys before us got caught trying to sneak cans of chewing tobacco. I don't even know who would want to dip while in the blistering sun, starving, and sleep deprived.

The instructor at the start point looked at SFC Tony and said, "Are you guys ready?" We all nodded and he said, "OK get outta here, and good luck gentlemen."

With our ruck sacks loaded, we headed into the forest not knowing what to expect in the days to follow. We were one of the last teams to leave the survival training site. The sun was scorching and beating down on us. The trek began through dense forest and everyone was sweating like crazy. After just a few hours we had already gone through all of our water. Although we weren't allowed to bring any more water than what was in our camel backs and canteens, we were given iodine tablets to purify our own water if we came across any. We must have covered eight miles by now and we were scouring the dense brush for any type of water source.

We finally came across a muddy divot with a pool of awful looking brown water. Without hesitation we all grabbed our canteens and began filling them up. SFC Tony handed everyone an iodine table. No one said anything. We all dropped the tablet in our canteens and began chugging. I swallowed several twigs and other weird textured clumps from the muddy water. It was delicious! After being so dehydrated it didn't matter what was in the water. After finishing the brackish canteen water, I realized how bad the rest of the course was going to suck. The suck factor had hit an all-time high. Another two miles through the dense southern woods and we finally made it to our hole-up site. Our site was pin pointed on our map and our designated place to remain for a few days. We were lucky because a mile from the site ran a stream.

We collectively built a shelter and started a fire while a few of the other guys walked out to the stream in search of food. To our surprise they returned with a bucket of freshwater muscles. Not only did they acquire food, but also found a useful bucket on the shoreline. We had a feast, consisting of the muscles from the stream and a few ears of feeder corn we came across on our hike to the site. Feeder corn was nothing like regular corn, it tasted a lot different, but still hit the spot.

That night some of us slept in the shelter and others just out on the forest floor. We made sure our camp was concealed before bedding down so we wouldn't get captured in the middle of the night. There was an opposition force searching for us and we had been trained in the art of covering our tracks. The team and I took two-hour watch shifts through the night so we could keep an eye out for any suspicious activity. I heard machine gun fire in the distance, and after waking up with the others I realized they heard the same. In the early morning, we concluded that another team had probably been captured.

Although the stew was good the night before, it wasn't very filling. Two guys on my team, SGT Andrew and SSG Mark headed toward a distant road to see if they could find the team some breakfast. Thirty minutes later they returned bearing gifts from a head on collision. SGT Andrew was holding a lifeless snake that had been run over by a car. We were all ecstatic since we were going to have some food to eat. SGT Andrew made quick work of getting the snake skinned and cooked. We portioned the meal and devoured our protein filled road kill. After the short lived meal, we went into defensive positions concealed from every angle in the forest. We split up throughout our impromptu hole-up site. However, we were all within a whistle or a shout away to alarm any of the team of a possible threat. We remained in our positions throughout the day staying concealed and covered, so as not to be seen by the enemy. We all agreed on a call that we would use if any of us saw or heard anything suspicious during the day. SSG Mark was closer to the road while I was perched 100 meters behind him in a bush. SFC Tony was behind me another 300 meters, SGT Andrew to my left 100 meters, and SGT Dan was 100 meters to my right. I heard a faint whistle from SSG Mark's position near the road. I relayed the call back to SFC Tony and everyone knew what was going on. A car was driving suspiciously slow past our site. Peering through my bush, I watched the car come to a complete stop. A young woman got out of the car and looked out into the forest in the direction of our site.

She yelled out, "Hello, are you guys out there?"

No one said a word and we all remained completely still. I hadn't seen her before as an instructor or somewhere in the previous classrooms. We didn't move an inch, and after looking into the woods and screaming out to us the woman got back in her car and drove away.

The sun was starting to go down now and even after she drove away we remained in our concealed positions. SFC Tony called me over to him and told me to grab the other guys to meet down by the stream, away from the road. I grabbed the others and we all met at the stream. It was dusk now and I could barely see across the slow moving stream. We gathered on the shoreline to discuss our options and what SSG Mark had seen at the road.

While he was describing the nefarious lady, we started to hear a low conversation in the distant forest. In a whispering huddle we all looked at each other and slowly ducked back into the woods away from the calm waters edge. The chatter stopped but the snapping of branches and footsteps were approaching from the road. We started to hear footsteps on either side of us as we laid still. We knew the enemy was close and if we moved we would be toast. While laying on the forest floor, I moved my head closer to the ground as the footsteps continued to approach our position. I could smell the dirt and pine needles in front of my face. With my eyes closed and not moving a muscle the footsteps were getting even closer and there were a lot more people than I thought. Almost like they had been watching us all day. We had been so cautious but must have slipped while our sleep deprived minds faded in and out. We had lost the edge while trying to fight off the sleep and hunger deprivation.

I felt a strong hand on my back grab my uniform, "Get the fuck up. All of you get up right now." A Middle Eastern accent yelled at me.

The heavy hand yanked me off the ground and I was brought to my feet. I was face to face with a guy in a black ski mask. The masked man staring me down yelled, "Who is your leader?"

I didn't say anything as I looked at him in shock. I was confused and I couldn't believe our team was captured. Another guy behind me jerked me left and right trying to get an answer out of me. Here we go I thought to myself, everything we had learned was about to begin. I didn't answer for the second time and the guy who was looking at me turned his attention to the rest of the team who were being held by more guys in ski masks. "Who is your leader?" He yelled through the forest while looking at everyone in the group.

His thick accent echoed through the wood line. No one answered, and he slowly walked over to SFC Tony. Without hesitation he delivered a devastating punch right to his stomach.

Then he said angrily, "We will take care of this back at the camp."

He looked at one of the guys that was holding SSG Mark by the neck and spoke to him in Pashto. I'm guessing he said something along the lines of, 'get these guys to the camp so we can beat the shit out of them.'

We stumbled our way through the forest back to the road while being steered like a drunk driver. Menacingly waiting for us at the road was a white truck pulling a white horse trailer. We were thrown in the hay littered enclosed trailer. The team and I started to devise a plan for when we came to a halt. The plan was to beat the shit out of whomever opened the door and make a run for it. The trailer ride felt long, but maybe it was short and felt long because there were so many variables running through our heads. I felt the trailer slow and finally come to a stop. We heard more voices outside of the trailer speaking Pashto again. Machine gun fire rang out, one gun after another then chanting and cheering from the enemy force. The trailer doors swung open and our plan of fighting our captors was quickly foiled when we exited the confined space. We were met with close to ten guys, all dressed in black robes and ski masks, pointing AK-47's at us. We were yanked out of the trailer and I was delivered a quick blow to the stomach by one of the AK wielding terrorists. A hood was put over my head and I had no idea where the rest of my team was taken. I was handed what felt like an ammo can and I heard someone shout, "Carry, carry." The heavy can must have been filled with sand, and I immediately dropped it.

The hood was yanked off my head and I was whacked in the face by a different guy, and he said, "Carry the fucking can!"

I decided after the stinging slap to the face I wasn't going to drop it again. While standing in the warm night's breeze with a hood over my head, I heard several guys yelling and more machine gun fire rang out. One of the enemy shit heads grabbed my wrists and yanked me until I hit the back of someone. I was told to grab the guy's hands in front of me. It must have been another guy from my team. I whispered every name of the guys on my team to whoever I was grabbing onto, but it didn't elicit any response.

I smelled myself underneath the black hood and it was disgustingly obvious I hadn't showered in days. My substantial beard whiskers poked through the hood. "Move," yelled a voice behind me.

The hands I was holding in front of me began to move and I followed behind him as cautiously as I could without tripping over him or anything else that might be in front of us. We walked for five minutes and my arm was starting to kill me from carrying the 50 lb. can. We continued to walk up an incline and I felt a pair of hands grip my shoulders, "No. You stay."

I was trying to make sense of everything but I couldn't comprehend what was going on. Yeah we were captured but where were we going? We were finally told to halt and I couldn't hold the heavy can anymore. I managed to maneuver the heavy object to my other hand.

After standing in place for another five minutes not knowing what was going to happen next, another unfamiliar Middle Eastern accent said, "Drop can."

I was relieved to let go, and without hesitation I dropped the can like it was on fire. Held on either arm by two guys, I was shoved. As they guided me I felt the air change. I knew I was in a room now. I couldn't hear the chirping birds and the unmistakable insect sounds in the woods. My hood was removed and I was face to face with a white bearded and round spectacled old man. Behind a grey desk, he was wearing a classy business suit and appeared to be Middle Eastern. The room was cement all around with no windows and a single light bulb hung from the ceiling. The dim flickering light highlighted the single gray hairs poking out of his balding head. He asked me a few questions that we had learned were OK to reveal when in enemy captivity.

After the simple to answer questions, I was ordered to strip down to nothing. The man threw me an old tattered light blue prison uniform and said, "You are war criminal number 41. Welcome to Pineland war criminal 41."

He was hovering over his desk filling out papers when he told me to put on the uniform. I put on the disgusting used outfit, and immediately a hood was put back over my head. I was yanked out of the room and tiny rocks pierced through the bottoms of my now shoeless feet. I was ordered to crouch as soon as the material beneath my feet turned from asphalt to sand, and what a relief that was. Crouching next to another prisoner, I was able to see glimpses of the same color uniform of the guy next to me underneath my burlap hood. I didn't try to call out any of the guy's names on my team anymore. It was pointless now. I knew we were under a cover, so maybe a room full of sand? ██████████████████████████████████████ ██ ███████████████████████████████████ and the suck factor shot through the roof. It was getting lighter out now and I hadn't had a lick of sleep. ██████████████████████████ ██ ██

██████ I felt the guy next to me drop to his knees and he was immediately yanked up. I heard several hand to face blows, then he crouched back down next to me. Finally, I was brought to my feet, and my knees couldn't have been happier.

I was shoved from all directions and led from one shitty experience right into the next. I felt us getting closer and getting shoved into what felt like a bigger room. By the sounds of the feet shuffling on the concrete floor there were a lot more than just the guys on my team in the room. My hood was yanked off my head and before the door slammed I could see everyone's faces. All of us wet, sandy, and standing in a tight confined room. We were all dressed in the same shitty prison attire. I was relieved to see a lot of the guys I met in the prior weeks. Several of their faces were red and some bloody from what I assumed was getting hit by the enemy. The room began getting hotter and it was getting harder to breathe. There were 50 or more guys in the room that was built for 20. Another 30 minutes went by and the door flung open. A bright light pierced through the doorway and we were pulled out of the muggy sweat and odor laden room. It was the first time in what felt like over a day I finally got to see my surroundings. The sight was reminiscent of a concentration camp as I exited the room. It was unreal, and I was so sleep deprived and hungry I forgot I was in SERE School. A sidewalk lined the outskirts of the building we were yanked from. Several other closed doors ran along the front of the building, and I definitely didn't want to know what was behind any of them. Tall chain link fences with razor wire at the tops surrounded the whole prison. In front of the concrete building was a large gate with two guard towers occupied by men in black shirts. Right past the tower and outside of the maximum security fence was another large single story building with no windows. A few doors ran the length of the dilapidated building. Between myself and the front gate was a courtyard full of rocks. A rocky path lead to the front gate and on either side were two large sunken pits that dropped down a half foot. The pits were filled with sand and littered with weeds throughout. Just before the left pit was a small brick building a little bigger than an outhouse. In front of the pit to the right was a shack, and to the far right of the shack was a large cage. The cage looked like a domicile fit for a large Great Dane. Guards in black shirts lined the entire fence perimeter. Every guard looked like they were wrestle mania superstars or Arnold Classic body building champions. Small isn't a word I would use to describe any of the 30 or so guards staring us down.

"Get in formation," one of the guards shouted. We hastily got in formation facing the building we just came out of. "About face," yelled the same guard.

As we turned another guard was raising an unfamiliar flag next to the right most guard tower. The guard who instructed us to turn around barreled through the formation and came to the front.

██

██

██

██

██

By now I realized the guy with the big full beard who had been ordering us around was the leader.

"Listen, we own you now and you're all war criminals.██████████
██████ You are the property of Pineland now." The bearded leader ordered.

██

██

██ We were finally released from the formation after the instructor finished ranting about how much better their country was compared to America.

As soon as we were released, the guards who just got done beating several of us, gave different prisoners orders. The instructions were vague ██████████████████████████████████ Five minutes passed and I felt like I was in an insane sick circus. ████████████████████

██

██

██

██

██ Any random sick and twisted thing you could think of; it was happening in this ridiculous prison camp circus. I looked around and noticed two guys inside of the cinder block building just before the left most sand pit. While on the ground pulling weeds, I realized the small structure was a bathroom. The door-less opening of the building greeted you with a concrete floor. I continued with my labor and noticed three holes drilled into the buildings floor. We had to squat to crap, but at this point I hadn't eaten in two days, so I didn't feel the urge to go. I was starving, and luckily word spread between the prisoners through the camp we were going to eat soon. We began to develop our own types of communication among the prisoners. It was the only way not to lose our minds. We all learned the, 'No talking to other prisoners,' lesson pretty quickly. Although we couldn't talk we always made sure the guy to the left and right was doing OK no matter how shitty we felt. While the shit show circus was going on I was ordered by another guard to complete a new task. I began cleaning metal dog bowls with dirty water in a shack next to the right most pit. We drank water out of the bowls, but had to get permission from a guard before refilling. Machine gun fire rang out from both towers and in the prior formation we were told to lay flat on the ground and not to move if we heard the guns rattle off. As I laid down on the cold concrete slab in the little shack I began to think for a moment. When was this going to end? I started losing track of how many days I had been in the camp. The course was only three weeks but could it go on longer? All these questions and more were running through my head.

One of the guards yelled, "All clear."

Everyone got up and went back to whatever absurd task they were doing. Two prisoners were marching back and forth in front of the main gate. Like zombies they were chanting something over and over again. Another set of prisoners were doing the same thing next to a chicken coop, which was just behind the outhouse.

The sun was the only thing that was keeping me going, and I wasn't sure how much more I could take. I thought about calling it quits while I washed the chrome bowls. I came to my senses and thought back to what SSG Kareem told me in the Alpha Company office. I remembered him mentioning other prior Alpha Company guys quitting SERE. I didn't want to be that guy; I couldn't be that guy. I remembered why I committed to the 160th journey and what my end goal was. A quick image popped in my mind while I was left to my thoughts in the miserable shack. The day on the flight line a year and a half ago. The mystery man behind that huge Gatling gun staring at me. That was my, 'Why.' That was the reason I was going to get through SERE. I was going to be the guy behind that gun and in charge of the giant special operations Chinook.

The main gates were swung open by the two prisoners guarding it. Two huge guards walked in carrying a large pot. Each of them holding a handle on either side. I could see steam pouring out of the pot, but couldn't make out what was inside. I tried to keep my head down while washing the bowls but stole glances at the men periodically. They were heading toward the shack. They got closer and finally laid the giant pot at my feet.

"Time to eat," the man said in an Eastern European accent.

I looked down in the pot to see a pile of rice with fish heads on top. I couldn't have been happier to see the sight of food. All the other prisoners took notice of our captors dropping the steaming meal off at the aged shack. I looked around the camp and everyone's faces lit up.

"You're going to feed everyone," the guard said to me sternly. "One scoop only."

The guards must have informed the other prisoners as I was drooling over the sight of the piping hot rice. A line started to form at the shack and I started to scoop rice out into the metal bowls. One by one I handed the delightful meal to the starving prisoners. Each prisoner the same as the last started shoving rice in their mouths as soon as I handed them the bowls. The line finally ended, and I scooped my own bowl of rice. The warm rice hit my mouth and I was in heaven. No Christmas dinner, or holiday feast could ever amount to the sensation of the warm taste of that rice. The rice was magical in my food deprived state and I just wanted to keep eating, but the huge rice pot was empty.

After consuming the rice and enduring countless interrogations, I had done it. I hit my breaking point. I looked around while standing in the shack at a group of grown men in their prison gowns, all crouching on the rocky littered courtyard. They were huddling over their bowls trying to get every last grain. Some were even licking the bottom of their bowls. I wanted to keep going but my mind was telling me otherwise. Several guys had already tossed in the towel that day and quit the course. At any time if you felt you couldn't go on anymore everyone had the ability to notify one of the guards. All I had to do was say, 'I quit,' and they would discreetly take me out of the prison. Fuck that! After everything I had to go through to get here, I had to dig deep and truly live the motto, 'Night Stalkers Don't Quit.' All the prisoners kept encouraging each other through our communication techniques when the guards weren't looking and it definitely helped.

"You," a guard shouted and looked in my direction while I pondered in the shack. I gave a dumb look while washing the recently used rice bowls. "Come with me," he finished fiercely.

I was a zombie and did whatever I was told. I followed the man who led me to another door on the main building inside the prison. He opened a large thick steel door and instructed me to go inside. Through the door was a narrow hallway leading to the back of the short building. On either side of the hallway were several doors, three on each side. The doors were low to the ground and just tall enough for a medium sized dog to squeeze through.

██

████████████████████████████████████ The small door shut behind me. I heard the man's footsteps shuffle down the tight hall, then finally exit the building. He slammed the door and it echoed through the torturous box.

██

██

██

████████████████████████████ I was miserable, and to make matters worse I had to pee. It didn't matter anymore, and while sitting in my isolated section of the camp I pissed myself. I had no emotions as my warm urine saturated my oversized prison pants. I watched my dark yellow pee pool up on the floor then slowly start to trickle through the bottom gap in the door. ███

██ I summoned my fortitude once more, not knowing how much I had left.

Hours passed and I must have fallen asleep. I opened my blurred and dead eyes only to wake up ████████████████████████ A guard was shoving me out of the door and the fresh air was sweet relief. It was pitch dark around the camp now, so I had no idea how long I was in the box. I was escorted back to the courtyard of the prison camp only to be greeted by the shit show circus once again. The guard pointed to a section of the courtyard and told me to start pulling weeds that were coming through the rocks. I was confused and exhausted. I didn't feel like myself anymore and I started to float. I watched my lifeless body in the camp from a bird's eye view. Hungry, tired, and hallucinating I was ready for SERE to end. I meandered to a section of rocks and started to pull weeds. Several other prisoners were doing the same mundane task as I crouched next to them. Feeling miserable as I yanked the thorny plants from the ground, machine gun fire rang out again. It was muscle memory by now so the rest of the prisoners and I laid flat on the rocks. I was ready to give in. I was mad, hungry, tired, and ready to punch the next guard who told me to do something.

After a few minutes laying on the ground while the guards walked around looking at everyone, we were told to continue with our labor. There was only one way to pick weeds in the prison camp and that was in the crouching position. My knees were never allowed to touch the ground. After picking weeds for 30 more minutes I couldn't bear to stay in the excruciating position any longer. I finally succumbed to the agonizing pain and sat down on the rocks. I told two prisoners who were near me to kick rocks my way if they saw a guard coming. With the heads up, I could sit up quickly before being caught in the seated position. The sun was coming up yet again and I didn't want to stay in the camp another day. I was in a daze and so depleted of energy and motivation. All I wanted to do was eat and rest my eyes. I felt like I was dying and I began to think about quitting again. The other two prisoners kicked rocks in my direction to alert me but I was so exhausted and out of it I had no idea what was going on. I felt a strong hand grab my right shoulder and pluck me from the ground.

Another guard who I had never been in contact with before asked, "What are you doing?"

I replied in a slow speech, "Pulling weeds." My answer must not have been good enough. ██

He sternly told me, "Don't ever let me catch you sitting down again or else it will be 10 times worse."

I felt like I had been in the prison camp for months, but in reality it had only been a few days. I was in the worst mental and physical state I had ever been in in my life. All of a sudden the leader of the guards called all the prisoners to formation. ██ █████████████████████████████ So like trained monkeys we all left our individual tasks and got into formation. We were moving a lot slower now compared to the first day in the camp.

Once in formation the bearded leader started yelling at us again. I don't know what we had done this time but he didn't sound happy. ███████████ ██

██████ He told us to turn around again. After the formation turned we looked at the lead guard and all the other guards of the prison at the front of the formation. They all looked irate and no one knew what had triggered their madness. ██ ██ ██ ██ Then the bearded leader ordered the guards back to the front of the formation.

He shouted out to the battered class, "About face."

███

██, we were
ordered to turn around again. We had never been in formation for this long
before. They must be playing another mind game. The tired, dead, lifeless
class faced the head of the camp again. I stared at the main building where
all the insane and awful interrogation techniques took place. I glanced at
the same door we were packed into like sardines on the very first day in
captivity.

He went on, telling us about how great their country was, how we are
all war criminals, and how we were never going to leave the prison camp.
After the ten-minute rant from the leader, he gave another thunderous
command, "About face."

As soon as we turned to face the guard towers, entrance gate, and flag
pole, I witnessed the most amazing sight. The most glorious thing I have
ever seen in my life. The enemy's country flag was no longer on the flagpole.
Instead a remarkable site, the United States flag was being raised on the
same pole we had come to hate. The United States National Anthem began
to play on the loudspeaker. The front fence perimeter we faced was lined
with instructors and staff who had taught us classes in the prior weeks.
All the instructors started to clap. I looked around the formation with my
eyes as everyone was saluting. The prisoners all perked up and stood tall
at attention. I had never seen so many grown men cry in my life. I was
overcome with emotion knowing that not one of us had to endure another
minute within the confines of the camp.

Seeing old glory lightly wisp at full staff was jaw dropping. Tears of joy ran
down our faces. It was the most amazing thing I had ever been a part of. The
National Anthem ended, everyone lowered their salute, and we all wiped
our eyes. All the instructors, from the survival teachers, to the interrogation
teachers, to everyone who had been a part of our training started walking
toward the formation. They congratulated us as we wiped our wet eyes.
██ were
now acting as if nothing had happened and they were our friends. It was
a mentally tough scenario to get over. Having been beaten and deprived
of food from these guys, I didn't want to shake any of their hands. It was
conflicting, and I had to remind myself that it was training. The course was
so intense and real I couldn't wrap my head around what was going on. The
only thing I knew was that it was finally over. We had been liberated from
Pineland and nothing I ever experienced was more rewarding. We exited
the entrance gate and the instructors had a buffet of food ready to serve. I

was going to feast. I took a scoop of everything and plopped it on my plate. When I began to eat I realized I hadn't eaten in days so I was only able to eat so much.

The meal concluded and military transport vehicles started to show up at the camp. We all loaded in the vehicles and headed back toward the SWCS compound where the journey began. We were released for the rest of the day after returning to the compound. Just like everyone else, I couldn't wait for a hot shower and a warm bed to sleep in.

The next morning the entire class had a long discussion in the same auditorium where we received our welcome brief. After the instructors concluded the SERE School debrief, a World War II POW (Prisoner of War) was front and center to tell his story. His tale impacted all of us sitting there. We all had a much greater appreciation now and we knew what he endured was far more agonizing. The old B-25 fighter pilot gave a very thoughtful speech. He ended his astonishing World War II story and we all rose to our feet to give him a standing ovation and pay our respects.

We were released and each one of us individually met with different psychologists. The psychologist I met with had a stack of notes regarding my whole time at the prison camp. I couldn't believe how many notes she had in front of her, but I guess during the entire time in the prison camp the guards were monitoring our mental health, our decisions, and essentially they were grading us. She went over things I could've done differently during my interrogations and my actions during the captivity. She concluded with the AAR (After Action Review), and told me that one of the instructors would take me to the military lodge on the base. Since I was the only one at the school from 160th, I was the only one that was going to leave that day. After the psychological session, I was instructed to gather my gear and get ready to leave.

Just like that, the best and worst school I ever had to endure in the Army was officially over. On the short five-minute drive to the lodge I had so many thoughts running through my head. The same guy who had driven me to the school three weeks ago was in the parking lot waiting for me to arrive. As I loaded my bags into the van the Alpha Company driver looked at me and asked, "How did it go?"

I just looked at him and gave a nod. He had been through the same course and knew exactly what I just went through. I hopped in the van and we departed Ft. Bragg, NC.

He asked, "Where do you want to eat?"

Excitedly, I replied, "Whatever you want to eat I don't care." After going through the week of hell and scrounging through the southern backwoods for a meal I couldn't care less where we ate. He chose Johnny Carino's, an Italian joint that sounded just right. After a hot steaming pile of Chicken Alfredo and an ice cold beer we wrapped up the meal and hit the road. I was headed back to Ft. Campbell, just one more step closer to becoming an Alpha Company crew chief.

I was excited but at the same time I was still trying to wrap my head around what I just went through. The drive home was quiet and I was left to my thoughts. Next, I was finally going to learn how to crew the MH-47G Chinook. The next school was the BMQ course. The course where I would finally learn all facets and to fly as a crew member. We drove through the night and finally arrived at Ft. Campbell. The van slowed to a stop in front of the barracks building that I left just three weeks ago. Although it was the barracks, I couldn't wait to sleep in that tiny twin bed, on my own sheets, in my own room. I took so many things for granted before finishing the mentally rigorous school. The ability to sleep on my own, eat what I wanted, and not have a prison guard barking orders was an amazing feeling.

The following day I drove through the 160th compound and headed toward the Alpha Company office. I walked into the crew office feeling like I had accomplished a lot and I was getting closer to being accepted in the company. SSG Kareem was in the office along with some new faces I had never seen. They must've just come back from a deployment or a training exercise. My speech was still a little slow and I was very cautious about how I answered everyone. I knew I wasn't at the prison camp anymore, but after completing the school I was now acclimated to tread lightly.

SSG Kareem looked at me and said, "Hey rookie, what's up? Long time no see. How was SERE School?"

I was out of my element and still making up for the physically demanding and mentally draining ordeal I had just gone through. I hesitantly replied, "I have a love hate relationship with the school."

SSG Kareem nodded his head in agreement and said, "You have a week to get ready rookie, BMQ starts soon."

He opened the upper cabinet of the crew desk and handed me a binder. It was titled, 'BMQ' and had my name written below. I grabbed the book from him and I couldn't wait to get started. SSG Kareem instructed me to go back to my barracks room and take the rest of the day off to get my gear ready for the course. It was a three month long course about flying and learning the specialized skills to become a 160th crew chief on the MH-47G Chinook. I'd been in the Army now for almost three years and still never flown in a helicopter. I worked on a bunch, but I was finally ready to fly. I recalled waving to the motionless 160th crew chief while the birds taxied by my maintenance section in Bagram. I finally reached the starting line and I couldn't wait to jump feet first into the new journey.

CHAPTER 7

BMQ

I started to learn and meet more of the guys in Alpha Company that week while I was waiting for the BMQ course to start. Of course, I was still the new guy and it was my FNG duty to run the Alpha Company grill. The company had an exterior covered outdoor patio area. It was sandwiched between the hangar and Bravo Company, another Chinook flight company on the compound. I guess you could say they were in some ways our rivals, from what I had heard. The outdoor space was decorated with spec ops memorabilia, aviation parts, and gifts from deployments. The seating area was a treasure trove of history. From Iraqi road signs to bullet riddled aircraft parts it was an unofficial Night Stalker museum. The grill was a way for us to sell burgers and hot dogs to make money for the Alpha Company fund. The money was usually spent on crew member's new born baby gifts or helping a guy in the company who was financially in need. Nothing like this ever existed in my old conventional Army unit. I learned fast how well the company took care of their own, no matter the situation.

Of course being the new guy still, I couldn't just be grilling over the hot flame in the treacherous summer heat, there had to be something more. I was told to wear a pink full face dirt bike helmet that was conveniently waiting for me by the grill once I got outside. Taped on the back of the helmet was a sticker that read, 'FNG.' This wasn't anything compared to what I had just gone through in SERE School so I welcomed the rite of passage. Some of the other crew chiefs gave me some encouragement while they were outside eating.

SSG Brian, one of the flight engineers, said, "Don't worry about the helmet, everyone has to go through it."

I started feeling a sense of belonging after making it through SERE. I held my head a little higher knowing not everyone passed the tough course. While grilling burgers for soldiers in other companies, and civilian contractors, I looked up over the flaming grill. Fifty feet in front of me the hangar's double doors swung open. The same muscle head that I now knew as SSG Atch was heading straight for me. I was expecting another mind fuck from him.

Making his way over, he said in a cordial manner, "What do you got ready Burnett?"

I gave a muffled reply through my full face pink helmet and said, "Just burgers Sergeant," all the while standing at parade rest with tongs in one hand and a spatula in the other.

He looked me up and down, then said, "Don't do that parade rest shit when you're talking to me, and call me Chris from now on."

The first name thing was still foreign, but I caught on that this was a family more than anything. A brotherhood that carried on under a different set of rules.

The grill was just outside the covered seating area, and SSG Atch headed in to grab a plate and fixings for his burger. While gathering his plate he was yelling out to me, in a thick southern accent. He asked me genuine questions about SERE School. I answered in a way as if we were friends. It was definitely nothing like my first interaction with him in the crew office a month ago. He came back out of the shack and held out his plate. I placed the overcooked hockey puck burger on his plate, and he headed back into the hangar without saying anything.

Two days later I found myself driving through the compound, but instead of heading to the Alpha Company office, my new place of duty was a classroom. The building was secure, and once inside the lady at the front desk knew who I was. She gave me very specific instructions on where to go for my first day of the BMQ course.

I placed my cell phone in a secure phone locker after she buzzed me in the fortified doors. I went up a long winding flight of stairs to the second floor. When I got to the top, I walked down a hallway with large windows on one side running the entire length. The windows overlooked several helicopter simulators. They were propped up high on giant hydraulic arms. I came to a door on the second floor labeled, 'BMQ Course.' It was the same sign the lady at the front desk told me to look for once I made it up the stairs. I walked into the classroom to see my new classmates all sitting down, two per table. Each table had a large stack of books in front of each seat. There was only one empty chair left, and fortunately the guy sitting at the table was an Alpha Company guy. I'd only worked with him a few times in the crew office and had a brief interaction with him about SERE School. Although I hadn't officially met him yet I knew we would take on the BMQ journey together.

I took my seat and a few minutes later a short plump man walked through the door and made his way to the front of the classroom. The rest of the students had arrived from other flight companies in other battalions. The teacher wrote his name on the dry erase board, and explained that he would be our instructor for the next month during the classroom portion. He went on to tell us that the three-month long program would start in the classroom and the remaining two months would be spent in the Chinook and at the BMQ trailer.

On each desk stood a pile of books and training manuals, all pertaining to the MH-47G special operations Chinook helicopter. I was in Heaven now that that first day had arrived. It was the same feeling a little kid would have if his mother had just told him, "Hey kid here is my credit card and there is the toy store, you can have whatever you want!"

After the day concluded, my excitement hadn't waned a bit. We learned not only what the course entailed, but also heard secret stories about special Chinook missions you would only fathom seeing on the big screen. The next days included tons of in class and out of class homework that culminated in a test at the end of each day. I slowly began to realize not everyone was cut out for the demanding role. Three of the ten guys who had started the course eventually flunked out. It was clear they wanted to weed out the shitbags before they actually put them in a helicopter. I was confused that after all the schools we had to complete before even taking a seat in the classroom, guys were failing. It was imperative that a Night Stalker trying out for a crew chief position was competent in the general mechanical, hydraulic, and electrical systems of the aircraft. For those reasons and constant test failures, not everyone made it through the first month of the course. I received passing marks through the class portion and also became good friends with the guy I sat next to everyday in class. His name was SGT Matt, a tall southern guy with a sincere criticism for anything you did. My new Alpha Company brother was always willing to help out anyone who needed it since he was very knowledgeable. Coincidentally, he went to the same junior college as I did before joining the Army. A very small school tucked away in the Rocky Mountains in a remote Colorado town, Steamboat Springs.

Close to the last week of the classroom portion, our short plump instructor who we came to know as Mr. Ski, told us to leave class early in order to meet him on the flight line later that night. We had been learning about NVG's (Night Vision Goggles) the whole day, and needed to grasp the concept of wearing them at night.

For the last few days we had been going over in-classroom instruction about every piece and part that made up a set of night vision goggles. While there were several different types throughout the military, all of 160th used a dual lens NVG known as the ANVIS (Aviator Night Vision Imaging System) 6. We were released from class a few hours earlier than normal in order to have time to do what we needed to do before sunset. The instructions were simple; grab chow, do whatever it is you need to do, and get back to the flight line to meet at the BMQ trailer at dark.

Later that night everyone reported to the BMQ trailer and met our instructor, Mr. Ski. We slowly trickled into the BMQ parking lot with a show time of 2100. Mr. Ski waited for everyone to gather around in the gravel lot just abreast of the BMQ double wide classroom trailer. Below his feet were several green canvas bags that looked like little green lunch boxes. He reached down over his belly and with a good deal of effort grabbed one of the bags by a long black nylon strap. He brought the bag to his waist and unzipped it. We all gazed inside the bag as he opened it. We were like kids at a zoo getting a glimpse inside a snake terrarium. Inside the bag were a pair of ANVIS 6's or NVG's, the device that made the Night Stalkers deadly during night time operations. The tool would become my everything over the next several years.

Mr. Ski began pulling different components out of the green canvas bag, and with poorly lit parking lot lights we relied on the bright moon to aid in seeing every item he pulled from the bag. After carefully pulling out every item and meticulously going over everything, all the students including myself huddled around him. It was tricky trying to learn the components in the classroom without actually seeing them and holding the NVG's. Ever eager, I thought loudly, enough with the components! We were all anxious to try them on and see what exactly depth perception meant. Below Mr. Ski's feet, not only stood the canvas bags, but also a foam Nerf football.

"OK get your helmets on and let's go play football," our instructor said enthusiastically.

We all hastily got our helmets on, then each grabbed a green canvas bag. I tried putting the strange new device on my helmet. Each one of us, being the Alpha type personality the unit embodied, we didn't want any help from the instructor to get the device securely locked on to our helmets. Reluctantly, we all inevitably had to get help from him. Soon enough, everyone became accustomed to putting on and taking off the device from our helmets. We followed the instructor out to the flight line. It was a glorious sight in the light of day, but even more astonishing in the darkness of night. Seeing rows and rows of black helicopters, at night, in their element, just gleaming off the exterior hangar lights was amazing. As if the Chinooks on the very far rows were saying, "You're getting close Burnett, don't give up now!"

I snapped back to reality as the class group meandered over to one of the training Chinooks primarily used for the course. While BMQ was an acronym used for crew chiefs, it was the same term used for new pilots just accepted into the elite program as well. The pilots started the BMQ flight portion of the program at the same time the crew chief students did. Everyone was learning while being taught by the most skilled individuals, whether it was in the cockpit or in the back of the bus. It didn't matter if you were a pilot or a crew chief, we were both there for the same heart longing desire to become a special operations aviator. There was a reason the unit had such a highly sought after reputation and it all started with the training.

We finally got a little farther away from the bright lights caressing the corrugated steel edges of the hangar's façade. We made it to a Chinook at the end of the flight line, and while SGT Matt and I were accustomed to the flight line some of the other classmates were not. Mr. Ski asked the class if anyone knew how to lower the ramp of the helicopter as it was closed and locked up, like every other bird on the flight line.

"I do," shouted SGT Matt and I over the loud rotor wash of two MH-60 Black Hawks and three AH-6 Little Birds taking off into night.

SGT Matt climbed in through the front cabin door and soon after, lowered the ramp and tongue assembly. As it lowered the whole class peered through the cabin. Without being asked I already ran around the side and plugged the battery in. SGT Matt and I had worked together on the flight line back at Alpha Company doing odd and end tasks. Having a good feel for how we worked with one another, as soon as the ramp fully dropped SGT Matt looked at me and said, "Dave did you get the battery?"

Joyfully, but keeping an even keel, I replied, "Roger." As soon as I responded, he turned the light switch on, illuminating the empty cabin. The rest of the class glared at us like, 'This is the kind of stuff Alpha Company has?' Alpha Company or A2, was known for being one of the top performing Chinook flight companies throughout 160th. Although SGT Matt and I were new, we held true to that accolade.

After the ramp was lowered, Mr. Ski told SGT Matt to turn off the lights and instructed us to lower our NVG's. After the class flipped down their NVG's, Mr. Ski pointed to each of us, asking us to retrieve something out of the aircraft. We would know the location of the item as it was standard equipment and would always be in the same place. Had we paid attention in class we would know exactly where the item was. I figured this was going to be easy, but after being instructed to retrieve the survival axe I slowly got discombobulated. Green fuzzy pixels appeared after I turned the battery switch on, located on the battery pack attached to the back of my helmet. I felt like Neil Armstrong walking on the moon. I was more concerned with where my feet were landing than the actual task I had to complete. I finally retrieved the survival axe and slowly walked out of the bird. I was instructed to hand it to another student to go return the axe in its rightful place. I began feeling nauseous and felt a headache starting to pulse. The whole new green vision was throwing me off. I would have never imagined wearing NVG's would be so intense for the first time. I had used night vision in basic training but only a monocular version. The dual lens ANVIS 6 was throwing my depth perception off and making me sick. I finally got over it after we started playing football on the flight line. With our NVG's on, the entire class must have looked like a bunch of aliens learning how to use their hands. Each one of us dropped the ball several times, but after some time we all started getting acclimated to the depth perception and the green glow.

After wrapping up the awkward football game we closed and locked up the bird for the night. Mr. Ski told us we would start the next morning in the doublewide trailers. Everyone was excited to start putting their skills to the test and see what being a crew chief was all about.

The next morning, we showed up to the trailer where we had departed from the night before. We had our big green kit bags for carrying large amounts of flight gear. Mr. Ski told us to bring all our flight gear so the new instructors could look over everything. Our flight vest and gear was critical, and the instructors needed to ensure we had everything set up properly. Five instructors came out of the trailer to greet us. Not knowing what type of demeanor to expect, they all introduced themselves and each gave a quick bio. A big barrel chested guy gave us the run down for what the day would look like as well as the following months. He must have been prior sumo wrestler turned body builder. I don't know how they made a flight suit big enough to accommodate his stature. I figured he was going to be a dick but after hearing him speak he was a genuine dude.

"We will be going over all components of the M-134 mini gun today and throughout the week," the beast of a dude said.

Oh man I could hear the symphony playing in my head with a beautiful choir singing hallelujah. I couldn't believe my ears. The very same weapon I saw the crew chief in BAF wielding behind the right gun door. I was again reminded I was closing in on the prize.

He went on to talk about the rest of the course then he paused, "Is everyone's gear good?" He glanced at all the students then over to the other instructors to get a verification nod. After receiving confirmation, he said, "Let's get inside."

We lined our aviator bags outside against the trailer wall and shuffled in the small single trailer door. The big guy, Mr. B, had to walk through the door sideways in order to fit. As we walked in I noticed several cubicles with other instructors sitting down. The cool air in the trailer was welcomed after feeling the Ft. Campbell sun starting to come out for the day. In front of the projector was a smaller table and on top of the table there she was. In all her beauty, it was the closest I had ever been to the M-134 mini gun. A giant 6-barrel Gatling gun. I had no idea what its capabilities were but I knew I would soon learn. I caught on that this was going to be a gentlemen's course with an emphasis on understanding and grasping concepts, techniques, and tactics, versus yelling and screaming like previous schools we had all endured.

The day continued in the trailer. We learned about the parts and components that made up the mini gun, the different jams we could expect while firing the weapon, and how to clear them. Most importantly we were briefed on when we were going to get to shoot the impressive weapon. We also learned what days we were going to attempt to qualify on the weapon system.

Mr. B continued with his briefing at the end of the day, "In the final weeks of the course we are going to fly cross country to New Mexico. You guys will be put to the test. You will demonstrate to the instructors all the skills you learned throughout the course."

We would have another trip during the course to Virginia Beach, VA where we would train for fast roping, ladders, and tactical landings. I got the hint early on that the Night Stalkers trained all over the United States and the world. As a single guy I couldn't be more excited for the two upcoming TDY trips. While I was showing a lot of excitement, I could tell that this was going to be a little more difficult for some of the married family guys in the class.

The week concluded and I knew everything there was to know about the 3,000 round a minute powerful M-134 mini gun. The weapon would become very useful in deployments to follow. The next week we learned how to start the aircraft and worked on calls and responses with the pilots going through the same course. I finally knew everything the crew chiefs were saying and doing when I saw them start those three birds on the flight line in Afghanistan. We did several dry runs during the week walking around the aircraft mimicking how we would respond to the pilots' calls.

A few days later on the flight line I stood on the left, or the number one side of the bird. I was ready to fire up the glorious Chinook for the very first time. All my flight gear was on and I could feel sweat slowly trickle down my back.

The loud APU (Auxiliary Power Unit) was screaming and the pilot called to me, "Clear to start number one?"

Referring to the number one engine, I responded, "Posted and ready on one, one is clear to start." As I stood next to the turbine engine I heard it start to whine and the blades above slowly started to turn. My fire retardant flight pants started to flap as the blades picked up speed.

"Good start on one," the pilot called over the radio.

"Roger, good start on one outside, moving to two," I called. My adrenaline was pumping and I couldn't believe my new responsibility. I hustled around behind the ramp dragging the ICS cord with me. The cord ran from a communication box inside the aircraft and connected to my flight helmet.

The cord afforded me and the rest of the crew the ability to communicate with the pilots and other crew members on board. I made my way around the back of the Chinook's ramp and finally to the other side where I could monitor the number two engine before it started.

"Number two clear to start, chief?" The BMQ pilot called.

Holy shit the pilot just called me chief! As in crew chief! I couldn't let my excitement get in the way, I needed to remain focused.

"Posted and ready on two, two is clear to start," I called back. I heard the second engine whine and the blades chopped through the air above. The rotor wash began to cool me down as I continued to monitor the exterior of the aircraft in my sweat soaked flight suit.

"Good start on two inside," the pilot exclaimed.

"Good start on number two outside," I quickly and confidently responded. I made my way back to the number one side next to the emergency APU shut off valve. I stood next to the shut off valve access flap on the exterior and waited for the pilots next call.

After the pilots went through some more checklist items in the cockpit he called over the ICS, "APU clear off?"

"Clear Off," I responded. The screaming of the APU slowly cut off. I grabbed the wheel chocks from the aft wheel after closing the APU emergency access panel.

After another several checklist items in the cockpit the pilot called back to me, "Chocks?"

I responded, "Removed and secured." I clipped the wheel chocks inside the cabin while the right ramp crew chief raised the ramp.

The pilot called back again, "Coming forward."

The crew chief at left gun called out, "Clear forward left."

Followed by another chief at right gun, "Clear forward right."

The bird began to creep forward and we were finally taxiing. I thought I did an OK first job with my call and responses with the pilots. I looked down the cabin at Mr. Zane, one of the instructors sitting on a troop seat. He looked at me and gave me a thumbs up. Just like that, I started my first MH-47G Chinook. A sense of relief pulsed over me followed by excitement and adrenaline. We taxied to Fury Sod, a large patch of grass next to the main runway where the entire unit's helicopter fleet conducted hover checks. After a quick hover check to make sure the weight and balance was appropriate for the flight, the flight received clearance from the Campbell Army Airfield tower. After the clearance call, wind, and weather conditions came from the tower, the pilot called, "Clear up?"

"Clear up left," left gun said.

Followed by right gun's call, "Clear up right."

We pulled power and the torque of the helicopter was heart pounding. The pilot pitched the nose down and we were flying. I was flying! The sheer power lifting off the ground was immense. Almost three years in the Army and I was finally flying on a Chinook. I didn't stop smiling the entire flight. The views, although just doing dummy circles around Ft. Campbell, were amazing. My new perspective from my new office was jaw dropping. It occurred to me I was finally a special operations aviator. Much like the rare 160th Chinook sighting I experienced in Bagram, it was a special occurrence on Ft. Campbell too. While flying I could see most people on the base below stop to look up to the sky. They were all probably thinking the same thing I was when I was on the flight line in Bagram. The flight was short and I wished for a moment it would never end. An hour later and we were back on Fury Sod.

We taxied back into our parking spot on the flight line and the same way I started the bird was the same way I shut It down, just in reverse order. Once the blades slowly came to a halt all the crew chiefs took their gear off and we started opening up the bird for a post flight. After every flight, the crew chiefs of the bird were in charge of looking over certain aircraft components to make sure there were no issues or areas of the helicopter that might warrant maintenance. In the event an issue arose during a post flight, it was the crew chief's duty to not only understand why the problem occurred, but also imperative to know how to fix the issue.

After the flight and every other flight to follow we would head back to the trailers to conduct a debrief. The instructors covered what we did, and what we could have done differently, only to improve in our new role. The crews were constantly learning from one another to better ourselves at our new coveted jobs. The job was meticulous and at the end of the day it could mean someone's life depending on how well or poorly we did. We concluded the day after a long debrief in the warm trailer. We learned we would continue flying day flights for the next few weeks.

We ventured and flew to different airfields and airports around Tennessee and Kentucky, and the class was getting better at the highly sought after Night Stalker position. Hoist and HAAR (Helicopter Air to Air Refueling) were the next qualifications we needed to learn and complete in the final month. In order to qualify in any crew served task on the Chinook, it had to be done during both day and night time.

We were reminded of our goal of mastery of the big 3 tasks, guns, HAAR, and hoist. It was critical to excel in the tasks during the day, but more importantly during night time operations under NVG's. We were the Night Stalkers after all. It is essential for any 160th aviator to function not only under high stress situations but also under the blanket of darkness with zero light. Relying on our NVG's was crucial to becoming part of the elite group of soldiers.

Now, it was time to transition into nights. The class was awarded a half day in order to aid in the shift change. One of the BMQ instructors, Mr. Zane, told us to show up at the trailers at 0100. The half day was filled with in-classroom power point presentations about range safety, proper mini gun clearing procedures, and techniques we might find useful when flying at night. We started at 0100 in the morning to get the birds ready for the aerial gunnery range. It was the first time the class would get to shoot the mini gun at night. We managed to do well at the aerial range during the day but the night time operation was sure to test us. We were all excited and eager because each one of us knew from stories, rarely did our job take place during the day. I was slowly starting to realize through stories, and talking with my other classmates, what the Night Stalker slogan truly meant. I often saw the slogan in discreet yet noticeable places throughout the compound, a slogan I would grasp the true meaning of on my first deployment with the unit, 'Death waits in the dark.'

Beep, beep, beep, beep, beep, beep, beep, beep. There it was again, that same annoying alarm clock my body had become a slave to after being in the Army for three years. It was the same beeping that woke me up every day since my first deployment. Only this time I was eager to wake up. It wasn't that first deployment where I had to get up and go work on an aircraft. It was midnight and I excitedly rolled over and shut the alarm clock off. I wasn't going to have to answer to SSG Chris in BAF. I was going to range ▮▮▮▮ the aerial gunnery range located on Ft. Campbell's vast acreage. I was going to train for something I was excited about. I was going to train to put bullets in bad guys. I was going to train for my first deployment with a team I wanted to be a part of. From the stories I overheard from the Alpha

Company guys and the instructors, I would be training for something that mattered. While maintaining the Chinook on deployment number one may have been contributing to the fight in some eyes, it wasn't to me. It was going to be my turn behind the mini gun now, and I knew I had to keep putting in the effort.

I slammed a quick bagel in my barracks room quietly as not to wake up everyone else sleeping on the same floor, then headed for the compound. I headed inside the trailer to see a few guys sitting down with the same shit eating grins on their faces. I knew it was going to be a long night but I also knew in the back of my head we were training for the real thing.

SGT Matt, another guy from our class, SGT Max, and I were told to go to the arms room to retrieve four mini guns. We were used to the routine after going through the day time iterations at range ███████ We jogged to the arms room which was 50 meters away, and into the next door hangar. We met the civilian who we came to know as Joe, because every time we would see him he would have a cup of joe in his hand. It wasn't even 0100 yet and sure enough there he was with a cup of steaming hot coffee. He always tried to keep us in the arms room to tell us stories from his SF days. We loaded the weapons on a wheeled push cart and headed out to the warm breezy flight line. The temperature was nice and all three of us rolled the weapons to the first and second birds we had been assigned the morning before. All of the other classmates were climbing over the birds like monkeys, getting everything opened up for the pilots to look at before taking off. This routine was known as a preflight.

Before each flight, as a crew chief, we were in charge of looking over all the main components of the aircraft. This standard was known as a PMCS (Preventative Maintenance Checks and Services). The process was extensive, but necessary in assuring the aircraft was airworthy. Knowing we were going to fly that night we had already done the PMCS the morning prior. This allowed the crews extra time to run through our weapons checks and get everything set up for the range. Each crew was at their respective bird when I heard some sort of diesel engine approaching the helicopter. Looking out the helicopter window where I was setting up one of the mini guns, I saw a fork lift carrying a massive pallet. The armament guys were dropping off ammunition for the night's training mission at the range. Each bird was getting 25,000 rounds of linked 7.62 ammo. The whole ammo loading process was a big undertaking and meant both crews from both birds helped one another getting the heavy load into the helicopter. We then carefully loaded the linked 7.62 rounds in the mini gun ammo cans, which could each hold up to 4,000 rounds. The mini gun's ammo cans were secured to the floor next to each weapon system. The rounds were electrically fed from the can through a long metal feed shoot and eventually into the powerful weapon. We managed to get both the left and right gun ammo cans topped off. We strapped the remaining ammo crates to the floor of the Chinook.

I heard a faint conversation coming toward the aircraft and looked out of the window again. The BMQ pilots were walking out to the flight line with flight gear slung over their shoulders. Almost like the sequence in the movie Armageddon, when the shuttle crews walked to their shuttle with dramatic music playing in the background.

Before every flight, the crew always has a brief detailing the mission, weather, timeline, and other pertinent information. I would soon learn this would get a lot more in depth on deployments, and for good reason. The pilots gathered at the back of one of the Chinooks. One by one the crew chiefs closed up all the helicopter panels after the pilots gave the OK, then trickled back to the ramp to meet the pilots for the brief. Before the brief started, the PIC (Pilot in Command) asked the FE to brief them on the log book and the overall status of the aircraft. The log book, which I became familiar with in the Alpha Company office, was used to record any faults with the aircraft, and track how many hours it had flown. This let the crew chiefs and everyone else know when it was time for the bird to go into a phase. The pilots concluded the 10-minute brief, and after each brief they went around the huddled crew asking each chief if they had any questions. If any of the crew had anything to add this was the time to do it. I started to feel like what I had to say meant something compared to my first deployment, where if I had a concern or suggestion everyone would just shrug off the inexperienced private. I was a SPC now, and had some experience under my belt on the maintenance side, and that was half of the job. The other half I was slowly learning, but it was at that moment I started feeling like a crew chief.

After the brief concluded we headed into our respective helicopters. The loud twin rotor dual turbine six bladed helicopters began to roar simultaneously. This was my favorite part, another movie-like scene. The position lights on each aircraft were glowing red and green under the darkness of the flight line. Radio checks between both helicopter pilots concluded, another routine part of the checklist before taxiing. If you couldn't talk to the chopper flying next to you then what was the point in flying two birds at all? We began taxiing, chalk one closely followed behind by chalk two, the bird that I was on. I was left ramp so I didn't have to make many calls while taxiing, that was the role of left and right gun. Both helicopters lifted off the flight line and landed back down onto Fury Sod. The crew and I were excited to lay lead into the various targets on the half mile stretched range. Everything from tanks, buildings, old vehicles, you name it. The same targets we were about to destroy were the same targets we had gotten accustomed to during the day. We got the clear to take off from the tower and in no time we were circling the target rich range.

"Range is hot," the pilot called over the ICS, as we made a banking turn in the night sky.

I flipped a switch on the mini gun spade grip and in an instant saw the light turn green on my weapon system. It was time to engage. Although I was excited, the instructors were standing right next to me ready to purposely jam the weapon. The training was to ensure we understood how to clear a malfunction of any kind. If we failed at clearing a jam and didn't qualify on the weapon system, there was no point in keeping you as a crew chief. This was the bread and butter of becoming a crew chief, it was our crew served weapon and it mattered to the crew, the job, and keeping our brothers protected.

"Left gun is cleared hot," the BMQ training pilot called over the radio.

"Roger, going hot." I called out. I had been instructed to change crew positions with the left gun crew chief while en route to range ███ I didn't know why the instructors wanted me to go first, but I wasn't about to argue. Left, left low, right, right high, was what we learned while executing the M-134 mini gun task during the day. While maneuvering the gun on target, the critical technique helped us aim by calculating air speed and trajectory of the projectiles. I took this to heart as this was my make or break run.

"Tank and smalls arms fire nine-o-clock," SSG Ted, another instructor called out over the radio.

I thumbed down the push button trigger and heard the loud electric growl, followed by rounds pelting into the tank he had called out on the giant range. I felt the sheer power pump through my hands on the spade grip as I made minor corrections to keep the rounds on target. As I monitored the target through my NVG's I saw tracer rounds impacting into and around the tank. The sound was beautiful and made my adrenaline pulse every time I let the six barreled beast rip and induce violent impacts on the targets below. Every time I pressed the trigger and watched tracer rounds barreling out of the mini gun I could only imagine what it would look like in combat. I felt like Pop-Eye to spinach every time I lit up the targets on the range. Only the mini gun was my spinach. As the tracer rounds bounced off the metal tank and shot straight in the sky the bullets stopped all of a sudden. A malfunction halted the firing and was purposely induced by one of the instructors. It was time to test my skill at clearing a jam inside the pitch black cabin. "Left gun jammed, left gun cold, working jam," I called over the radio. After a quick correction under the dim illumination of my lip light attached to my mic boom, the jam was cleared. I clicked the feed chute back into the feeder de-linker and called, "Left gun operational, left gun clear to engage?"

One of the pilots came back over the radio, "Clear to engage."

I gave another five second burst before the pilots called, "Cease fire, cease fire, left side cold," at the end of the range route.

I thought I had cleared the jam in a quick fashion. I only hoped I impressed the instructors enough to get the qual. The Night Stalkers were all about precision and, 'Good enough,' just didn't cut it. The unit prided itself on being the best and just squeaking by would ensure you didn't make the cut.

The mini guns blared all through the night with the other crew chiefs and me switching in and out of left and right gun positions. We had to load the 4,000 round mini gun cans when the guns were ████ or out of ammo. It was a hard task to accomplish in the pitch dark cabin while the pilots were yanking and banking. Loading the rounds in the can was a back breaker to say the least. Two chiefs would slump over a can; one would load while the other fed the linked belt of ammo. Doing the task with a 60-pound kit on was exhausting.

"Range two nine is cold," a call came from the PIC. Countless iterations, jams, and bullets destroying targets, and the exhausting and fun night was over.

The sun was starting to come up. Dead tired and ready for bed we were all eager to find out who passed the qualification. Back in the trailer we would not only receive the debrief but also learn who qualified and who didn't. The instructor read off the list of who made the qualification, luckily I was one of the names. Not so lucky were three of my classmates. Fortunately, they would have one more chance to qualify during our one week trip to WSMR (White Sands Missile Range) in New Mexico. We were all told to head home and be back the next night to begin hoisting operations. Again, a very hard task during the day that we had already covered would prove to be a lot more difficult at night.

The hoisting operation was imperative to learn as it would aid in rescuing soldiers on the battle field during emergency evacuation scenarios. The class arrived at the trailer the next night, and the look on everyone's faces resembled a zombie. From the heavy lifting of all the ammo cans, and transitioning into the night flying, we were all starting to feel it. Maybe this was one reason we had to go through SERE School before starting the course. Either way, with the end of the entire BMQ course in sight, the class wasn't about to let a little grogginess get in our way.

We trickled into the trailer and the instructors let us know that the daytime instructors had already completed a PMCS on the helicopter. The brief was written on the dry erase board in the trailer and told us critical information. Some important things to know before getting the bird opened up were written on the board. How much fuel was needed for the mission, and what birds we were assigned.

Just like the gun qualification, we had already done hoisting operations during the day and everyone in the class received the day qualification. We wouldn't get to do live body hoisting until we finished the course and got back to our individual companies. While some regular Army units may have an external hoist, the majority didn't. The hoist gave us all kinds of capabilities to perform rescue operations on land or at sea. We practiced hoisting on the flight line several times before taking off from Campbell Army airfield.

The pilot banked left immediately after take-off and we headed to a training site to go locate Rescue Randy, our 225 lb. test dummy. We arrived at the training site ten minutes later and proceeded to scour the training village, comprised of shipping containers and random wrecked vehicles. The pilot spotted Randy at our twelve-o-clock and he proceeded to hover toward him. Some of the other instructors had driven to the site to set up Rescue Randy and the ground hoisting operation. During the operation the right gun had to be swung inside or outside the helicopter to maneuver the hoist cable. The right lower gun door had to be removed as well. The hoist was located above the right gun door and boasted an incredible 250 feet of hoist cable. Not only did the class have to qualify on the task, but also learn about every component of the hoist. From how to trouble shoot issues, to fixing the hoist, it was ingrained in our heads before we even got to operate the thing. The operation and qualification of the hoist required two crew chiefs. One chief laid down on his stomach with his head and half of his body hanging outside the helicopter door. While the other chief stood over top straddling the other chief's waist with his feet. The chief standing was in charge of making calls to the pilots and controlling the hoist grip. The hoist grip was the controller for the hoist and had the ability to lower and raise the 250 feet of cable. 250 feet was the max so it was imperative to learn to gauge how high the bird was off the ground. The pilot called over the radio the distance the dummy was at the twelve-o-clock. During the task the pilot called the distance and direction of the target or dummy until the crew chief operating the hoist grip was able to see him.

"Twelve-o-clock 50 meters," called the pilot.

"Roger continue forward. I don't have the target in sight." I called while trying to locate Randy below.

A brief pause and the pilot managed to make another call. "Survivor at the twelve-o-clock moving to the three, twenty meters."

As I hung out of the gun door scanning to locate the dummy, the wind from the rotor wash was beating across my face. The green pixelated town through my NVG's was clear from the mock town's lights. At last, I saw the target and Randy was laying lifeless on the ground next to two instructors. "Continue forward 10," I called. As the pilot inched forward I began to lower the hoist cable. The task had to be timed perfectly all while giving the pilot commands over the radio. "Continue forward 9,8,7,6,5,4,3,2,1. Hold your forward. Positioned over survivor, hoisting out," I said abruptly.

The whole job of a crew chief, and one of the most important was to keep the pilots informed of what was going on at all times. During any task, silence over the radio wasn't a good sign. I learned this concept pretty quickly. Continuing to lower the hydraulically operated cable, I suddenly felt a thud on the back of my helmet. The instructor hit me with something then he started talking over the radio, informing me to make certain calls that I wasn't making. I must have been mesmerized by the cable lowering down to the mannequin on the ground. Not only was I not making the proper hoist calls to the pilot, but the pilot had drifted forward away from the survivor. After the thud on the back of my helmet I understood it was all up to me to position the helicopter directly over Randy so we could get him hooked up and rescued. "Come back 5," I called. "Hold you position; hoist is half way down. Good height good hover." I exclaimed not wanting to get hit in the back of the head again. "Hoist is on the ground, hooking up hoist."

The instructors ran over to rescue Randy and managed to secure the hoist hook to the dummy's vest. I received the hand signal from the instructors on the ground. "Survivor is hooked, hoisting up." I toggled the up switch on the hoist grip and monitored the training dummy making his ascent off the ground through my green and black vision. I continued to make calls into the mic boom over the loud rotor wash. SGT Max was laying on his stomach just below me. With both hands on the cable he made sure Randy wasn't being slung around violently during the rescue. "Hoist is half way up," I managed to inform the pilots. Followed shortly after by, "Survivor at the cabin door. Working on securing survivor." SGT Max began to come to his feet as we were met by Randy at the cabin door. He and I pulled the lifeless dummy into the aircraft and managed to unhook him from the end of the hoist cable. While handling the dummy I managed to continually make calls over the radio. We drug him to one of the troop seats while making sure not to get our ICS cords tangled in the cable or caught on Randy.

While I finished securing Randy to one of the troop seats, SGT Max began to secure the lower cabin door. "Door secured!" SGT Max, called over the radio.

I continued to reel in the cable and finally got it sucked back into the hoist and called, "Hoist secured."

One of the chiefs in the back of the aircraft called out over the ICS, "Aft ready."

Followed by my, "Forward ready" call.

"Coming forward," the pilot called.

"Clear forward left." SGT Max said.

Followed by my, "Clear forward right."

The pilots headed away from the training site so we could regroup in the back. SGT Max and I switched positions with the crew chiefs on the ramp. It was time for the other crew members to attempt their qualification. I made my way to the ramp of the Chinook while the aircraft made a banking right turn. I clipped my monkey tail to a tie down on the floor. I sat down at the right ramp position seat and just hoped I got my qualification. I was certain the thud to the back of my helmet meant I wasn't going to get the qualification. While sitting at the right ramp position SGT Max turned around, tapped me, and put out his fist for a fist bump. A bit of encouragement went a long way in the unit and that was what I needed.

The next chiefs were up, and they did really well from my perspective while I monitored the operation off the leveled ramp. I was kneeling out on the stubby wing keeping a watchful eye over the rescue while listening to their calls. After the iterations of rescue hoist operations concluded the 2nd bird came in from the south to begin their qualification. Chalk one had been practicing roll on landings while we were doing our hoisting qualifications. After concluding the hoisting operations at the training site both birds switched places and we headed back to the airfield to practice roll on landings. After at least three dozen landings, the night was finally coming to an end and we headed back to the house. A common phrase that would stick with me for the rest of my crew chief career.

We landed back on the flight line, which was a small jump away from where we were practicing roll on landings. Chalk two followed closely behind us and both birds taxied to their parking spots. Right gun was in charge of calling the bird into the parking spot. While in the course we all received a chance to hold the coveted right gun position on the bird. However, once back at Alpha Company the position was held by the FE, which was the highest crew member position. Each helicopter in Alpha Company was specifically assigned to an FE. I had a long way to go to get to that level.

"Continue forward 25, 20, 15, 10,9,8,7,6,5,4,3,2," right gun continued to call over the radio, "Hold your forward."

The pilots slammed on the brakes instantly after hearing the call. During the beginning of the class so many of us messed the call up, either telling the pilot to stop too soon or too late. By now, we all had gotten the parking and calling the aircraft into place down.

Both birds shut down after running through the process and all of the chiefs began to put the birds to bed. Another crew chief term used to describe locking and closing everything up on the aircraft. We closed up the birds while the pilots and instructors headed into the trailer. The birds became our babies and I slowly began to learn the 54-million-dollar aircraft was my responsibility, this was the crew chief's responsibility. Not only to make sure she was always up to par maintenance wise, but also guiding her through the night safely. The crew chief was the sorcerer to the dragon. I was becoming less and less expendable the further along I got in the role. I was truly becoming a crew chief and enjoying the shit out of it.

We finished putting the birds to bed. We always waited on the last guy ensuring everyone else was good to go inside and didn't need any help. While we would soon depart the course and the other chiefs would go back to their companies I could see the brotherhood mentality starting to form. The cool night air was still as we walked to the trailer. I could hear the buzzing of summer bugs as I looked up at the bright flight line lights. The walk was a mere 300 feet to the trailer, and the entire walk all I could think about was if I received the hoist qualification or not. We finally managed to drag our tired bodies into the trailer to receive the debrief. Just like the mini gun qualification the instructor went down the list naming off the guys who had passed.

"Burnett," he sounded off.

Yes! He called my name. The debrief continued and I learned from the instructor that my ability to adapt after the helmet smack is why I received the qualification. We all left the trailer knowing the rest of the week consisted of putting our new qualification to the test, with some hoisting rescue missions more challenging than others. While getting the qualifications may have been tough, it was a constant challenge trying to keep the qualification. Just like we were awarded the qualification it could just as easily be taken away.

A month remained in the course. All we had left was; a week of HAAR (Helicopter Air to Air Refueling), a trip to Virginia, and a trip to New Mexico. We were almost done and I was getting eager to get back to Alpha Company. Traveling cross country didn't seem like the most fun time for some, but I was beyond thrilled to go.

HAAR was equally important as any other BMQ task. HAAR allowed us the ability to refuel during long range missions while in flight. The notorious long refueling probe was one easy way to determine a Special Operations MH-47 from a regular Army Chinook. The task not only allowed us to fill the oversized fuel tanks so we didn't have to land, but would also tie into another task I would later learn. Much like all the other tasks, HAAR was just as challenging.

It was 0100 and just like a rhythm we were all waiting in front of the BMQ trailer for an instructor to open the door so we could check out the dry erase board and get to work. We were all sweating from the humid summer air. Although it was the middle of the night it was still ungodly hot. An instructor showed up and let us into the trailer. Once everyone knew what bird they were assigned to and who we would be working with, we were like a well-oiled machine. It was a beautiful sight, and for the first time I felt like everyone knew what had to be done.

We all headed out to the flight line while two chiefs stayed behind to get the gas cards and helicopter keys from the flight ops office. Yes, helicopters have keys just like a car. As we all walked out to the flight line with our gear slung over our shoulders and carrying a helmet bag in the other hand I felt like a million bucks. There wasn't much that needed to be set up for HAAR inside the bird, like some of the other qualifications. After we got the bird open and ready for the pilots to look at we began to go over the refuel panel with one another. Once in flight and the pilot made a clean connection to the fuel hose coming off the tanker, the balancing of fuel in each tank fell on our shoulders. The panel allowed the right gun crew chief to distribute fuel evenly between both the left and right tank. Several switches on the panel allowed us to open and close different valves depending on how much fuel the pilot wanted on board. The amount of fuel we would take on would normally be discussed before taking off so everyone was on the same page.

While we were all out on the flight line going over the panel, we were also going over call and responses that would need to take place between the crew chief and the pilot. Communication during this task was imperative just like every other task.

Within an hour we were wheels up. The call was made over the radio to flight ops after taking off and we were en route to the target. Or in this case, en route to a pre-distinguished flight pattern. The pre-determined air space was coordinated with the Air Force prior to wheels up, but that was pilot shit. Although the instructors educated us on crew chief duties, it never hurt to know what going on with the pilots either. Constantly communicating was the secret to having the best operating crew.

The flight to the pre-determined pattern was boring. Finally, one of the pilots came over the radio and said, "I have the tanker in sight." I peered out of the opened right gun window and through my pixelated NVG's, all I could see were clouds. I sat in my chair and waited for the next call.

Shortly after the first call the pilot came back over the radio and said, "Tanker one-o-clock half a mile." I peered out of the right gun window again and I saw the giant KC-130 as we moved closer to position.

I came over the radio, "Roger tally on tanker." As we got closer the pilot and I began to go over the pre-refueling checklist. After a short one minute back and forth, we finished going over the panel and made sure everything was set up properly to take on the accurate amount of fuel. Just like the

Chinook, the KC-130 had a crew chief as well. The KC-130 chief's job during the operation was to flash different color lights from his window. One window was located just aft of each wing. Each color meant something different and was just one of the many things we learned about HAAR in class.

I looked outside the window again and saw one of the colored lights. The pilot called, "Moving to pre-contact position."

We were on the left side of the KC-130 and just before moving to the pre-contact position I called over the radio, "All misses up and left."

The pilot came over the radio immediately after my call, "Roger, all misses up and left." The call was used to make sure both the pilot and the crew had that engrained in their heads in case of a missed contact attempt.

HAAR was not the easiest thing in the world and was one of the many reasons only 160th Chinook companies had the midair refuel capability. We were the best. We moved into the pre-contact position and I looked out the window only to see how close our helicopter was to the massive KC-130. Any slight move by either the KC-130 or the Chinook could be catastrophic.

"Moving to contact," the pilot called over the radio. I came inside the helicopter for a brief second to look through the front windshield. What a magnificent sight! The refueling probe was lined up in the center of the drogue and we began inching closer to the refueling hose coming off of the KC-130. Flying just behind the KC-130 in perfect formation was nerve wracking, but exhilarating at the same time.

As the pilots inched the Chinook closer to the probe I heard a faint connection noise. The refueling probe stuck the hose first time. "Contact," the radio call came from the cockpit.

I followed with my response and got to work, "Roger refueling check list in progress." After going over the refueling checklist we began taking on fuel.

When the fueling was complete the pilot called to the crew in the back, "Moving to disconnect."

Left ramp replied, "Clear back left."

Then I called, "Clear back right." The aircraft slowed down and broke away from the hose.

I thought I did a good job going through my checklists and refueling the bird all while balancing the tanks on either side. It was a little more difficult than doing the task in the daylight, but that was the nature of my new unit.

While the pilot was in the stern position still flying next to and slightly behind the tanker, chalk two came over the radio. "Moving to contact."

As I looked across the sky, brightened through my green goggles, I saw chalk two on the other side of the KC-130. While we were just refueling one helicopter at a time the KC-130 had the capability to refuel two birds at once from both the left and right wings. This was why the, 'All misses up and left/right,' call was so important. You could be on either side of the tanker when conducting refueling operations.

As chalk two was continuing with the refuel operation, I switched positions with SGT Max, who was headed to Bravo Company after the course. He would stay at Ft. Campbell but he would be in a different company. The night went on and my fun was over. I sat at right ramp the rest of the night while the other three chiefs rotated out of the right gun position. The BMQ pilot on our bird was CW3 Ryan, a former Ranger, and an all-around good guy. He always took time to learn something about the crew on board and never took his job lightly. He was also heading back to Alpha Company after the demanding course. Most of the pilots treated the chiefs with a lot more respect than my previous unit. CW3 Ryan had a good night with only one miss out of ten contact attempts during the HAAR operation.

As I sat in the back listening to the other chiefs make calls, I started to think about what lie ahead. I felt like I was doing well in the course and I knew it would be less than a month before I was back at Alpha Company. I was so close to flying on missions down range and actually taking the fight to the enemy. I was nervous and excited at the same time. Millions of questions started running through my head. Will I be ready? Will I have all the knowledge to contribute in a valuable way? These and countless other questions started swirling in my mind.

Before I knew it I was coming out of my daze and we were on our final approach to Campbell Army Airfield about to land for the night. The night concluded and I was eager for the final portion of the course. My first TDY trip. We were headed to Virginia Beach, VA for more training and to go over a culmination of tasks we had already learned. We would be learning new over water tasks too, and hoped to God I wouldn't have to use my Dunker School training.

After landing, we went through the same routine we all had come to memorize. The after landing ritual that would continue throughout the rest of our crew chief careers was hasty. Close the birds up, debrief, and get the bird ready for the next mission. I found out like all the other chiefs that everyone passed the qualification, except me. I thought I had done a good job, but I learned from the debriefing instructor, Mr. Zane, that I had messed up a few of my checklist calls. He went on to tell me that I would have another opportunity to attempt the HAAR night time qualification in New Mexico. With all the crew chiefs huddled in the trailer I felt a sense of failure sink in.

Mr. Zane addressed the entire BMQ class after I learned about my failed qualification attempt. "We are heading to Virginia next and you guys all need to bring your A-game."

He gave us a quick timeline and we left the trailer. We had less than 24 hours to pack our bags for the trip to Virginia Beach. The trip was going to be closely followed by the New Mexico TDY trip. The New Mexico trip was talked up a lot because representatives from all the companies were going to be there. Different FE's from all three battalions were going to make sure the chiefs from their companies were up to speed and would be a valuable asset to them.

CHAPTER 8
BEACHES AND DESERT

★ ★ ★

We were nearing the end of the course and while I was excited about how far I had come I knew it was just the beginning. On the drive home after leaving the BMQ trailer debrief I received a text message from my platoon sergeant. It wasn't a very long message but I got the gist shortly after reading it. The text said, 'Burnett, you're headed to the sand box on the November rotation.'

Shit! The news I had been waiting for. I was going to deploy with Alpha Company shortly after graduating BMQ. A rush of emotions ran through me. I was ecstatic, and I couldn't wait to put bullets in the bad guys and finally contribute in a meaningful way to the fight. While I was excited to deploy and work behind the mini gun, I was nervous too. I didn't know how the guys at my new company would accept me, since nearly all of the Alpha Company guys had never met me. I had to get through the final portions of the BMQ course first then I could start worrying about my first big boy deployment.

On my way back to my barracks room I noticed the sun starting to rise after flying all night. On my way back I noticed several regular Army units running in formations and doing PT on the giant parade field I passed everyday driving to and from the compound. It was the exact same field where I learned the importance of always having your dog tags on you. Seeing all the soldiers running and yelling cadences reminded me how far

I made it and how different the new special operations unit I was a part of really was. I made it back to my barracks and wanted to fight how tired I was, and get all the packing done for the upcoming TDY trip. The trip to VA was just around the corner and it was prime tourist beach season. I don't know if I was more excited about bikinis, beach fly overs, or just going on my first TDY trip in general. Either way I had to get packed so I could get some sleep before the cross country flight. I crashed at noon and didn't wake up until 0300 the next morning. I could have slept a few more hours, but I knew my body didn't want to sleep anymore. It was time to fly!

I arrived at the flight line at 0700 and the instructors already had the birds opened. I saw several of them loading the aircraft with bags and gear for the trip. Another critical crew chief role was being able to load the aircraft while maintaining a sustainable CG (Center of Gravity). This insured the aircraft was within proper weight and balance criteria. If the helicopter were too heavy and loaded down with fuel, passengers, and gear that could pose a real issue. CG also played a pivotal role in how the helicopter handled in flight. The pilots counted on us to achieve the crucial loading standard. I hustled to the birds on the flight line to help the instructors.

Since we were going to conduct over water tasks, we had to bring our over water gear. The gear was used when conducting any operation over the water for long periods of time. The gear I'm referring to is a MAC (Mustang-buoyant Aviation Coverall) suit, LPF, and a HEED's bottle. All of the equipment was introduced to us in Dunker School. We learned how imperative the gear was while over a large body of water. After hearing about the tasks we would be executing I was thankful for the Dunker School pre-requisite. The MAC suit was a giant marshmallow man wet suit. Depending on the water temperature would determine if we had to wear the suit or not. However, even during the summer, if an instructor wanted to punish you, then you got to wear the suit no matter what. The LPF was a concealed life vest worn around the neck and one I struggled to inflate in the Dunker course during the swim test. The last piece of over water equipment was the HEED's bottle or a bottle filled with compressed oxygen. This was another over water item I became very familiar with during Dunker School roll overs. This was the one piece of equipment stressed and engrained in our minds while at the school. Being accountable was taught to all of us early in basic training and only continued on throughout the Army. It was crucial when flying as a crew chief to know what equipment was required for each task.

"Chocks," the pilot called over the radio.

Followed by SGT Matt, "Removed and secured."

It was always better flying with a crew in the class you liked, and fortunately that was the case for the trip to VA. I was in the back, on the ramp with SGT Matt and as soon as he made the call, he flung the chocks onto the back of the ramp so he could focus on coiling his long 50 foot ICS cord. I grabbed the wheel chocks and hung them on the internal fuselage wall. At right ramp, I needed to continually watch the maintenance panel, while constantly checking for aggressive vibrations and making sure all systems inside the aircraft were operating properly.

We began to taxi behind chalk one and two. Three massive MH-47G Chinook's began their taxi to Fury Sod. I was excited to be flying in a flight of three. While I thought two giant 160th Chinooks flying in formation was cool, being in a flight of three was magnificent. All birds finished hover checks at Fury Sod and after a brief pause with all the birds chomping at the bit and ready to take to the sky, we got the call from tower. "You're clear for take-off."

Whoosh, whoosh, whoosh, the rotor wash was unreal and all three birds began to lift off the ground. Chalk one, then two, then us in the final bird, all in synchronized harmony. I felt the monstrous power underneath me. The nose pitched forward and after passing the tower we made a hard right bank. I looked out of the right ramp window to see the two birds in front of us making the same right turn. It was the most beautiful thing I had ever witnessed, and we were off.

Several hours later I began to see more buildings out of the open ramp window. As we transitioned from flying over rural communities and fields, then into densely populated towns everyone in the aircraft began to perk up.

"We are about 30 minutes out, gentlemen," the PIC came over the radio. Everyone already knew that as we had been listening to the back and forth radio calls between the pilot and certain towers in the area.

Another ten minutes and the lead instructor pilot from chalk one called over the radio, "We are going to do a beach fly over before we go in to land boys."

Holy shit, I was thinking to myself, now this is some real Hollywood shit!

Another ten minutes and I gazed over the level ramp to look down below. We made it to the end of the beach and left the houses below to witness the dark blue ocean. All of a sudden I could see chalk one and two making a hard banking left turn to line up with the beach.

"Coming left," our pilot called eagerly over the radio.

"Clear left," SGT Max, who was standing at left gun called out.

Closely following behind chalk two we began making our hard banking left turn. We lined up with the shoreline and I could see all the tourists baking in the sun prop up off their beach towels. All eyes were on us.

The lead bird came over the radio, "Coming down to 50 feet AWL (Above Water Level)."

In sync, all helicopters descended and we were gaining speed above the ocean parallel with the tourist littered beach. The entire packed beach came to a halt. Beach balls, Frisbees, and beer drinking ceased. The entire beach was looking at the three bird formation. It was the coolest thing I had been a part of. I imagine this is what the crew chief was feeling when the other regular Army guys and I were looking at him on the flight line in Afghanistan. We were so low to the water I could feel mist on my face from the rotor wash blowing up the salty ocean water. Thousands of people were waving and just awestruck about the amazing scene they were witnessing. I thought about waving as we were so close, the beach goers would surely see me. Then I thought back to the time when I waved to the masked man behind the mini gun in Bagram. I recalled he never waved and it was a lot cooler that way. I grasped the feeling from the other side of the tinted visor now. I refrained from waving as I watched from my completely shielded flight helmet. I was almost a BMQ crew chief and I could taste the finish line. The beach came to an end and all three birds pulled thrust and we all began to climb again. The minute-long Hollywood flyover was over.

After the long trip we finally landed at NAS (Naval Air Station) Oceana. A Navy Master jet base. Rental cars were there waiting for us as a liaison had flown commercial to get the logistical stuff set up. Three brand new black Suburbans, one for each crew awaited. I felt like the CIA or part of an elite special operations unit. Oh wait, we were. I had to keep reminding myself that I was in an elite unit now and these are the kinds of things that happen. From the most intense training to the most blacked out Suburbans, I had to start grasping I was a part of one of those units I used to dream about. My regular Army days were over.

The crew that I flew with began to unload the helicopter while I went to grab a Suburban. After getting the birds closed up we loaded up the vehicles and headed to our hotel on the main VA Beach strip. Just a short drive, and we were unloading our gear and checking in at the front desk. Twenty Night Stalkers gathered in the lobby waiting for the frantic lady at the front desk to check us in. Tourists and civilians alike passed through the lobby trying to meander through the maze of soldiers. The civilians passing through were curious and interested as to who we were and what we were doing. Although the unit made it a point to appear as inconspicuous as possible when out in public, it was kind of hard to hide all of the military looking bags and the dozen or so black hard cases. After everyone was checked in, the pilots went to occupy a ballroom to set up their planning gear and erect an impromptu ready room. The ballroom would turn into the mission planning headquarters for the duration of the trip.

After getting settled into my room with SGT Matt as my roommate, all the chiefs headed to the lobby after showering. We knew our show time for the morning and we all decided to hit the strip and grab something to eat for dinner. Strolling through crowds of people and taking deep breaths of cool ocean air, we finally settled on an upscale pizza joint. We shared different pizzas among the table and exchanged stories about flying, crewing, and our different companies back home. The brotherhood was more real to me than ever. As we were exchanging stories I realized I didn't have this type of bond with my old unit. We carried on, discussing the upcoming tasks we had to perform. Although we had gone over them time and time again in class back at Campbell, we hadn't actually performed them yet. Tomorrow would be filled with a series of repetitions of a task called ladders. We wouldn't actually be able to obtain the qualification because we didn't have live body customers on board to go through the iterations with us. Instead, we were told, we would be going through all the motions without supporting another elite team.

The next day we were back at NAS Oceana prepping the birds for our over water ladder mission. The giant Jacobs Ladder was tied in at the ramp and was used to extract operators out of the water. Whether extracting a dive team or an SBT (Special Boat Team), this task was ideal for getting a large team out of the water. While we were training using the ladder on the ramp it could also be configured to be lowered out of the hell hole. The hell hole was a square door in the center of the helicopter used primarily for center hook sling load operations. The Chinook was capable and well known for lifting aircraft during a rescue situation or just carrying large shipping containers from base to base. Although this was cool, this was where the regular Army excelled. The 160th didn't focus on or do many sling load operations. We would often fly without the center hook installed in order to perform different center hole operations like extracting teams with the Jacobs Ladder.

With the ladder hooked up to the proper ramp tie down points we pulled thrust and we were off toward the blue ocean water. After increasing altitude to 100 feet AWL the water was clear and so was our flight path. The further we got out into the blue ocean abyss the more uneasy I felt. The beach was so distant. I couldn't see it anymore and within ten minutes we were out over the open water without a boat or parcel of land in sight. Dunker School training kept running through my head, and I definitely didn't want to use it.

We were all wearing our MAC suits, and not because the water was below a certain temperature, but rather to train and get the feel for wearing the suit while conducting overwater operations. Chalk one and two began the approach to simulate a ladder extraction and let us do our thing in the back of the bird. We began the descent to the ocean below and SGT Matt lowered the ramp. SGT Matt and I positioned ourselves on the stubby wings of the ramp.

"Good height good hover," SGT Matt called over the radio as the misty water covered my visor and face.

The goal of the ladder task was to call the pilot to the proper height over the water. Ten feet was the targeted height before tossing the ladder into the water below. Once we got the pilots down to an acceptable height we let them know.

"Got you off ten, looking good sir," SGT Matt called over the radio.

"Ladders, Ladders, Ladders," the pilot responded.

SGT Matt and I reached for the coiled ladder and rolled it off the ramp. I looked down and watched it splash into the water.

"Ladders in the water," SGT Matt called.

One of our BMQ instructors came over the radio and took over simulating what the call and response would sound like if we were actually extracting a team. "Team swimming toward the ladder. Good height good hover. First man on the ladder." The instructor continued.

The calls needed to constantly be verbalized to let the pilots know what was going on in the back while they continued to hover. The instructors got on to us if we paused for too long and weren't relaying what was happening from moment to moment. I learned that the hard way during my hoisting qualification.

SGT Matt picked up the call after an on looking instructor pointed to him, "Last man on the ladder." The imaginary team was almost retrieved from the water as SGT Matt continued, "Last man on board, working on retrieving ladder."

As I heard the call I began to help SGT Matt pull the ladder back on board as quickly as possible. "Ladder retrieved, ramps up aft ready," SGT Matt exhaled into his mic.

Soon after SGT Matt raised up the ramp the pilot said, "Chalk three coming out, chalk three coming out."

"Clear forward left," the left gun chief said.

Followed by a, "Clear forward right," from right gun. The day continued, switching through different crew chiefs so everyone got several turns making the ladder calls.

After simulating ropes, ladders, and hoisting over water, the trip finally came to an end. The week was exciting and nothing short of exhausting. While there were no qualifications taking place at Virginia Beach, the BMQ class and I were getting better at our jobs. We would all eventually have to get qualified in the tasks we learned, but not until returning back to our companies. We weren't able to work with any live bodies and actually extract, hoist, or rope guys from the helicopter during the trip. This was the main reason no one received a qualification completion for any of the practiced tasks. Nonetheless, we were heading home more prepared for the next opportunity to attempt the real qualification. After a long TDY trip we were en route to Campbell Army Airfield just to prepare for New Mexico.

We landed at Ft. Campbell and began unloading bags and equipment we strapped down for the flight. Downloading, closing up, and getting the bird ready for the next trip took a little longer than just a normal night or day flight. After three hours of getting everything straight and ready to roll for the New Mexico trip, the crews, once again, headed to the BMQ trailer. After an hour long debrief and receiving the timeline for the next trip, I headed home to get some rest. I had a day off and used my time to clean my uniforms and get packed for the final BMQ TDY trip. I was excited to finish the course, and although becoming a crew chief was my long term goal I began to feel nervous. After finishing the course, it wouldn't be long before I headed back to Afghanistan. Only this time I would be going to the familiar land with a new title under my belt representing an entirely different unit.

After going through the same packing and loading routine as Virginia the crew and I were ten minutes out from Double Eagle Airport in Albuquerque, NM. We stopped at a few regional airports for gas on the way down from Campbell. We received so many intriguing looks from the regional airport patrons. It was a cool feeling being such a spectacle to someone who had never seen the mystical beasts before. I knew the feeling quite well.

After the long flight, we finally landed in New Mexico at Double Eagle Airport. The crew immediately began unloading the birds. Again, three black Suburbans were waiting for us. All I could think about was who was coming from Alpha Company to critique SGT Matt's and my progress. It was critical that we didn't mess anything up during the training exercise while being overlooked by an Alpha Company representative. Whoever was there to monitor our every crew chief move would surely report back to the company once we were complete with the trip. Neither of us wanted to represent ourselves to be unworthy for a crew chief spot within Alpha Company. We knew we had to bring our A-game. This TDY trip was the super bowl for all the chiefs in the course, to prove to their companies they had what it took. We were confident in our skills but it wasn't over 'til it was over. We drove to our hotel and unloaded, again setting up another impromptu ready room. We were set and primed to do HAAR the following night after a day long range day at one of the biggest aerial gunnery ranges in North America. After my roommate and I ordered some pizza I went through the ARSOA (Army Special Operations Aviation) manual. I made sure to read and re-read the HAAR task. It was my last chance to qualify in this task.

"All right, we are crossing into the WSMR air space. Take a look at the targets and your sectors of fire," the training PIC called over the ICS, as we flew over the vast aerial gunnery range. The size and variety of targets were nothing like range ███ back at Campbell. I was at left gun, and as I hunched over the gun to look out and down over the range I could feel the Alpha Company FE standing directly behind me. Alpha Company had sent SSG Chris F. to monitor and observe my knowledge and skill set during the short TDY trip. As we descended to get a visual of what we would be shooting at, I noticed tanks, buildings, airplane relics, satellites, hidden bunkers, and even a submarine. It was mind blowing how many bullet riddled targets lay on the sandy dunes below. The PIC had the entire crew convinced after telling an elaborate story mid-flight, that we were flying over an old submarine training lake.

"Bullshit," a 3rd battalion FE who was observing another guy in the class said.

The PIC continued the story, "Yeah, they drained the lake to turn it into this range. That's how that massive submarine got out there." Everyone in the cabin looked at each other all shaking our heads.

"OK sir." SSG Chris F. the FE from Alpha Company chimed in.

"Coming right." the well liked and very accredited training PIC said.

"Clear right," another chief in the course responded from right gun.

"Range is hot, both left and right sides are cleared hot," the pilot sounded off. The right gun and I had to work as a team and not clog up the ICS or interrupt one another while making gun calls. This was a new concept since back at the Campbell range only one side was able to shoot at a time. At WSMR it was completely different. The range was massive and allowed for both the left and right side guns to be fired at the same time.

"Left guns hot, left guns engaging," I spat into the mic boom trying to talk over the already firing right gun.

"Clear to engage." The PIC responded. I flipped the mini gun on and pressed both thumb triggers as I aimed at an old rusty satellite. The loud hum of the six barrels spinning followed by the notorious mini gun sound ensued. I watched bullets impact the sand to the left of my target. Dust flew everywhere making a large sand cloud. I began to turn the gun slightly walking the rounds to the target. Before they could impact my designated target I heard a loud click over all the aircraft noise. My gun seized and I pressed the trigger again with my naïve thumbs. I felt the electronic relay click inside the spade grip as we passed more littered targets.

"Left gun jammed, left gun cold working jam." I informed the pilots. I ran through the procedures and realizing I had a double feed, I dropped the feeder de-linker and began the procedure. I turned the rotor inside the assembly as SSG Chris F. stood over me watching my every move. I continued to spin the gear freeing the bent, mangled casing inside. I lifted the gun's de-linker underneath the weapon with one hand and lined up the quick release pin I pulled out with the other. After clicking the component into place I looked out the window and realized we were still over the range.

"Left gun hot, left gun engaging," I relayed to the cockpit.

"Clear to engage," the familiar pilot answered. I flipped the toggle switch from off to on and depressed the trigger buttons. I anxiously waited for the rounds to start exiting the barrels and destroy an old wrecked airplane below. I hoped I cleared the jam and would be shooting again since I was being watched closely. Braaaaaaaaaaap, the mini gun let out its infamous shout. I released the trigger and searched for a new target after obliterating the plane. "Left gun engaging," I called again. I let thousands of rounds pierce through a tall two story building.

SSG Chris F. induced three more jams over the range and I was able to successfully clear them, some faster than others. I felt confident in my ability to clear and utilize the M-134 mini gun to its full potential. After a long day over the range we landed back at Double Eagle Airport, just to get reset for the night time HAAR flight. SSG Chris F. took me over to a hangar that the airport allowed us to use to store equipment for the trip. I knew he was about to debrief me on my mini gun proficiency. We pulled up two vacant chairs next to a gleaming twin prop airplane in the hangar.

"Well you did OK," he said staring directly at me. I nodded and he proceeded to quiz me on the different weapon ROE's (Rule of Engagement). It was critical to know the three different ROE's that pertained to the armament on the aircraft. While deployed the mission and combat environment would dictate how and when we could use our weapons. Weapons free, weapons tight, and weapons hold were imperative ROE's to understand and a key in maintaining the M-134 mini gun qualification. Having already received the qualification at Campbell I was grateful to learn I was keeping the coveted gun qualification. After the debrief and revisiting lessons learned from my gun time over the range I headed back to the aircraft to help the rest of the crew. There wasn't much to do on the helicopter, other than lug the empty ammo containers off, dis-mount the mini guns, and get the HAAR refuel panel set.

We took off and linked up with the KC-130 tanker to begin the night time HAAR operation. The pilots made several successful refueling attempts through the night and the last attempt was my time to shine. After a crew change in the back I was eager and ready at the right gun position.

"Moving to disconnect," one of the BMQ pilots interjected over the ICS.

After shutting both valves off on the refueling panel, I responded, "Roger."

A post refueling checklist was rambled off between both pilots in the cockpit for a few short minutes after the refueling probe broke away from the tanker's fuel hose. They finished up front and I began spitting the post refueling checklist out into my mic boom.

I finished the checklist and felt a lot more confident about my calls, and after a long night we headed back to the airport. The bird began to shut down after landing at the quaint regional New Mexico airport. While the guys in the back began to shut the bird down I unplugged from my ICS connection and began opening critical access panels at the front of the aircraft. I opened one just above the hallway that led into the cockpit. The access panel I removed revealed the bottom of the forward transmission, which was a critical component to look at during the post flight inspection. Running along the side of the small through way was another access panel which revealed the flight control closet. I heard the blades begin to slow as I finished opening up the panels. I began to grab the crew's NVG's to put them in their appropriate storage cases. I had a routine now and I was beginning to get the hang of the job. I was excited and I wanted to excel as a crew chief. The rotation of the blades came to a sudden halt as the pilots engaged the rotor brake in the cockpit. The APU cut off, and I removed my smelly, sweat soaked flight helmet.

"Burnett, come with me," an instructor called from the back of the aircraft. I made my way through the maze of guys taking off their flight gear in the cabin and finally to the back where the instructor was standing. He pulled me off to the side of the aircraft and began to debrief me since everyone else on board had already successfully completed the HAAR qualification. "You got the HAAR qualification," a tired and sweaty BMQ instructor informed me on the flight line. He finished by going over a few more things I could have done better. The quick brief concluded and we were both back in the bird putting sensitive gear away.

The next few days in New Mexico were filled with pinnacle and slope landings. A pinnacle landing gave us just another edge when supporting ground forces in a combat role. On an HLZ (Helicopter Landing Zone) that couldn't accommodate the large Chinook, a pinnacle was the backup procedure. The task was utilized while infilling or exfilling guys onto a building or a mountain cliff. The crew learned how to position the aft wheels over the landing zone before calling the aircraft down to the ground. The pilots would then balance the beast on the aft wheels, while guys on loaded or off loaded. The landing was a bit nerve wracking when executing the task on a rocky surface. If a rock slipped out from underneath the wheels, the bird would lose balance and we would have to reposition the aircraft again. The class got tons of practice during the last days and after receiving a wealth of crewing knowledge we were headed back to Ft. Campbell. Just like we had become so accustomed, we unloaded all the gear, cleaned up the bird, closed the bird, and headed into the BMQ trailer. It was bitter sweet walking to the trailer leaving the three glorious BMQ Chinooks on the flight line. It was the last time the class would fly on those three birds we all got to know so well. The instructors gave a final debrief in the trailer followed by talking about the crew chief role and what we needed to do in order to constantly improve our craft.

We met back at the trailer the next day after some long overdue rest. After the instructors gave a final brief, everyone shook hands and said our goodbyes. The class took in the final sights and sounds of the trailer, accepted our completion certificates, and exited the trailer one last time. After making my exit I headed to the Alpha Company office. There was no long drive to ponder what I had just gone through. No dramatic scene here, I literally took a thirty second walk to the hangar next to the trailer and I was in the Alpha Company office. With my completion certificate in hand I walked into the PSG's office and handed it over to SFC Dave. He was hunched over the desk looking over a handful of papers. SFC Jayson who I had been dealing with was deployed, and SFC Dave had just gotten back from a deployment. "Congrats now it's time to put your training to work. You ready to go?" He energetically asked me.

"Roger," I timidly and half excitedly said. From school after school, and nonstop training after completing Green Platoon, I caught on that the pace of my new unit was no joke. The pre-requisite training I endured after Green Platoon had taken me almost a year, and now I could finally deploy as an Alpha Company crew chief. It was a long journey but I was eager to start logging some flight hours in a combat role with my brothers.

CHAPTER 9
FIRE PAY

I learned a lot over the last year of training, but it was finally time to head across the pond and be a part of something new. When I was a kid I always watched war movies. I developed a deep rooted love for how a man or woman could put themselves in harm's way in order to protect his or her homeland. Maybe this concept I felt early on is what led me to embark on this journey. I didn't feel like I was contributing to the fight, or anything for that matter on my first deployment. I knew deep down that my first 160th deployment was going to be a lot different. Over the last year I had learned a lot of new skills. Skills that were only taught to a carefully selected group of guys. More importantly, I learned the true meaning of brotherhood in the last year, or so I thought. Even though I was still the new guy, I knew the guys in my company would share the same mindset. The inherent thought process after all the training was to look after everyone on the aircraft no matter the situation. The idea that laying down your own life for your brothers was the only option. I was eager, nervous, and hopeful that I would perform at my highest level in order to meet the highest standards.

It was 1900, I looked at my barracks room one last time, turned off the lights, and headed out the door. At 1915 I rolled into the compound with a lot of emotions running through me. We were rolling out with six guys from Alpha Company to replace guys in the company who had been down range for the last 60 days. As the new guy I was automatically going to be putting in a 90-day deployment. This compared to my last 13-month deployment a year ago was going to be a walk in the park, or so I thought. It was mid-October now and from what the more senior guys were telling me, I wouldn't see much action. They informed me things tended to slow down in the winter months. This was kind of a disappointment but at the same time it was probably a good thing. I could learn the ins and outs of deploying with the unit without getting shot at right away.

I pulled up to the front of the Alpha Company office to drop off my bags and go park my truck way in the back where everyone who was deployed parked. Getting to Afghanistan with 160th was going to be far different from deploying with the regular Army. On my last deployment it took the unit months to prepare to head over there because we had to bring everything, and because we were replacing an entire division. We flew over in a nice 777 flown by United all the way to Germany and then switched over to a C-17.

Back at the Alpha Company office I was briefed that we were not only taking six guys but a Chinook as well, to replace another Chinook that had been over there for some time. Just like guys getting rotated in and out of the country, 160th did the same with their helicopters. Since the chiefs were in charge of the birds we were responsible for loading it on the C-17. Instead of having a magnificent send off like I remembered from my regular Army days this was far different. Sure there were a few families bringing their husbands and sending them off with a kiss. But there was definitely no sign holding or popcorn machines for the kids and crazy balloons. This was simply get to the office, grab your shit, and go baby go. We tugged the 54,000-pound beast across the flight line to the other side of the runway where a C-17 was parked and waiting for us to begin the loading process. I was new to this, but several of the guys I was with had gotten used to the routine.

Coincidentally, SSG Atch was also on the deployment and it was his 12th with the company, so he knew everything that needed to happen to a T. As the senior ranking enlisted guy among the crew dogs I took all my direction from him during the loading process. What an amazing thing to behold, seeing a giant helicopter being winched into another aircraft to be flown across the world and eventually be put in harm's way. After the Air Force load masters and all the crew dogs got the Chinook loaded inside the aircraft, we winched up the forward and aft transmissions. The crucial aircraft components were mounted on their own transportation dollies after they were removed from the aircraft. After winching the final aircraft components on board, everyone started scrambling around like mice to a block of cheese. The guys I would learn to call my brothers were snatching chains and shackles from pre-determined cutouts of the C-17. There were diagrams taped on both sides of the Chinook, depicting how the chains were supposed to be oriented in order to strap the 54,000-pound helicopter in place. While the other guys didn't need to glance at the cheat sheet once, having done it so many times, I found myself staring at the diagram often. Everything was finally strapped in, and since the crew flying with the helicopter had to get everything on the C-17 we also got first choice of seats, which was a big deal.

All the seats would eventually be filled with a bus load of 160th personnel that were ordered to cross over the runway once the helicopter was done being loaded. I had no idea where the best seats were as I had never experienced this type of configuration or deployment.

On my first big Army deployment we flew from Germany to Afghanistan in the very type of aircraft we just loaded a helicopter into. However, the configuration was much different. Instead of having a giant Chinook in the belly of the massive Air Force cargo plane, there were rows and rows of seats. Imagine theater seats, but a lot closer and a lot more uncomfortable. It was at my regular Army unit's discretion at the time to make certain we wore full armor while on the 6-hour leg to Afghanistan. On the contrary, since the Chinook took up the majority of space in the center of the plane the only seats available ran along each side of the fuselage which gave us a lot more room to spread out. Alpha Company had our spots picked out, and while I was busy learning how to strap the aircraft down, another crew dog had snagged me a prime seat.

After finishing loading and strapping down the MH-47G Chinook and all the main components, the crew went over all the tie downs again to make sure everything was locked in place and tied down to specifications. When we concluded the once over, SSG Atch, who was the NCOIC (Non Commissioned Officer in Charge) for the deployment, called us all out of the C-17 on to the flight line. The sun was setting over the trees in the distance and I could see all the fierce black helicopters across the flight line oriented perfectly in their parking spots. A cold breeze drifted across my face as the last few crew chiefs came out of the airplane's cargo bay to meet the rest of the Alpha Company guys on the flight line. In the distance I could see the big white school bus picking up the remaining guys to cross over the runway and then board the C-17 for departure.

SSG Atch began to speak. I was still the new guy but in the team huddle before the big game I didn't feel like the benched 3rd stringer anymore. I was a starter on this team of freedom. I felt like I was about to be a part of something I couldn't even grasp quite yet, I just knew it was going to be huge. SSG Atch began to tell us that the missions aren't as often, meaning every day, because it was in the midst of a slow season, and I suppose that was due to the winter months. He went on, "Although the guys down range aren't going out on mission every night, they have taken some small arms fire over the last month." I perked up all of a sudden and leaned in a little closer. I was excited, eager, and nervous all at the same time. I knew from stories that our birds got shot at frequently since my new company was always deep behind enemy lines and right up close where the fighting was hard. This felt different though, instead of hearing stories being exchanged in the crew office I was being briefed on what to expect when I was crewing. The one thing I had set out to do almost two years ago. "Remember boys, we just need to get shot at once a month to get Fire Pay," SSG Atch added.

The group nodded in acknowledgement since we already became aware of the new rule. Just weeks before, deployed aircrews would receive an extra stipend on each pay check called, 'Fire Pay,' regardless if they took enemy fire or not. The new rule stipulated that aircrews must take enemy fire in flight at least once a month to be paid the stipend. I knew I signed up for this hard hitting action and welcomed the monthly stipend.

The time had arrived to go do what I had dreamed of doing ever since I saw the 160th crew chief taxiing along the flight line in BAF. SSG Atch singled me out in the team huddle and made sure I damn well knew this wasn't training anymore and the stakes were high.

He added, "We are expecting a lot from you so don't fuck anything up or it will be your ass. We all have each other's backs over there. I don't care what crew chief is shooting, but if you're on the same side of the aircraft as the person shooting you damn well better be shooting in the same place as the guy next to you. This is not training anymore Burnett," he reiterated, "We always have one another's back no matter what, you understand?" He glared in my direction not blinking once.

"Roger that," I said as my voice cracked finishing confidently.

"Alright men let's get the job done and come home in one piece." SSG Atch concluded.

Everyone in the circle nodded in SSG Atch's direction, and we headed back into the C-17 to take our seats. As I took my seat I looked around the massive cargo bay. In front of me was a giant Chinook that we just loaded. More amazing was, I would be flying the same helicopter in a war torn country in the next three days. All the other guys sitting to the left and right of me all had their head phones in. The senior guys already had routines down from several prior load outs. This way of deploying was all new to me. No sendoff ceremony, no hugs and kisses good bye from loved ones, no cushy passenger airline to take us to Germany. This was far different and felt much more real and substantive versus the last time I left the country. We waited for the sun to go down, and wouldn't take off until night fall. Leaving under the cover of darkness was what the unit dictated. The change from a big Army deployment brought an inexplicable excitement. I was now a crew chief in special operations, about to go do special operations shit. As I continued to ponder, the white school bus pulled up behind the giant C-17. More 160th personnel started filling the remaining seats while I continued to imagine what the deployment would hold for me.

Before I knew it the pilot came over the loud speaker, "We are about to push off, buckle up." While the pilot came over the radio one of the load masters in the back of the plane was leaning over a station at the back of the aircraft equipped with buttons and gauges. He depressed one of the buttons and the aft ramp of the C-17 slowly began to close. I watched hangars, a faint tree line, and the Ft. Campbell silhouette begin to disappear. That would be the last time I would see US soil for the next 90 days. Engines 1, 2, 3, and 4 all began to whine starting chronologically. The power of the aircraft engines resonated through the large cargo bay. I put in some ear plugs and looked over at the guys to my left and right. I had no idea what I was about to get myself into, but I did know that no matter what these were my brothers. Some of them had earphones in and others earplugs with eyes closed, some reading books. I had a million things running through my mind constantly. Luckily we were all given Ambien for the flight to Germany, which was another thing I didn't get to experience on my first deployment.

There were no flight attendants announcing a, 'Prepare for take-off,' call. It was just a bunch of Air Force load masters walking around the cabin making final checks on the secured cargo. After a quick taxi and U-turn on the runway, we were airborne. The hydraulic landing gear retracted and the cabin lights dimmed. The cabin was dark with a few exit sign lights glowing above cabin doors. I popped my Ambien and dozed off. Next stop Germany for a pit stop, fuel, and a meal, then to put bullets in bad guys, or so I thought.

The 10-hour flight to Germany didn't seem very long and thankfully the Ambien had done its job. I woke up to a call over the speaker system and the bright lights in the cabin turned on overhead. We were ten minutes out from landing at Ramstein Air Base in Germany. Once on the ground I looked through the well-lit cabin and everyone was still in a groggy daze from the Ambien. I unbuckled and began to follow everyone out the cabin door. As I walked out of the door and down the aircraft steps to the flight line pavement I was greeted with a misty rain and clouds that mimicked my groggy state.

Two white busses, identical to the ones at Campbell, were parked at the bottom of the stairs, waiting to transport us to our new lay over home. From what I was told we were staying in Germany for a day before flying out to Afghanistan. This transition allowed the aircrew of the C-17 to get their proper crew rest before flying again. We packed the busses and in the short 20-minute drive I got to see some of the German country side as the location of our sleeping quarters were off the main post. The busses slowly approached a check point where a gate was guarded by both German and US forces. As we pulled up to the check point the bus came to a halt. A German man boarded the bus and asked everyone to hold up their identification cards in a thick German accent. We obliged and he made his way down the narrow walk way checking everyone's ID's. One by one he stepped through the aisle. He said something to the driver after confirming the Night Stalker's identities and the busses air brakes released. We proceeded into a holocaust looking compound, which seemed fitting.

We off loaded the bus and headed toward a single door at the front of a green warehouse structure. Inside, we were met by an older German man at the front counter. He made his way around the counter to greet us. The inside of the building was filled with bunk beds to house soldiers coming from or going to Afghanistan, much like Manas, Kyrgyzstan. There was a pool table, ping pong table, and a room equipped with a giant screen to watch movies. The floor was concrete and it had a, 'musty horror film,' type feel. There was a small kitchen area where we could enjoy bottled water and disgusting microwavable meals that were included in the 4-star bed and breakfast. I wasn't complaining by any means. I was excited to be in Alpha Company and grateful to deploy with the guys I was with now.

The older man began to brief us about the holocaust structure. He pointed to an older lady behind the desk and we were instructed to sign out a set of sheets, blanket, and a pillow for our selected bunk beds. After retrieving my bedding all the Alpha Company guys walked past the open kitchen area to be welcomed by hundreds of sprawling bunk beds. They were all in separate rows with nothing separating them. Just an open warehouse full of bunkbeds. The other Alpha Company guys and I selected our bunks and we were on our own for the night. Some of us went to take a shower and grab chow while others laid down to relax. I chose the latter and didn't wake up until the following morning. It was either the jet lag or the hangover effect from the Ambien, but I just passed out.

"Burnett, wake up," a violent shake brought me back from my coma. I opened my eyes and SSG Atch was hovering over me. He said, "It's time to go man." I hadn't even changed out of my uniform nor my boots. I slowly came to a seated position on my lower bunk as the springs creaked underneath me. I gathered my things together and removed the sheets off my bed. I headed toward the gathering of deadly looking Night Stalkers exiting the warehouse. They were dropping their sheets and pillows off in giant bins at the door. I tossed my sheets in the bin and headed out the door. We boarded the same white busses and returned to the flight line. The group loaded into the C-17 where we were greeted by the same helicopter and equipment. The engines spooled up and just the way we left Campbell we were wheels up in no time.

The last leg to Afghanistan was long but a lot shorter than the first leg of the flight. I tried to fall asleep again for the last portion, but my Germany coma wouldn't let me get there. Most of the guys were asleep on the floor during the flight. Through my headphones, while listening to the Johnny Cash classic, I Won't Back Down, I heard the load master come over the intercom system. "OK we are about 30 minutes from KAF (Kandahar Air Field), start getting your things together." He went on to say that we would be going in blacked out. The lights didn't come on in the cabin like before. A loud thud echoed in the cabin, after the wheels hit the ground. Although there weren't many windows on board, I could feel the aircraft start to slow then finally stop. The ramp started to lower at the rear of the aircraft and I gazed out to catch a glimpse of KAF for the first time. As the ramp continued to lower I started to see a convoy of vehicles from Humvees to various armored and non-armored Toyota pick-up trucks. There was an odd looking short foreign white bus too. All the vehicles had their hazards on, which was common practice on military flight lines back home. Several personnel were standing outside the vehicles and the amber lights from the hazards were bouncing off of their unknown faces. Some guys were wearing civilian clothes and others in military uniform. By the looks of what all the guys were wearing I knew it was going to be a cold first deployment. I gathered my gear and headed toward the forward door of the aircraft.

CHAPTER 10
TO THE X

★ ★ ★

As I deplaned the aircraft there was a recognizable Alpha Company face at the bottom of the steps. Some of the other guys from the trip were already starting to gather around him. He wasn't hard to miss, it was SFC Jayson, the big PSG who recruited me close to a year ago in Green Platoon. He had been in KAF for a while, and SSG Atch was about to slap hands with him to take his place. I made it to the bottom of the stairs, and without missing a beat, he looked at me and said, "Burnett, are you fucking ready?"

I replied, "Roger Sergeant."

He glanced away as he said, "You fucking better be," in an arrogant you're still the FNG kind of manner. He addressed everyone after the attack the new guy ploy and told us to get the C-17 unloaded. We made our way back into the aircraft after throwing our gear in the foreign white bus next to the giant C-17. Like ants to a dead carcass we began unstrapping the chained aircraft and equipment in the plane. The bright lights in the cabin cast their glow over the entire cavernous space in the darkness of the cold Afghanistan flight line. Some of the guys I had flown over with started chatting with different guys from our company and other companies who had been in KAF for the last two months. This was all new to me, being in a unit that does such short deployments and just replacing a guy. The guys getting replaced helped us unload the aircraft and load another one that had been flying in Afghanistan.

After winching the Chinook out of the C-17 I watched a maintenance guy drive an aircraft tug around toward the back of the Chinook. I must have been the only one there that didn't know the routine. It was seamless and incredible. A few other maintenance guys hooked up a tow bar to the aft wheel of the Chinook then guided the tug to it. After hooking up the tow bar to the tug the driver began to push the aircraft toward an open lit hangar on the flight line.

The hangar was 200 meters away from the nose of the C-17. Maintenance guys, flight guys, and avionics guys, all with different companies within 2nd battalion 160th followed the aircraft and other equipment toward the hangar. As another maintenance guy guided the tug driver and aircraft into the hangar I watched the left side of the hangar to make sure everything was going to clear.

SSG Atch pulled all the Alpha Company guys aside in the dark, just outside the hangar. "I know you guys are tired, but you know how this shit goes." He went on to tell us that we would be assisting the maintenance guys on putting the aircraft together until the day crew relieved us. The local time was 2300, and you could see the fatigue on everyone's faces. He said he was going to tell someone to go grab us hot plates from the chow hall so we could get some well needed calories before putting the helicopter back together.

After breaking from the huddle we headed into the hangar to see several maintenance guys going to town on the Chinook. They were putting major components together all working on different parts of the aircraft. From my maintenance days in the regular Army I knew a great deal about the process so I wasn't concerned about helping out. SSG Atch asked me if I had any maintenance background earlier during the trip over. I was able to give him a brief background of my maintenance days. Some guys went straight from AIT to Green Platoon, and then to flight company without having ever worked on the helicopter but in AIT. Luckily this wasn't the case for me and I could add some value in putting the Chinook back together again.

The night dragged on fighting sleep deprivation while trying to assemble the aircraft. The sun started to come up and I started to see my surroundings. The place I would call home for the next three months was a familiar scene. As the sun started to rise there was a haze across the flight line and runway. The clouds obstructed my view to see to the end of one of the runways. I saw military compounds lining both sides of the flight line, with several different aircraft parked on either side. From foreign aircraft to US, and from rotary to fixed wing, the airport was vast. Just at the end of the runway that wasn't obstructed by the hazy mist, I could see mud huts and little towns past the double razor wire perimeter. The perimeter was lined with guard towers about one every half mile.

"You guys ready to go grab chow?" SSG Atch asked all of us as we sipped rip its and admired the sunrise while taking a break outside the hangar. The day time maintenance guys started to trickle into the hangar housing the currently half assembled Chinook.

We loaded on the Alpha Company bus and SSG Atch jumped in the driver seat. He proceeded to take us to the compound where we would be living before heading to chow. The sun was starting to reveal itself from behind a few mountains across the Red Desert. A short drive through the windy FOB roads and we pulled in front of a heavily fortified compound. We were met with a gate that I couldn't see past. The two US civilian guards stepped onto the bus and asked for everyone's compound badges. I received a special badge prior to deploying and I had it at the ready. After glancing at everyone's badges a third guard rolled the gate open. As the gate began to open I noticed a few guys in civilian clothes walking around inside the gated area that SSG Atch began to drive us through.

The compound was comprised of two long rows of shipping containers stacked on top of each other with stairs leading to the second floor of the containers. A common cost effective way for the government to build housing for deployed personnel was to convert shipping containers into bedrooms, and that's exactly what they were. My new shipping container home awaited me as SSG Atch stopped the bus alongside the row of containers. I was excited for the living situation since it was a huge upgrade compared to my last deployment in the shoddy eight-man B-hut. We grabbed our gear that we had wedged in the extra seats on the bus.

I walked out of the bus and SSG Atch told me I was rooming with SPC Andrew. He gave me my room assignment and said, "You're on the second floor."

My new upgraded room arrangement all of a sudden turned into a buzz kill once I heard the name. Ever since AIT this guy had been a pain in my ass. I didn't see him after AIT since I was assigned to a regular Army unit. SPC Andrew on the other hand, went straight to 160th. He was also a prick during the few encounters I had with him in the Alpha Company office. SSG Atch told me to head up stairs to download my gear, then we would head to chow.

I navigated my way up the janky metal stair case to the second floor of the shipping containers. I walked down a long wide hall open to the elements but covered with a roof overhead. As I lugged my gear to the last door on the left, I found the names on the door that read my name, along with SPC Andrew. I sighed before opening the door and heading into my new living quarters. SPC Andrew had been at the C-17 for the download, but I didn't see him after that. I guess he was helping another senior enlisted guy with some logistical stuff somewhere else. SPC Andrew and I were the same rank, but I learned pretty quickly that although rank meant a lot in the big Army, experience and time as a crew chief on the aircraft were superior in Alpha Company.

I walked into the elongated shipping container equipped with a vacant bed and dresser in the first half. In what appeared to be an occupied back half of the container, SPC Andrew appeared from behind a large armoire that acted as a divider between the two sleeping areas.

"What's up dude?" A chipper SPC Andrew greeted me. This was nothing like the SPC Andrew I remembered. He was welcoming and we immediately dove into a conversation about the deployment. SPC Andrew had been in KAF for a month and had another two months before he would head back to the states. "You're on my crew." He said, and began giving me a brief run-down of how things worked in the desert.

It was a lot of information to take in all at once, but I was excited be a part of the fight no matter how cold it was during the winter months. He went on to tell me he was the number two man on the crew. The FE was the go to guy for the pilots, and the number two guy was the go to guy for the FE. The number two role among the crew was afforded to someone who showed discipline and a great understanding of the aircraft. The number two not only had a wide knowledge base of the Chinook, but also knew what needed to get done before critical missions. The role was normally only given to a more senior crew chief who had a few deployments under their belt. I respected SPC Andrew for having the role and I would learn the majority of crewing on the deployment from him.

Mid conversation while going over the aircraft and what SPC Andrew and the crew expected from me, there was a knock at the door. I opened it and SSG Atch in his country accent said, "You fuckers ready? Let's go to chow." I was still in uniform while SPC Andrew was in civilian clothes and to my confusion so was SSG Atch.

"Hurry up and change," SSG Atch said while looking at me.

During my regular Army deployment, it was mandatory to be in military uniform at all times. We were only allowed to wear civilian clothes while in our cramped rooms. If at any time we left our rooms, we had to be in full uniform. Yet another thing I had to get used to was wearing civilian clothes to chow and around the FOB when we weren't preparing for a mission. This special operations caveat was just one more rule that made the unit different from other conventional units. At the end of the day what mattered the most was the missions and how precisely they were executed. The unit was too focused on winning to worry about making sure you wore a certain uniform everywhere you went. Not to mention, civilian clothes were a lot more comfortable.

We headed out of our new sleeping quarters and jumped into the bus for some chow. After a quick bus ride to one of the chow halls on KAF, I was standing in line waiting to eat breakfast for dinner. I had to learn to get used to the interesting meal ritual since all of our operations took place at night. Hence the name Night Stalkers. In a sea of Army and Air Force uniforms the only group of guys in civilian clothes stood out like a sore thumb, and as we walked over to a large table eyes peered at us and whispers echoed through the chow hall. I knew they were speculating and thinking who the hell are those guys? I felt different and important. It was an odd feeling and one that is hard to describe, but while among the most elite group of guys I felt it. I had never felt anything like it while walking through the other tables to find a seat.

We inhaled our meals and everyone waited for the last guy to finish. SSG Atch looked at every crew member at the table in the eye and gave a nod. After a brief pause, and realizing everyone was finished, all at once we sat up and walked out together like we owned the chow hall.

We headed back to the compound to bed down for the day. After a decent night of sleep, I woke up to catch the sun going down. I was about to experience, for the first time, what it's actually like to go outside the wire on an actual mission. No more wake up and work on a helicopter for 12 hours, it was finally time to wake up and go out on mission. To actually be the guy I had until today only aspired to be. To be that guy I saw on the flight line a year ago. It was game time.

After waking up to SPC Andrew's annoying siren alarm clock, I was pumped. It was 1600 local and I only hoped we were going to leave the wire. After a quick shower and shave I put on my slick uniform. Another thing the company did while deployed was remove our unit identifying patches we normally wore on either shoulder. This only added to our secret unit concealment while deployed. We all met at the bottom of the shipping container steps where SSG Atch was standing. "Burnett you're the new guy and you will be the first one down here every morning no matter what," he sternly ordered.

"Roger Sergeant," I said in an, I just woke up, kind of voice.

"Alright the plan is to go get chow and head to the flight line to get the birds ready. SPC Andrew be sure to bring Burnett up to speed as quick as possible because we are rolling out tonight." SSG Atch had already been up for the last hour and received word from the pilots in the TOC (Tactical Operations Center) that we would be hitting a target compound that night. "We are going after a HVT (High Value Target) suspected of manufacturing IED's (Improvised Explosive Device)." My heart started racing when I heard we were going to fly. "SPC Andrew," SSG Atch looked over at SPC Andrew and continued, "Burnett is going to be at left gun on our bird, so make sure you get him squared away." Then he looked over at a dark skinned guy who I had never seen before. "SGT Andre you will be with me in the TOC going through your FE training." As I listened during the impromptu meeting I got the gist of the crew I would be flying with. SSG Atch, SGT Andre, SPC Andrew and I were all going to be crewing chalk one, or the lead bird. The number two guy's role was even more critical and put a lot more on SPC Andrew and I since SGT Andre was going through his FE training. For the duration of the deployment SGT Andre was going to be quizzed, tested, and learning from SSG Atch to see if he had what it took to become an Alpha Company FE.

The FE's job was much more demanding and garnered a lot more responsibility than a CE (Crew Chief/ Crew Engineer). In order to even be considered for the prestigious position you had to show a lot of drive, discipline, and knowledge of the aircraft as a senior FMQ (Fully Mission Qualified) crew chief.

We all jumped on the bus and headed to chow to have dinner for breakfast. The base didn't cater to our special operations schedule by serving us breakfast at night, but we dealt with it.

After chow and back on the bus, we headed toward the flight line as the sun started to set into the cold Afghan night. It was clear out but cold as shit. I brought an extra bag full of warm weather gear because something told me that flying at night in the cold with all the windows open was definitely going to warrant the extra layers. As we pulled up to the flight line I could see three MH-47G Chinooks parked side by side in their own barrier like parking stalls.

"Chalk two," SSG Atch yelled out in a humorous way as he stopped the bus behind the bird in the last stall. The chalk two crew filed out of the bus and over to their beautifully sleeping bird. "Next stop, chalk awesome," he finished. I assumed he was referring to chalk one since that was the bird that the remaining guys on the bus were crewing. SPC Andrew and I got off the bus while SGT Andre, SSG Atch, and the Bravo Company chalk two FE, stayed on. I was slowly learning that while the crew chiefs got the birds ready for the night's mission, the FE's went to talk with the maintenance guys to make sure everything was mechanically sound on the bird. They needed to know if they had worked on it during the day, and if anything was wrong with their assigned helicopters. The FE was also responsible for going to the TOC, to meet with the pilots and get briefed on the night's mission. While the FE's drove off in the bus, SPC Andrew and I started opening up the bird and getting it ready for the night.

Prepping the aircraft was something I knew how to do and did thousands of times during the BMQ course. From taking the blade ropes off to opening up the doors and ramp of the aircraft, this stuff was a piece of cake. In combat everything after that to get the aircraft ready was far different than what I was used to doing. After removing all the blade ropes SPC Andrew unlocked the right cabin door and climbed in the aircraft while I waited at the back of the ramp. The sun was gone now with just a glimmer of light left over the hazy runway. "Ramp clear down?" SPC Andrew yelled out through the aircraft.

"Clear," I yelled back. As the ramp began to lower I looked into the aircraft cabin expecting a different looking interior than what I was used to. Maybe a sort of combat looking interior. The ramp finished opening and it wasn't much different, except for all the gear strung up along the internal fuselage walls. Both the left and right door mini guns were swung inside, which was different than back at Campbell. We would leave the mini guns on board and attached to the aircraft throughout the deployment. This allowed us to quickly get them set up in case we had to execute a TST (Time Sensitive

Target). Whatever combat smelled like that's what the inside of the aircraft emitted. It reeked of dust and tattered uniforms almost like walking into an Army surplus store. The red canvas troop seats were lined up and locked in on either side of the cabin. The cabin was dusty and there looked to be a dark brown blood stain on one of the seats. Two US flags adorned the ceiling and were attached with zip ties at each corner. The floors were dusty much like the seats. ICS cords were placed and coiled neatly throughout the cabin. The pilot's helmets were hanging in the cockpit on either seat. Just past the narrow walk way to get to the cockpit, I noticed the dashboard. It was covered with dust along with tattered mission essential checklists. A large Yeti Cooler was strapped down to the floor in the center of the aircraft all the way at the front, separating both mini gun stations. As I made my way toward the forward most part of the aircraft where SPC Andrew was next to the mini guns, he told me to come over to where he was standing. He motioned to the left mini gun, "That is your new crew station. Start setting up your gun." He informed me the left gun crew station was the customary new guy position.

All other crew positions had a bit more responsibility than left gun, although I would still have a very specialized responsibility to crew. It was the best position for the FE to train me from since he would be right behind me on right gun. I pulled the handle on the left gun window and popped the window out. I swung the mini gun arm outside the aircraft and locked it in place. I heard a loud click as I locked the gun arm into the bracket on the window frame. I made sure all the electrical connections were hooked up, the ammo can feed tray was locked down, and all the safety pins were installed. I flipped the kill switch on the spade grip of the M-134 to see if I had a green light. Boom, green light was on and I made sure the feed chute was disconnected from the feeder de-linker. This insured when I tested the operation I wasn't actually shooting bullets. That would make for a sure way to go home and get kicked out of the unit.

"Left gun spinning barrels," I yelled outside of the aircraft window as I peered to the left and right of the dark Afghanistan flight line. I pressed the trigger and watched the barrel's spin on the deadly weapon system. Sweet, I thought to myself, my first task as a crew chief in combat, and I did it with ease. I turned the activation switch off and watched the green light go out. I felt something heavy on my boots and when I looked down I noticed a long chain of linked 7.62 rounds piled at my feet. I followed the trail of the rounds and realized I forgot to disconnect the electrical connection to the ammo can. Disconnecting the connection prevented rounds from being electrically fed through while testing the weapon's operation. Son of a bitch I thought to myself. I looked at SPC Andrew and he gave me a look like, 'don't worry about it dude it happens to all of us at least once.'

As I fed the rounds back into the ammo can and got the gun sorted, I asked SPC Andrew, "What's next?" He had been busy working on every other station getting it prepped for the mission. He walked me to every station and gave me the run down on how everything needed to be configured for combat. He showed me what was mandatory at every station, how SGT Andre liked his NVG's set, here versus there. I felt like a hospitality manager at a hotel knowing everything about the guests staying the night and what they liked and didn't like. SPC Andrew informed me that this is how the bird needed to be set up every night for the remainder of the deployment. Just as we had gotten everything complete in the bird, the bus pulled up behind the aircraft and honked.

As SPC Andrew and I walked toward the lights of the bus we couldn't make out much else from the lit Chinook cabin looking out to the dark flight line. As we got closer toward the ramp both SGT Andre and SSG Atch appeared and headed into the aircraft. "We all good?" SSG Atch asked SPC Andrew.

"Yep," he said.

SSG Atch had a small stack of papers in one hand and went on to say, "This is going to be a bad ass first mission for you Burnett." My eyes lit up like a kid watching a stupid fountain on the fourth of July. He walked past SPC Andrew and I, then sat down on one of the troop seats while SGT Andre sat next to him. SPC Andrew and I sat directly across from the two on another troop seat.

"Alright boys! Operation Liquid Ice," he said while unfolding the papers and laying them flat on his leg. I hunched over to get a closer look. It was imagery of the target compound and the location of where we were going to land. As I continued to try and decipher the imagery, SSG Atch went on to point out certain things to look out for when landing at the HLZ.

Before SSG Atch could continue with the brief, SPC Andrew eagerly chimed in, "To the X?" Me being the FNG, I had no idea what the hell he was talking about.

"Yes," SSG Atch exclaimed.

I chimed in right after, "What is the X?"

Everyone looked at SSG Atch then back at me in a profound look of disgust. "We are landing within 300 meters of the target compound, versus landing to the Y which is an HLZ 300 meters outside of the target." SSG Atch went on, "We are literally landing in this dude's front yard. On our final approach, the target building will be off the left side of the aircraft." He finished pointing to the black and white pictured target building on the piece of paper laying on his knee. I pondered for half a second before I truly understood why SSG Atch had said this was going to be a good first mission for me. Target building was on the left side, my crew position left side, oh shit, this was it. This was the moment I had been waiting for. SSG Atch continued with the brief as I stayed hunched over looking at the different sheets of paper depicting the target compound, the landing zone, and sleepers. The term sleeper was used to describe guys sleeping on rooftops waiting for someone or something to shoot at.

The intel officer in the brief had told SSG Atch and SGT Andre about potential small arms fire in the area. As SSG Atch concluded the brief he looked at SPC Andrew and told him to get the bird up level two. Then, he looked at SGT Andre and told him that we needed 4,500 lbs. of fuel for the mission and that the fuel truck would be arriving shortly. The brief concluded and we all sat up and went in different directions. I followed closely behind SPC Andrew, and we made our way up front into the cockpit of the aircraft. He took out a checklist and began going through the steps to get the bird up to level two. Level two meant everything was ready to go in the cockpit. All the pilots had to do when they came out was get in their seats, go through a few more checks, then crank the aircraft. Having the crew get the bird up to level two saved the pilots at least ten minutes in the lengthy start up process. This was useful in a combat scenario just in case the time line to hit the target shifted to the left, or if the targeted individual we were going after started to move from one area to another. It was important the aircraft was ready for the pilots to get in and get moving quickly regardless of the situation. While sitting in the cockpit, SPC Andrew went through the steps to get the aircraft to level two, he described each thing he was doing and why he was doing it. It took him seven minutes to get the radios, PTU's (Power Transfer Units), and other imperative items set up on the glass MFD's (Multi-Function Displays). We were level two and he looked at me and said, "When you start doing this I don't expect you to do it that fast. Be sure to take your time and go through the check list." He finished instructing me through the David Clarke headsets we were wearing. The APU was on and running. Getting the APU running was the first step in the level two process. The APU allowed all the systems and electronics in the aircraft to receive power and begin functioning.

After completing the level two process, one by one we exited the cockpit and crouched out through the narrow walkway and back into the cabin. I glanced around and took it all in as SPC Andrew, ahead of me, headed toward the back of the aircraft's ramp. He waved me to come over as I snapped out of my excitement. During the set-up, SPC Andrew mentioned how several boxes of chem-lights or glow sticks always needed to be stocked and kept in a certain spot on the helicopter. The box was placed against one of the walls and secured with a bungee cord. He grabbed a green one, opened it, and cracked it to activate the glowing stick. He grabbed a roll of 100 mile an hour tape, or super strong duct tape, which was located on the hydraulic ramp's pump handle. He walked off the ramp and out toward the flight line directly behind the aircraft. He placed the chem-light on the ground and taped it to the dusty concrete with the single piece of tape he had ripped off the roll. "What is that for?" I asked.

"This lets the customers know which bird is which so they don't get on the wrong aircraft. A single chem-light behind our aircraft lets the customer know that we are chalk one." As he said that I looked to my right down the flight line 50 meters to see two green chem-lights already illuminated behind chalk two.

After taping the light to the concrete we headed back toward the ramp. The light from the cabin was glowing out into the dark cold Afghanistan night. I wasn't about to let the chilly night penetrate my excitement to experience first-hand, what it's actually like to land at the target compound and go get the bad guys. At the back of the aircraft hung two coiled 60 foot fast ropes, one attached to the aircraft walls on both sides. The ropes were used for fast roping operations and would remain on the aircraft for the whole deployment for a mission configured combat ready helicopter. Although I learned about fast rope operations during the BMQ course back home, I wasn't qualified yet. I hadn't actually instructed guys to rope down while hovering over a target. This was another reason my air crew member position was left gun. If for any reason we started to land at an HLZ and there was an obstruction in the way, we might need to drop the ropes and fast rope our passengers onto a building or the ground. Since I wasn't qualified I couldn't maintain the right or left ramp positions yet. Some missions were briefed beforehand knowing that fast roping was the only way in, while others might call for it once we got there without knowing prior to the operation. It was a really think on your feet type of job, and I needed to know everything about the aircraft and the operations we could perform. Being a crew chief wasn't just standing behind a gun and shooting at the bad guys when the time came. I learned this was a very common misconception. I even over heard a guy refer to us as door gunners in passing at the compound where we lived. The term door gunner pretty much bothered every crew chief I worked with so far. It was like a slap in the face. The regular Army had door gunners and I can recall very vividly from my last unit that some helicopter crews pulled guys from different jobs, whether cooks, welders, or diesel mechanics, to be a door gunner. That was a gunner, not a crew chief. Aside from that, we were doing the job in the most unforgiving environments working with the best operators on the most dangerous missions. Door gunner? Get the fuck outta here with that bullshit.

SPC Andrew and I passed the ropes on the ramp and as he sat down on one of the seats I followed suit and sat across from him. He started grilling me with questions about things that we had gone over throughout the evening. While drilling me with questions and answering as many as I knew answers to, I heard a noise approach the right side of the aircraft. I looked out a circular window just behind my right shoulder and noticed a large fuel truck pulling up next to the aircraft. As I monitored outside the window I could see SGT Andre exchanging conversation with a 160th fueler. I heard the diesel truck go from a low rumbling to a loud pitched diesel noise, which meant we were taking on gas. I was accustomed to getting gas and learned about it and the entire fuel system during the BMQ course. The fuel truck quieted down as I sat in my seat and pondered about the night ahead. The air brakes of the diesel fuel truck chirped and it circled around and lined up next to chalk two. Just then the pilots boarded the helicopter from the ramp. One of the pilots, CW5 Frank, who everyone referred to as the Godfather, made his way toward the cockpit. He was the highest rank of CWO (Chief Warrant Officer) there was. I heard a lot about him from the other crew chiefs but wouldn't fully grasp what they were talking about until I actually flew with him. The other pilot, CW4 Ray, was a goofy guy but was serious when mission time came. Everyone in the unit was very professional, but we weren't all robots and we actually did have personalities. As they passed us the Godfather looked at SPC Andrew and said, "How is everything looking boys?" then glancing to me at the end of his sentence.

"Good sir," SPC Andrew replied.

He then looked back at me as he hunched into the cockpit and said, "You all good Burnett?"

"Roger that sir," I exclaimed.

Shortly after, SSG Atch and SGT Andre emerged from the dark flight line and walked into the aircraft.

SSG Atch yelled a thunderous, "Wooooooooo, its go time mother fuckers."

It was getting closer and soon the aircraft would be weighed down with 33 highly trained Rangers all kitted up and ready to assault the target compound. The crew and I donned our flight vests. My kit was a 65 lb. ballistic vest that held all necessary gear needed while in flight. A full combat load of ammo, which was seven magazines consisting of 210 rounds of 5.56 NATO ammo. A first aid kit, knife, survival gear, and whatever else I needed to make me feel the most comfortable and completely prepared for war adorned my kit. I was able to break my kit in quite well during the BMQ course, and I was ready. SGT Andre, the most senior crew chief and almost FE, was at right ramp while SPC Andrew took the left ramp position. The crew stations and helicopter configuration were talked about prior to the mission. After our vests, we all put our flight helmets on followed by our night vision goggles. I attached the NVG's to my helmet but wouldn't fold them down until taxiing on the runway. I was used to this practice after a few hundred flight hours in BMQ. When we were all situated and plugged into the ICS, everyone announced when they were up and on comms. After getting my helmet and NVG's situated I put the mic boom close to my lips. I pressed firmly on my PTT (Push to Talk) button attached to my vest, and said. "Left guns up."

"Left seat," the Godfather exclaimed.

"Right seat," CW4 Ray said.

Then SSG Atch, who was right next to me said, "Right gun."

"Left ramp," SPC Andrew followed.

Then SGT Andre said, "Right ramp."

Everyone one chimed in and we were all ready to rock and roll. The pilots completed a few last minute checklist items and then asked, "You guys ready to fire this thing up?"

SPC Andrew at left ramp, who was in charge of starting the aircraft said, "Roger that sir, let's do this!"

"One clear to start?" The Godfather said.

"Posted ready on one, one is clear to start." Andrew said over the intercom with haste.

While I was standing at left gun inside the aircraft I looked out the window to see SPC Andrew shining his Surefire Flashlight at the number one engine. I monitored his movements while he communicated to the pilots. I was always learning and watching other crew chiefs, how they did something versus how I did it. How could I do better and what could I improve on as a crew chief. As the blades started to turn and SPC Andrew made his way to the number two engine, I saw him walk behind the ramp. The aircraft began to shake back and forth as the bird picked up power from the starting engine. As he was walking past the ramp I noticed a large group of heavily armed dudes start to line up at the green chem we placed off the back of the aircraft.

"Two clear to start?" The Godfather called out.

"Posted ready on two, two is clear to start," said SPC Andrew. The engines started to whine and pick up more speed. The blades started turning faster and faster and the aircraft began to shake from side to side more turbulently.

SPC Andrew made his way back in the aircraft and called out to the pilots. "The guys are here and starting to form at the ramp." Although I had never heard that call before, I was certain it would become very familiar in the following months.

"Roger, I will let you know when we are clear to load," exclaimed the Godfather.

While the rest of the startup checklist continued between SPC Andrew and the pilots, more comms chatter started coming through my helmet. Another thing I had to start getting used to was monitoring 7-9 different radio conversations. While listening to all the assets communicate in my helmet, I still had to accurately perform my crew member duties. The other communication I started to hear were different aircraft that were a part of the same mission. The other aircraft platforms, or CAS (Close Air Support), were referred to as the stack. A stack of different aircraft platforms were already flying above the targeted buildings at different elevations. They are the Rangers eyes and ears and provided anything from surveillance to fire support during the mission. The stack could be any number of aircraft but normally consisted of 2-8 different aerial platforms above the target at the same time. Tonight's mission consisted of five aircraft in the stack, which had already been discussed during the brief in the TOC. SSG Atch told us what aircraft had which call signs so when we were monitoring the comms we knew who was talking.

"Alright Andrew you're clear to load," the Godfather said after finishing the last preflight check list item.

"Roger, loading," SPC Andrew said. To ensure an accurate head count, SPC Andrew and SGT Andre stood on either side of the ramp creating a funnel so the guys had to get on one by one. I looked back toward the ramp and watched the Ranger team begin to load the aircraft. With helmets on, a full kit, and the most superior weapons, they boarded one by one. Seeing and working with the Ranger Battalion 2/75 for the first time was exhilarating. The leadership of the team boarded first, and as they approached the front of the aircraft, SSG Atch gestured to one of them while handing the Ranger an ICS cord. He plugged in and took a seat just behind SSG Atch on the large Yeti Cooler. The cabin was filling up with several Rangers, some carrying ladders, others sniper rifles, and a few with heavy machine guns.

A call came over the radio from SGT Andre, "Three-three ███████, one dog," he finished. We referred to the customers on board as ███████, the bad guys as ███████, and the dog, was well, a dog. This insured the pilots could get an accurate count while flying to and from the target.

"Roger, three, three, and one," the Godfather said over the radio.

"Ramps up aft ready," SGT Andre said.

As I looked through the sea of Army Rangers seated in the middle of the cabin and occupying all troop seats, I saw the ramp start to raise. SGT Andre dimmed the cabin lights from a bright white down to pitch dark. I could still make out silhouettes of bodies in the cabin from the lights of the flight line piercing through the ramp's opening. The bird was loud and we were at full speed. My adrenaline started to pump as I flipped the NVG's down from my helmet.

"Forward ready," SSG Atch said.

"Coming forward," the call came from one of the pilots in the cockpit. Followed by my, "Clear forward left," call.

Then SSG Atch with a quick, "Clear forward right."

We began to taxi forward. The bird was loaded down with the crew and handfuls of hard charging Rangers. I could feel the power of the helicopter pulse through my entire body. I held the mini gun and looked out the window through the green and black lenses of my NVG's.

"Coming left," the Godfather said.

"Nose clear left," I said.

Then SSG Atch muttered, "Tail clear right."

As we began to turn onto the main runway to conduct final checks before take-off, I could see chalk two taxiing right behind us loaded down just like us, with a total of 28 ▮▮▮▮ and all crew including the flight medic. The medic always flew on chalk two I learned, and they would be the ones to go in, in case of a CASEVAC (Casualty Evacuation).

The target compound was 15 minutes away, and after our aircraft and chalk two completed a quick hover check to make sure the weight and balance was good, we got the all clear from tower. "Clear up?" The Godfather said. I glanced up to the sky and glared around to make sure nothing was landing or taking off around us.

"Clear up left," I replied.

"Clear up right," SSG Atch said.

The engines growled and the bird lifted from the ground. I looked toward the back of the aircraft to see the distinct outline of chalk two start to pick up and follow right behind us. "Chalk two is off the ground and in formation," SPC Andrew said over the ICS.

"Roger," said CW4 Ray, the right seater. The cold air again, was beating across my face as we picked up speed and the aircraft pitched forward. All I could think about as I looked out at the mud hut riddled town below, was what's going to happen when we get closer. I knew from the brief that SSG Atch had given us, that there was a high possibility of taking small arms fire, but I had no idea if that would lead to anything or even happen for that matter.

"Left and right side you're cleared hot for test fire." CW5 Frank informed the crew we were above a suitable test fire area. This wasn't range ▮▮▮▮ at Ft. Campbell anymore, this was the real deal. It was combat now, and more imperative than ever that all the guns on the aircraft were set up properly and completely functional.

"All guns hot, all guns test firing." SSG Atch responded to the Godfather. SSG Atch had briefed us before the flight on how he wanted the test fire to be communicated to the pilots. After he made his call I flipped my mini gun to kill mode. The green light peeked through a piece of black electrical tape that had been taped over the light to conceal its glow. I pressed the two buttons on the spade grip like I had done so many times in BMQ. The gun roared and pelted the dusty sand below. The other weapons on board were being fired on either side by the other chiefs. The two M-240's blasted and echoed from the rear of the cabin. I heard SSG Atch's mini gun behind me boast the same unforgiving sound as my M-134. After a short three second burst and releasing my firmly pressed thumbs from the gun, I called, "Left gun cold, operational." The calls made it around each station in a hurry.

"Left ramp cold operational," SPC Andrew said.

Without pause SGT Andre chimed in, "Right ramp cold operational."

"Right gun cold, operational. All guns cold operational." SSG Atch concluded the calls after the quick test fire.

He barely finished his call and CW5 Frank came over the radio through all the other chatter from the different players in the stack. "Roger guys, 10 minutes out," he said in an elevated tone.

"10 minutes aft ready," SGT Andre said.

Then SSG Atch replied, "10 minutes forward ready." As we heard the call, each one of us looked back in the cabin and held up both hands showing ten fingers while yelling to the barrel chested Rangers.

"10 minutes." I yelled as loud as I could over the noise of the engines and the blades cutting through the sky. My adrenaline started racing furiously as I turned back toward my gun and perched my head out of the window. I tried to get a glimpse in front of the helicopter to look for anything noticeable from the imagery that SSG Atch shared with us earlier.

The 6-minute call followed shortly after from the pilots and we all did the same thing as the ten-minute call, only holding up six fingers and yelling, "six minutes," inside the cabin. Then the 3-minute call came, I felt the pitch of the aircraft change from a nose down attitude to an upwards one, slowing the aircraft dramatically. While slowing down we crested over buildings and they were so clear. Probably because we were only 30-40 feet above them. I switched my gun from off to on and saw the green light illuminate underneath the tape. I didn't want any light shining off of me to give the enemy a better target.

"One minute," the Godfather said.

I turned around holding up one finger and yelled, "One minute."

The Rangers heard the loud call and they began to prop up from their seated positions, eager to race off the helicopter upon landing.

CW5 Frank called to the AC-130 gunship in the stack, "Sparkle on." The aircraft started slowing dramatically. I looked out the window in front of the aircraft to see a giant infrared spot light illuminating the HLZ. The bright light, only visible under NVG's, lit up several buildings around it. We were landing in the bad guy's front yard. The, 'Sparkle On,' command from our pilot let the AC-130 know to light up the HLZ, and it did just that. Buildings started getting closer and a lot clearer below the vicious heart pounding aircraft. I started to make out clothes lines, window planters, and random toys in courtyards. As we began to descend even lower to land on the HLZ, I spotted a man on one of the mud constructed building roof tops. I continued to monitor the man and noticed three other guys by his side. As we continued the descent he became more clear and he was holding what appeared to be an RPG (Rocket Propelled Grenade). Before I could react in time he fired the weapon at chalk two and a plume of smoke left his shoulder.

"Contact left," SPC Andrew hastily called over the ICS as the pilots continued their final approach to the HLZ. The entire left side of chalk two began to fire violent mini gun and M-240 rounds at the men on the roof top. Luckily, the RPG had missed the helicopter. A smell of burning matches and spent ammo overtook my sense of smell. SPC Andrew followed his contact left call with, "Left side engaging." I turned my mini gun as far to the left as I could and began firing in the same direction the RPG was shot from. SPC Andrew, who was on left ramp, started putting bullets down onto the roof top too. Between chalk two, SPC Andrew, and me, we turned the dirt building and the men on it into Swiss Cheese. We could only get so many rounds on the target before reaching the max distance our weapons could be turned to the left. Chalk two came over the radio and relayed everything I just witnessed and said all systems on their bird were good. We were on our final approach and both birds were good to land. The ground was getting closer and just like that we took care of a bad guy and now we were about to land in a dirt field. "Clear down?" the pilot asked. I looked toward the ground as dust and debris kicked up.

It became difficult to see through the dust and sand, but I was able to give the call, "Clear down left."

After realizing everything looked good and nothing was going to hinder the landing down below, SSG Atch followed with, "Clear down right." We continued to descend to the field. I scanned my sectors of fire looking left and right outside my window while we descended. I saw more mud huts with windows and doors. I kept my eyes on the buildings while dust pelted me in the face. I squinted my eyes as we got closer to the ground continuing to monitor the vacant buildings now directly out of my window.

SSG Atch came over the ICS, "I've got you off 10, 9, 8, 7, 6, 5, 4, 3, 2, 1. Contact." The aircraft stomped into the dirt field and I began to scan roof tops, a courtyard, an alleyway, and the windows and doors of the buildings in front of me. Our bird was feet away from the ancient looking huts and someone could pop out at any minute.

"Ramp, ramp, ramp," the Godfather said.

"Ramps coming down," SGT Andre replied. I knew the target compound was on the left side and it was looking me right in the face. I shined my mini gun mounted IR (Infrared) spotlight on a single door cut out in a small mud hut. The IR spotlight lit up the building like a professional sports stadium. I scanned the building with the light, slowly moving the gun left and right as the Rangers continued to exit the aircraft. While I was scanning, SGT Andre was constantly relaying to the pilots how the offload was going.

"Half way done." SGT Andre said, followed by a short pause then, "Last man on the ramp," and in a matter of seconds SGT Andre came over the ICS and said, "Ramps up aft ready."

Without hesitation SSG Atch said "Forward ready."

"Chalk one is coming out, chalk one is coming out," the Godfather relayed to chalk two who had landed behind us to our seven-o-clock position. "Clear up?" He asked after letting chalk two know we were coming out of the HLZ.

"Clear up left," I said while keeping my IR laser pointed on the target building door.

"Clear up right," SSG Atch followed. As we began to pick up I kept my mini gun and IR spotlight trained on the small mud hut to make sure anyone who came out of the opening showing hostile intent would get lit the fuck up.

As we pulled up with glorious raw power the Godfather said, "Clear left?"

I responded with a quick, "Clear left." The landing zone and target compound began to fade into the dark Afghanistan night. My heart was still racing from what had just transpired and I could see chalk two still on the ground. IR lasers were shining every which direction from the team of guys we just dropped off.

"Chalk two coming out, chalk two coming out," a call came over the radio. A dust plume engulfed the distant helicopter below as it began to pull power. I watched the giant aircraft as we proceeded in our left banking turn. The helicopter disappeared into the cloud of dust. I continued to look on as the scene unfolded in front of me while maintaining situational awareness of the surrounding buildings below. I looked on through the darkness and finally the big black Chinook blasted through the cloud of moon dust and pitched nose forward to gain speed and regain formation with us.

"Good landing boys, and nice shooting," the Godfather chimed in over the radio.

"Roger," SSG Atch muttered. I thought to myself, wow praise from the pilots, that was awesome. Never in my entire Army career had I been acknowledged from such a high ranking person, let alone a CW5 in 160th. Sure, I had been awarded a few ribbons in my prior unit but nothing compared to that. I wasn't a Fobit anymore and I could actually say I was a 160th special operations Chinook crew chief taking the fight to the enemy outside the wire. In a matter of minutes chalk two was linked up in formation with us again.

SGT Andre relayed to our pilots from right ramp, "Chalk two in formation, seven-o-clock, two discs."

After infilling the ground pounding Rangers, we headed back to KAF to park. This was called logerring, or waiting for the guys on the ground to complete the mission. Once complete they would call us when they were ready for exfill. What had taken almost 30 minutes felt like three. Everything happened so fast and just like that it was done. We touched down at KAF. After the bird was shut down and back to level two, the pilots began to ask me and SPC Andrew questions about what transpired after getting shot at during our final approach.

"What happened Burnett?" The Godfather asked. With the lights in the cabin on now and the rest of the crew sitting down on the troop seats eating a snack, I looked back toward SPC Andrew. He gave me a gesture with his arm like, 'dude tell him, he just asked you a question.'

I hesitantly started, "Well sir, I saw a man on a roof top with an RPG and before I could say or do anything he fired a rocket toward chalk two. After SPC Andrew made the, 'Contact Left' call we both began to fire. I believe they were all killed." I looked back at SPC Andrew and he was casually eating some beef jerky. I was thinking to myself, man this dude is calm and relaxed and I'm over here with my heart still trying to lunge out of my chest. This was SPC Andrew's 3rd deployment, so I imagined he had probably seen and dealt with the same situation many times in the past. For me however, it was the first time I ever experienced real combat, not only on the receiving end, but on the returning end too. The mortar and rocket attacks on base during my first tour were nothing compared to the recent rooftop shenanigans.

"Next time that happens Burnett, I need you to call out where the contact is coming from, so I can try and adjust course prior to landing if necessary," the Godfather said. I knew I had fucked up and I froze in the moment. We had gone over it time and time again in training while in BMQ. Always calling out the enemy's position was crucial and everyone on the aircraft should have known what was going on. Even though SPC Andrew had made some calls, I failed to relay the distance and direction of the threat before engaging.

I felt I let the crew down. "Roger sir, I won't let it happen again." I presume the fog of war blanketed over me after seeing someone with so much hate. Someone that wanted to kill me and my brothers. I reacted out of adrenaline and nerves, but I knew I needed to do better.

"Don't get me wrong Burnett, you did the right thing, I just need to know what is going on back there, and where the enemy is," the Godfather finished.

With a bit more pep I replied, "Roger."

During my conversation with the Godfather I was slumped over, sitting on one of the troop seats and looking at the ground. After finishing the conversation with CW5 Frank, I looked up toward the back of the aircraft. SPC Andrew, SSG Atch, and SGT Andre were all standing in the middle of the cabin acting like they were holding machine guns and shooting them all over the place. Just like that, when I thought I let the guys down they made light of the situation and started portraying me out to be some machine gun wielding dude on Schwarzenegger's team in Predator. I laughed and lunged forward to grab a water out of the cooler. As I went to grab the water and still in my full kit I started hearing comms through my helmet. From the sounds of it, the team of Rangers had captured the enemy and then some. They relayed through the comms to the TOC, "████████" and that they would be ready for exfill soon.

"Prepare to copy loadout plan." The lead Ranger on the ground concluded. Two minutes passed and the same guy came over the radio, I knew by his call sign. The muffled but clear voice came through the radio, "We are ready for exfill, prepare to copy," he called to our bird.

The Godfather was the PIC, and all exfill plans were coordinated with him from the JTAC (Joint Terminal Attack Controller). The JTAC was the one guy on the ground who communicated with all the aircraft in the stack on every mission. His voice became easily recognizable. Chalk two could hear everything being passed over the net, so any other suggestions or mission changes that the Godfather wanted to make would be passed to chalk two accordingly.

"Roger, ready to copy," the Godfather replied.

"Chalk one, three-three ███████, one dog, two ███████. Left door load. Heavy brown out. HLZ will be marked with pulse sparkle. Break." The JTAC paused and continued after catching his breath, "Chalk two, two-eight ███████, four ███████. Left door load. Heavy brown out. HLZ will be marked with steady sparkle. How copy?" The JTAC finished passing the loadout plan to the Crazy Horse flight.

"Roger copy all. Will call when one minute out," the Godfather responded. While the exfill plan was being relayed, CW4 Ray had been going through the checklist and starting up the helicopter. When the guys on the ground were ready to go it was time to go and it was time to go now.

"APU clear off?" CW4 Ray said just as the Godfather finished receiving the load out plan.

"Clear off," answered SPC Andrew.

SGT Andre's, "Ramps up aft ready," call followed. The bird was at 100% operating speed with all six blades turning and both engines burning we were ready to pick our guys up.

Then SSG Atch responded "Forward ready."

"We are all set to go, are you guys ready?" The Godfather radioed to chalk two.

"Let's rock n roll," one of the pilots from chalk two replied. SGT Andre turned off the cabin lights and I peered through SSG Atch's gun window to see chalk two in their parking stall at full RPM. I watched all their cabin lights shut off and go completely dark.

"Coming forward," the Godfather said. and just like that we began taxiing the same way we had left just hours ago. Within minutes we were airborne after the clear up left and clear up right calls came from SSG Atch and I.

I surveyed the dismal town below as we left the wire. More intercom chatter came through my flight helmet. It was from one of the ISR (Intelligence Surveillance Reconnaissance) planes that had been above the target compound all night guiding the guys on the ground and relaying to them any important information about potential threats in the area.

"Crazy 54 how copy?" from the ISR platform to us.

"Good copy, send your traffic," said the Godfather.

"We have Icom chatter in the AO (Area of Operations). Chatter is, prepare for the black helicopters with the circle guns and shoot them down when they come back."

The surveillance plane above monitored cell phone calls and communication from the enemy all through the night. Icom chatter was radio traffic between enemy forces. Not only were they talking, but they were talking about us and the exact helicopters we were on.

If the RPG being fired at us a few hours earlier wasn't enough, now they were saying, "Shoot down the helicopters when they come back." Fuck I was thinking to myself, what a way to start off the deployment and on my very first mission with 160th.

"Copy all," Godfather said to the surveillance plane.

"Alright boys keep your eyes peeled when we go in to land. These guys aren't playing around tonight." CW4 Ray said.

"Roger," SSG Atch responded. The short brisk and chilly flight was just that, quick.

"All players all players, this is Crazy flight, we are one minute out."

"Roger one minute," SSG Atch said, then all the other aircraft in the stack chimed in as our bird began to slow. I could see the buildings get closer as we descended once again. We were landing at a different HLZ for exfill, but that didn't excuse any of us from not scanning for any potential threats in the area.

"Sparkle on," the Godfather called over the radio.

The JTAC on the ground echoed back, "Sparkle on." I peered out the window as dust and debris started to kick up from the ground below. I saw a pulsating IR laser on the ground. I followed its trail to a man on the ground.

As we made our approach and got closer to the IR laser I could see a line of 33 guys that were about to board our aircraft.

"Team in sight," I said over the radio. It was my job to call the pilots past the entire team to get the aircraft's ramp close to the first guy in the line and land it to the ground once positioned. "Continue forward 50," I called to the Godfather. "25," I continued as I looked at all the guys in line passing on the left side. We continued to descend closer to the ground. They passed by with a few blinking strobes on their helmets, I continued with the calls, "Continue forward 10, 9, 8, 7, 6, 5, 4, 3, 2, 1, clear down left."

Followed by SSG Atch's, "Clear down right," and we began to descend to the ground. SSG Atch finished calling the pilots to the ground while my face was getting pelted by tiny rocks, dust, and sand. I could hardly see anything. Then all wheels contacted the ground and the dust still present cleared enough for me to see the team of guys start running toward the back of the aircraft.

"Ramp, ramp, ramp," the Godfather exclaimed. SGT Andre lowered the ramp and I kept scanning the buildings surrounding us while we waited on the ground for everyone to get on.

"Three-three ███████, one dog, two ███████. Ramps up aft ready," SGT Andre came over the radio hastily after the entire Ranger element boarded.

"Roger. 54 coming out, 54 coming out," the Godfather said. Clear up left and right came from both SSG Atch and I. The engines began to roar as the pilots pulled power and we began to pick up off the ground. The buildings started to become unclear through all the dust and debris again. We cleared the dust cloud and I looked down at the ground to see chalk two lifting off the HLZ. We began to gain elevation and we were headed home.

As we continued to climb an unknown voice came over the radio. "Nice landing sir. Thanks for getting close to our guys so we didn't have to run so far." It was the team lead of all the Rangers who just boarded the aircraft and plugged into the ICS.

"That was all left gun," the Godfather said.

"Right on, thanks chief." As those words were muttered through the ICS I felt a pat on my back. I thought SSG Atch was trying to get my attention as he had done earlier in the night. No, it was the team lead slapping my back and thanking me. No amount of awards or high fives would ever be as rewarding as the team lead saying, 'Thanks chief.' I couldn't let that go to my head though as everyone on the aircraft was equally responsible for crewing the violent Chinook.

"You get the bad guy?" The Godfather said to the Ranger team lead.

"Yeah, we got him, and a few of his shit head buddies. Oh and a couple hundred pounds of black tar heroin."

"Nice work, now let's get you guys home! Three minutes." The Godfather responded, and just like that we were three minutes out from landing back at KAF.

A cool morning running around the flight line and still getting used to the glorious violent fleet of MH-47G's. Photo courtesy of Nate M.

Flight Engineer SGT Andre looking over his M-134 before flight.

SSG Brian surveying his sectors of fire over Afghan villages below after a long night in Kandahar.

A view looking down on the fleet at KAF coming home from a daylight exfil.

Beach flyover Virginia beach during TDY with Doc while in the BMQ course.

The crew of chalk awesome on my first deployment with Alpha Company.

SPC Arron taking in the gorgeous Afghan views after a long night in Helmand province

A view from right gun over the vast Afghan mountain ranges. Photo courtesy of Jose D.

Chalk 2 plugging in to take on gas along the HAR track.

Helo cast training with another hard hitting elite team.

Heading home after a 4 ship flight into the Kajakai Dam, Afghanistan. Photo courtesy of Richard P.

Desert mountain training in New Mexico during the BMQ course.

After a long night in the Kajakai Dam, Afghanistan, spent 7.62 rounds litter the Chinooks floor. Photo courtesy of Andrew M.

Rangers from 2/75 wait patiently to get on board to ensure bad things happen to bad people. Photo courtesy of Joe T.

Right ramp CE monitors a village below after hearing small arms fire pop shots en route back to KAF.

Three MH-60's and Three MH-47's line up for departure in Afghanistan eager to take to the skies.

Two CE's sit on the ramp and ponder what the next mission will hold. Photo courtesy of SOAR medic.

Taking in the views heading back after day time overwater training in VA. Photo courtesy of Jose D.

While I looked serious, this was right before my first taste of overwater operations during the BMQ course.

CE monitors the height from the stubby wing position during over water training. Photo courtesy of SOAR medic.

CHAPTER 11
WELCOME TO THE CLUB

★ ★

The clear down left and right call came from SSG Atch and I, and we taxied the aircraft back into our parking spot. The mission was over, but my heart was still racing. I was hooked and I couldn't wait for more, but after landing there was still more work to be done. As the cabin lights came on I looked through the dusty cabin to see a group of tired and worn out Rangers. As they started to exit the aircraft, sitting up one by one, I felt a sense of accomplishment. Although just a small contribution to the overall mission it was still a victory. The small victory resonated with me as it was a saying that held true and one I learned while at SERE School. This mission felt a lot more rewarding than just turning wrenches and fixing an aircraft, like I had done at my old unit.

As SPC Andrew was shutting down the aircraft and the customers were getting off, SSG Atch and I began policing up our stations. When the guys were getting off I noticed the or bad guys the Rangers had captured from the target compound. They were wearing black and white robes with nothing but sandals on. They were escorted by two Rangers, one on either side gripping an arm. Black hoods over their heads covered up their faces, and zip cuffs secured their hands. They were shuffled off to a white windowless van parked just behind the aircraft. I thought to myself, now the battlefield is just a little safer with these IED manufacturers captured. We began putting our NVG's in their proper carrying cases, clearing our M4 rifles, and making sure the mini guns were safe and cleared before swinging them inside the aircraft. The blades of the aircraft began to slow. I could hear the distinct wisp and cutting through the air sound they made as I continued to clean up inside the aircraft.

SPC Andrew made the final call to the pilot, "APU clear off." As the whine of the APU slowed and eventually shut off, I removed my helmet which had been on all night. The NVG's and weight of the helmet was straining on my neck but I was used to it by now, and it didn't bother me as much as it had during BMQ. The entire crew including myself were gathering up weapons, putting gear away, and opening up key access panels of components that needed to be looked over before heading to chow.

As I made my way outside of the aircraft to climb on top and start opening access panels, the rest of the crew began taking petty jabs at me. They started calling me machine gun Burnie and everyone had a good laugh. I guess the hasty engagement behind the mini gun warranted it. I started to feel accepted as an Alpha Company crew chief. The pilots started walking behind SSG Atch and SGT Andre around the lower access panels while SPC Andrew and I continued to inspect critical components inside the forward and aft pylons on top of the helicopter.

After inspection on the bottom concluded the pilots climbed up onto the aircraft and began to go through the same routine as on bottom, and SPC Andrew and I closed the bird up top. The last thing to do before putting the aircraft to bed was to put blade ropes on each blade and tie them down to the wheel shackles accordingly. SPC Andrew stayed up top while I clambered my way down to the front of the aircraft where I was able to grab onto the very end of one of the blades. After I clipped the blade rope into the pre-drilled hole on the bottom side of the blade, SPC Andrew was doing the same to the aft blades. After the two of us attached the blade ropes on each forward and aft blade I yelled, "Turning blades."

"Clear," SPC Andrew yelled from on top of the aircraft. I grabbed the blade I just clipped the rope into and began to push it so the next blade would be directly over the nose and the aft blade over the tunnel cover. I lined up both blades so SPC Andrew could clip his blade rope in. The process continued until all six blades had ropes attached and we could begin tying them to the wheel shackles.

As I finished tying the last blade rope, SSG Atch came up behind me and said, "We are meeting behind the ramp after you finish."

"Roger," I said. This being my first mission and just trying to learn the daily routine I thought it was just that, routine.

After tying the final rope, I meandered to the back of the aircraft where everyone from both chalk one and two were huddled, minus the pilots. The pilots, I assumed, had already taken off to get chow and head to bed. "Great work tonight guys, and Burnie you went to the X for the first time, so job well done," SSG Atch said in a mentorship type tone. "We have all been there and we all know what that first time is like," he went on. "There is something else that goes along with going to the X for your first time." Right as he finished the sentence both the chalk one and two crews were on me like a hungry pack of wolves. I was swarmed, and as I tried to fight for my escape all the hands and arms grabbing and wrapping around me got tighter.

"Just best if you don't fight it Burnie," a voice from a crew member of chalk two chimed in. All tied up, the seven guys carried me from the back of the aircraft all the way to the tip of the aerial refuel probe. They balanced me on top of the probe while others began duct taping me to it. I had been used to the initiation and hazing before coming out here, but this was pretty creative I had to give them that. The duct taping operations finished, and I thought to myself, this wasn't so bad, now get me off this thing so we can go eat. I strained my neck to look up as I dangled on the probe. I saw someone holding clippers and then I heard the buzzing sound as they turned on. Shit, I thought.

"Welcome to the club Burnie," someone exclaimed. I guess going to the X for your first time was a big deal and one that warranted an X being shaved into my head. After the worst haircut in the history of haircuts was finished, the guys cut me free from the probe and everyone shook my hand or gave me a hug. The feeling of brotherhood hit home and I knew, although I still had a lot to learn, I found my new family. A group of guys who exuded excellence and constantly lived by the Night Stalker Creed, but also knew when to have a good time.

We walked back toward the ready room which was just off of the flight line. We gathered our things left from the night prior before leaving the wire. Everyone boarded the infamous foreign bus and we were off to chow. Stories of the night's mission were exchanged between both crews on the short ride down the narrow dirt roads to the chow hall. A friendly argument broke out between both chalk one and chalk two crews about who killed the deceased RPG wielding terrorist and his buddies. Chalk two was comprised of a few Bravo Company guys.

One of them exclaimed, "SGT Max got that kill!"

Not one to back down from an argument, friendly or not, SPC Andrew chimed in, "Bullshit that kill was either me or Burnie." The argument went back and forth as I gazed outside of one of the cloudy bus windows. I saw regular Army units and other conventional military units in PT uniforms running in formations on either side of the tight road. Running in formation was not something we did while we were deployed. We ran and worked out every day to maintain a peak physical fitness level but in no way did it look like that.

I laughed as all the guys did on the bus when SSG Atch pointed them out abruptly interrupting the, 'Who got the kill?' argument. I had a deep rooted meaning for my laugh as I had come from a unit just like the one running by us. Some of the other guys went straight into 160th, but I wasn't as fortunate. I had been that guy before, running in formation, dressed in PT's, but I was now part of a much different unit and family. I could see every day the minimal and large contrasts between the two units conventional versus special ops.

We made it to the chow hall and if we weren't a site to behold from everyone else eating, due to our completely slicked out uniforms. The shaved X in my hair made it even more of a display. We didn't want to bring attention to ourselves, that's just how it was, but the X didn't help. After chow we made our way back to the heavily secured compound and it was shower and bed for me. The sun was still on the rise and after enjoying my first mini gun action, scrambled eggs for dinner, and the new brotherhood induction, I thought to myself, I fucking did it. I set out to complete a goal and here I was a year and some change later making it happen. I was proud of what I had done but didn't really realize the magnitude of it until writing this book.

CHAPTER 12
TRAIN LIKE YOU FIGHT

★ ★ ★

I woke up the next morning, well morning for us but getting ready for bed for the rest of the units on FOB KAF. I was up before SPC Andrew and made sure to be quiet, as I crept out the door and then down the hallway to indulge in a hot shower. I opened the door to the confined shipping container turned locker room. The container had been converted into a row of six showers lining the wall with three sinks, and mirrors splitting between the showers. The confined space was empty judging by the lack of towels or clothes hanging on the hooks just across from each shower stall. I turned the water on before stripping down to realize there was no water. I tried the shower next to it, then the one next to that. No water at all. Before giving up all hope I walked to the sinks and tried the water there. Just as I had thought, no water there either. Discouraged, I grabbed my shower bag and headed back to my room. As I shuffled in disappointment back to my room I noticed one of the day shift maintenance guys coming up the stairs at the end of the hallway. I scream whispered over to him, "Hey, do you know why the showers aren't working?"

"Mortar attack earlier today busted one of the water lines, there is a pallet of water over there that is pretty warm you can use," as he pointed down the stairs. I was still in the hallway and where he was pointing was blocked, but I knew what pallet of water he was talking about. All around the base there were pallets of bottled water. Normally the pallets were out in the open and not covered. So the bottles of water he pointed to were baking in the sun all day. I turned around and headed back to the showers to put my stuff down then headed to grab a case of warm water. I always woke up early, not only because I was the new guy and I wanted to be ready and prepared, or because I was excited for the next mission, but for situations like this. I woke up early enough to adapt to the new deployment circumstances and overcome the lack of a shower. A shower was a luxury in the Army anyway. I brought the case of bottled water in the shower with me and had my first ever warm bottled water shower. Never again will I take a hot shower for granted. Back in the room I started putting on my uniform and tidying up my sleeping area. I heard SPC Andrew starting to wake up and I cut the light on while turning my red lensed head lamp off.

"It's a new day machine gun Burnie," SPC Andrew exclaimed while jumping out of his bunk.

I smiled and said, "Yeah, oh and there is no water."

"Oh well who needs a shower anyways," SPC Andrew said enthusiastically.

"Not you I guess," I said in a serious tone. I always had a way of making a joke but maintaining a straight face. Those who hadn't quite gotten to know me that well yet didn't know what to think when I tried cracking a joke. I would often be met with the phrase, 'Wait, are you serious?' I would then have to crack a smile to indicate I wasn't being serious whatever the joke may have been. "I'll meet you at the bus," I said to SPC Andrew.

I walked out the door and down the stairs to see SSG Atch standing at the swinging door of the bus. This wasn't a good sign since just the other day he told me to be the first one at the bus from now on. I looked around the rest of the special operations compound to see a few Rangers walking to their shipping container buildings or coming out of Average Joe's Gym. We were all waking up and getting started at the same time since we worked together. We were the 2nd Ranger battalion's direct aviation support on the majority of the missions. Normally SSG Atch was up before everybody and most always had already talked to the pilots about what mission was on the burner for the night. So while all of us slept during the day, intel guys and surveillance planes were preparing, monitoring, gathering, and discussing potential missions for the night. Normally by the time we woke up SSG Atch already received word from the pilots or someone in the TOC, what exactly we would be doing that night and where we would be going.

After glancing around the compound while I walked toward SSG Atch I focused my attention back on him and just before coming to a complete stop in front of him I asked, "So what bad guys are we getting tonight?" I finished the sentence, stopping three feet away from him.

"Well Burnie, we aren't going out on mission tonight, but I'm going to try and get you vehicle qualified since we have a down day." I was excited but at the same time I was hoping for another mission like the night prior.

The next crew title, and what every new Alpha Company crew chief was striving to become was FMQ. Although I was new I wasn't the only BMQ crew chief in the company. The designation of becoming an FMQ crew chief took a lot of time and wasn't the easiest to obtain. In order to be considered an FMQ crew chief, you needed to be proficient and signed off in eight special operations tasks critical in crewing the MH-47G Chinook helicopter. The tasks consisted of FARP (Forward Arming and Refueling Point), HAAR (Helicopter Air to Air Refueling), Decks, Amphib 1's, Fast Ropes, Hoist, Guns, and Vehicles. I already accomplished three of the eight qualifications in the BMQ course, which designated me as a BMQ crew chief. I had five more qualifications to complete before obtaining the FMQ title, and from the sounds of it I would be crossing one of those off the list tonight.

SSG Atch went on to say, "Have you done any vehicle training back at the house?"

"Negative, as soon as I finished BMQ I came out here with you," I said. Although Alpha Company was small, the guys were constantly deploying, coming home, then training, and then deploying again in a tiresome cycle throughout the year. I could easily understand why SSG Atch didn't know I hadn't received any vehicle training or introduction to the qualification yet. In learning about all the qualifications needed to become FMQ, I easily understood why the task, while deployed, was so important. The vehicle qualification was the ability to load a vehicle inside the Chinook by guiding the driver under NVG's. The task would be easy if I were guiding a Razor or dirt bike driver, but in order to get signed off on the qualification it had to be a Humvee. I couldn't even comprehend a Humvee fitting inside the helicopter, but the interior cabin of the Chinook was just wide and tall enough to fit a slick Humvee. Meaning it wasn't armored and had antennas and anything else sticking off of it removed. After the quick discussion at the bus with SSG Atch he headed into the TOC again. After a brief minute he came back to the bus where everyone from chalk one and two were gathered. He told us that after we ate we needed to configure chalk one for vehicle training. Everyone acknowledged and we boarded the bus. On the short ride to the chow hall a plan was devised as to who was going to do what, and what needed to happen in order to configure the bird for the qualification. The plan was to train me on guiding the Humvee into a shipping container while the other crew configured chalk one for the vehicle qualification. The pilots knew the training was going to take place for me and set a hard take off time for 0100 local. That would give us ample time to set up the bird and for SSG Atch and SGT Andre to train me on how to guide the vehicle onto the bird. We finished chow and headed to the flight line to complete the mission we had discussed. SSG Atch slammed on the brakes as we pulled behind chalk one.

SGT Max whom I had gotten to know in the BMQ course, was in Bravo Company and one of the chalk two crew guys. Depending on the mission op tempo, we often split deployment rotations with Bravo Company. They were on chalk two while the Alpha Company crew flew on chalk one. Although we had a rivalry, at the end of the day we were in the same fight and on the same team. Back in our minds though we knew Alpha Company was the better company to crew for.

The ramp came down and SGT Max emerged from the cabin, and the bright cabin lights were already on. Everyone started pulling out the troop seats and getting the bird configured properly to accept a four ton Humvee. While I looked on from the back of the ramp SSG Atch was talking me through some critical things I needed to remember during the qualification. After a brief pep talk, we walked to the hangar. The hangar was 100 meters away from the three Chinook parking stalls. On the side of the hangar, a slick Humvee awaited us. The vehicle was used for transporting gear and equipment to and from the aircraft during the day when the maintenance guys were working on the helicopter. I navigated to the passenger seat with my headlamp shining in front of me. We always had a headlamp dangling from our necks. It pretty much was a part of our uniform while deployed, seeing as how everything we did took place at night. It was no different than always having a knife on your person. SSG Atch cranked the engine and we drove toward a shipping container on the flight line. We were still within sight of the parked 47's. Headlamps were moving in the night as we got closer to the container. The Humvee came to a halt as we parked in front of the container, both SPC Andrew and SGT Andre were standing there waiting for the next instruction from SSG Atch. He got out of the door-less Humvee and walked over to SGT Andre and SPC Andrew as I followed closely behind. He reached in his cargo pocket and pulled out a box of IR chem-lights and handed them to SGT Andre. He told SGT Andre that he would be the one training me for the vehicle qualification as he handed the box to him. SGT Andre was going through FE training and needed to know the mechanics of every qualification. He also had to be able to train the qualifications to lower rated crew chiefs. This was important and one of the many responsibilities as an FE. SGT Andre was training for the coveted FE role, and after seeing SSG Atch get on his ass for multiple things I could tell the role was taken very seriously. I learned from a lot of the other guys to never cross SSG Atch in any way shape or form. He was by the book and if something wasn't right or you fucked up he would let you know it quick and in a hurry.

After a short briefing, SGT Andre asked me where my flight gear was, and I told him, "In the connex." A military term used for shipping container.

"OK we won't worry about that until it's time to practice loading on the bird," he said.

Hovering over SGT Andre's every interaction with me, SSG Atch yelled, "The fuck you won't. Train like you fight, c'mon you know better than that Andre." SSG Atch looked at me and said, "Burnie go get your fucking flight gear now."

I said, "Roger," and darted off in the direction of the connex where the flight gear was kept when we weren't flying. After retrieving my flight gear and sprinting back to the shipping container, I noticed the Humvee had moved and SGT Andre was in the push up position with SSG Atch standing over him. When I got to the container SSG Atch told SGT Andre to get up. I guess he had to remain in the position until I returned from getting my helmet and vest. I learned quickly that SSG Atch didn't play around when it came to training or anything to do with combat readiness. A simple screw up while out on a mission could cost lives and SSG Atch drove that philosophy home when training too. He told me that SGT Andre and he would run through the vehicle task first, and for me to watch how it was done.

They put their flight helmets on and folded their NVG's down in front of their eyes. SSG Atch was standing in front of the vehicle on the front passenger side, while SGT Andre with helmet and NVG's down, stood on the other side. SPC Andrew was driving the Humvee and would take all directions from SGT Andre. With two IR chem-lights in either hand he gave the signal to start the Humvee. He pointed the chem-light at SPC Andrew in the driver seat and moved it in a circular motion. The loud starter of the ignition turned over the diesel engine. With the Humvee backed up eight feet away from the opening of the shipping container SGT Andre began by holding the chem-lights horizontally in either hand and in a continuous pushing motion moved the lights from his chest out toward the vehicle. He continued the repetitive motion and the Humvee slowly began to back up toward the container opening.

"Good on my side good up top," SSG Atch hollered to SGT Andre over the low growl of the diesel engine. As the rear of the Humvee started to enter into the shipping container the calls changed. SSG Atch was meticulously looking down the passenger side of the Humvee to make sure it didn't contact the internal shipping container walls. "3 inches my side, good up top," another call came from SSG Atch as I continued to view from the side. SGT Andre gave the all stop signal. An X crossed in front of his body with the two chem-lights. SPC Andrew hit the brakes. SGT Andre instructed SPC Andrew to turn the wheels to the left with another glowing chem-light signal. The signal was followed by a backup, stop, then straighten the wheels out again. The calls continued coming from SSG Atch always keeping SGT Andre informed of how much room he had on the passenger side of the vehicle.

The front of the vehicle cleared the opening and was all the way in the shipping container. SGT Andre and SSG Atch both closed the container doors and SGT Andre called out, "Ramps up aft ready." The whole iteration took them two minutes.

After giving the kill the engine signal and shutting the container doors, SSG Atch looked at me and said, "You ready Burnie?"

I hesitantly nodded and said, "Roger."

SSG Atch flung the container doors open to reveal the Humvee they just guided in. He and SGT Andre guided SPC Andrew out of the container much like they guided him in. Bringing the vehicle out of the make believe Chinook went a lot quicker than guiding it in. The Humvee was out and after the kill engine signal, to SPC Andrew, which was a chem-light being motioned across the throat, SPC Andrew hopped out.

After a short brief of who would be in charge of what position during my iteration, SSG Atch handed me the two IR chem-lights and said, "Let's see it." SGT Andre was on the passenger side of the vehicle ready to give me concise information about how close his side was to hitting the inside of the container. SPC Andrew was once again the driver, and SSG Atch was looking on to make sure I was doing everything to standard.

I pointed the chem-light at the driver and made a circular motion.

Right as the engine fired up I started to hear a loud metal clanking noise. I peered under my NVG's over the Humvee to try and figure out what the noise was. It was coming from the shipping container. I looked quickly so I didn't lose focus with the task at hand. I noticed SSG Atch was throwing rocks at the side of the shipping container. I knew what he was doing and it wasn't anything new. Every type of training in 160th up to this point always included something a little extra. The unit wanted to always be prepared and have that, 'train like you fight,' mindset. SSG Atch, I assumed, was simulating someone shooting at us while I was guiding the vehicle onto the Chinook. "Just focus," SGT Andre confidently told me while yelling over the metal dinging. I continued with the hand signals slowly backing the vehicle into the shipping container. I made SPC Andrew stop several times to correct my mistakes.

After what seemed like an eternity and rocks constantly being slung at the side of the container I finally guided the vehicle safely into the container. I gave the, 'Kill Engine,' signal, shut the container doors, and shouted in frustration, "Ramps up aft ready."

We proceeded with a simulated landing and I guided SPC Andrew back out of the container. Once the vehicle was out of the container I looked at SSG Atch for some sort of acknowledgment or next instruction. He looked at SGT Andre and I, then muttered three words, "Do it again." He repeated the same words ten more times before he finally acknowledged I was ready to do a dry run on the Chinook. We policed up the shipping container AO and headed over to our bird where the chalk two crew was nowhere in sight. I hurried into the cabin after our short walk from the shipping container and flipped on the lights. Everything had been removed to make room for the giant Humvee. The seats, go bags, fries' bars, and fast ropes were gone. The bird was all set up and ready for me to hopefully get signed off and qualified on the vehicles task. Just like at the shipping container, SSG Atch made me run through a few dry runs, getting the Humvee in and out of the helicopter. The aircraft was a bit tighter than the shipping container, but luckily all the lights in the cabin were on. SSG Atch wanted me to get the feel for doing the task on the helicopter before actually donning all my flight gear and doing the actual full blown task under NVG's. Once SSG Atch was confident enough in my ability to guide the vehicle onto the aircraft it was time to get on my flight gear, helmet, NVG's, and gloves. Only this time instead of my partner yelling over to me how close the vehicle was to the other side of the aircraft, we were hooked into the ICS.

The vehicle was out of the aircraft and SSG Atch looked over at SGT Andre as we huddled around the back of the ramp waiting for the next instruction. "Go crank the APU," he said to SGT Andre, then glanced at me and instructed, "Burnie. SPC Andrew is going to be your partner during this iteration and don't fuck up!" As SSG Atch finished his brief conversation with us, two F-18's took off overhead and I watched the blue afterburners disappear in the night sky. The igniter of the APU clicked and the slow whine turned into a high pitched scream. SSG Atch jumped in the Humvee and peeled away off into the distant flight line.

SGT Andre emerged from the cockpit after firing the APU, and headed toward SPC Andrew and I. Before he exited the aircraft he killed the white cabin lights and yelled to us over the loud APU. "Be prepared for when he pulls up to the aircraft to give him instruction and treat him like he doesn't know anything about the loading process."

"Roger," I yelled back to him from the flight line, while he waited around the aft ramp area. SPC Andrew and I simultaneously flipped our NVG's down and scanned the flight line looking for the Humvee that just took off. Another minute passed looking for the Humvee, while SPC Andrew and I had minimal conversation through the ICS, both wondering the same thing. Where the hell was SSG Atch? Another minute passed and the Humvee darted out of the maintenance hangar. With the headlights off, the vehicle began to pick up speed, and as it got closer to the aircraft I started to give the signal to show SSG Atch where to line up the vehicle. I was standing 20 meters from the ramp and centered with the aircraft as I signaled. The vehicle started to slow down as it headed straight toward me. Since I knew my body was centered with the aircraft I gave SSG Atch small corrections to center the vehicle as best I could with the ramp of the aircraft. I gave the crossed X signal to stop the vehicle and as I heard the squeal of the brakes the Humvee came to a stop.

The ICS cord wasn't long enough for me to stay plugged in and walk to the driver side door to give instructions. I un-plugged the cord from my helmet and walked over to SSG Atch. I gave him a 2-minute brief and explained what the hand signals meant. The first iteration would be guiding the vehicle in forward and then the final iteration would be backing the vehicle in. Going through both ways of loading the vehicle several times in the shipping container I was confident this was going to be a walk in the park. After yelling the quick instructions to SSG Atch over the loud APU, I plugged back in, gave the, 'start your engine,' signal, and began moving the

IR chem-lights back and forth toward my chest. I was on the driver side of the vehicle and on the left side of the aircraft. I managed to stay about 5 to 10 meters in front of the Humvee at all times.

As the vehicle started to enter into the aircraft I began to receive calls over the ICS from SPC Andrew, "Three inches my side good up top," as the front of the vehicle entered the aircraft. The hood raised up into the cabin as the front tires gripped the rear loading ramps. I realized the vehicle was coming in crooked. "Two inches my side good up top," another call came from SPC Andrew. Shit, I thought to myself. SPC Andrew was on the rear passenger side walking behind the Humvee, while I was guiding SSG Atch from the driver front. I couldn't keep guiding the vehicle in without correcting the wheels which is why I immediately realized this wasn't the easiest task. I grasped the practice shipping container was a lot bigger inside than the inside of this Chinook. I stopped the vehicle, gave a hand signal to correct the wheels by holding one arm up and pointing the chem-light in the direction I wanted SSG Atch to turn the wheels.

After the correction I started guiding it into the aircraft again. "Three inches my side good up top. Four inches my side good up top. Five inches my side good up top." Several calls came from SPC Andrew through my flight helmet, letting me know that the passenger side of the vehicle was slowly moving away from the inside wall on his side. I stopped the Humvee again and had the driver straighten the wheels. I pulled and whipped my ICS cord back before continuing to guide the vehicle on to the aircraft. I didn't want the cord to get run over and have to back up the vehicle.

"Vehicle is clear of the ramp," the call came from SPC Andrew as I continued to guide the vehicle in, waiting for his call to let me know that the vehicle was in the correct position to begin strapping it down. "Continue forward 3, 2, 1, hold your forward," the call came from SPC Andrew at the ramp area. I gave the vehicle the, 'halt' signal followed by the, 'kill engine,' signal. SPC Andrew and I crawled under the Humvee and began strapping the vehicle down, hooking into pre-determined shackles. This was the standard and I had been shown how and where to strap the vehicle by SGT Andre prior inside the shipping container.

"Forward straps secured," I called over the ICS while I was trying to maneuver out from under the vehicle.

"Back straps are secured, vehicle secured, ramp is up aft ready," SPC Andrew said.

Then I called to SGT Andre who was monitoring our task the whole time, "Forward ready."

SGT Andre, who was plugged into the ICS said, "Good job Burnie, now guide it back off; I will imitate the landing calls," he concluded.

"Roger," I said while looking over the vehicle to get an acknowledgment from SPC Andrew. Under the green glow of the night vision I saw SPC Andrew give SGT Andre and I a thumbs up from the back of the bird.

The ICS was silent for a minute, then SGT Andre came over the headset. "Got you off 10,9,8,7,6,5,4,3,2,1, contact. Ramp, ramp, ramp."

"Ramps coming down," SPC Andrew responded.

I followed with, "Working on un-securing vehicle." I lunged toward the ground and low crawled under the vehicle to release the straps. I tried to make myself skinnier under the vehicle but my flight vest was so cumbersome. I had to force my way to reach the straps. Finally, I reached the first and then the second, and unhooked both from the Humvee's shackles. "Forward straps released," I called back to SPC Andrew.

A few seconds passed and as soon as I heard the call, "Rear straps released," I pointed my IR chem-light at the driver, SSG Atch, and moved the chem-light in a circular motion giving him the, 'start engine' signal. I began to guide SSG Atch out meticulously, carefully, and quickly just like I had gotten the vehicle in the aircraft. "Good on my side good up top." Numerous situational distance calls came from SPC Andrew as the vehicle started creeping off the ramp. I continued giving the driver the backup hand signals holding the chem-lights horizontally and pushing them away from my body. The Humvee's front wheels crept to the ground emerging from the back of the MH-47G. I kept backing the vehicle up to get it clear away from the aircraft. "Vehicle clear," SPC Andrew called. Gripping both chem-lights with one hand I gave the clear of aircraft, continue mission signal. I pointed in a direction other than the aircraft and the Humvee cranked its wheels and took off. SPC Andrew and I picked up the loading ramps which were hinged to the ramp of the aircraft, and flipped them inside. They made a loud thud that could be heard even with our helmets on. We jumped in the helicopter and SPC Andrew raised the ramp and said, "Ramps up aft ready."

"Forward ready," I said, and just like that it was over.

"Turn the lights on," SGT Andre said through the ICS, looking at us from the front of the helicopter. As SPC Andrew turned the lights on I could see

SGT Andre reaching inside the cockpit. The APU cut off and it was quiet again. I pulled my helmet off and my hair was soaked. I was sweating my ass off and I was eager to take off all my gear. I thought it was going to be a cold night, so I wore long underwear and several other layers underneath my uniform. Right as SGT Andre was about to say something to us, he paused after hearing something. It was unmistakable and we all paused, hearing the same infamous sound. A loud blast rang out through the FOB and it sounded pretty close. "Mortar?" he looked at SPC Andrew and I with a questioning grin.

"Probably," I said.

The loud speaker wired throughout the whole base, echoed in a British voice, "Rocket attack, Rocket attack, Rocket Attack."

SSG Atch pulled up to the back of the ramp in the Humvee and all three of us standing in the middle of the Chinook, looked at him as he exited the vehicle. "Shit man that one was close," he said, referring to the mortar. He made it up onto the ramp and then paused in confusion and curiosity. We all stood in place not saying a word. A whistle sound soared through the sky followed by a thunderous BOOM. Shrapnel, rocks, and debris cascaded over the aircraft, and it sounded like we were in the middle of a hail storm. "Well damn," SSG Atch said in a calm and collected country tone. He went on, "That one was pretty close, let's get the fuck outta here." We ran out of the aircraft and jumped in the Humvee, taking off to the closet bunker on the flight line. We got out of the vehicle and holed up in the bunker as two more mortars hit the flight line. We had a clear line of sight of the aircraft in the parking stalls and the next two mortars rained down even closer than the first two.

Another ten minutes passed by and the loud speaker echoed, "All clear, All clear." We were all used to mortar attacks, but the base we were on was so big they were rarely that close. SSG Atch would later find out from the TOC that the mortars were targeting the black helicopters with the circle guns. Al Qaeda's worst nightmare was their number one target.

We headed back to the Aircraft after a brief pause in the bunker, to be greeted by the Godfather and CW4 Ray. "What's up guys," the Godfather looked at all of us. "We are on a stand down right now, there is a UXO (Unexploded Ordinance) on the flight line." He pointed to a spot some ways down the runway and I could see several emergency vehicles, Humvees, and fire trucks as I looked past the Chinook's parking spot. One of the mortars hadn't exploded on impact so it was still considered live. It needed to be taken care of before we could take off and I could get this damn vehicle qualification.

The crew and I made sure the straps were set up properly, and went over key points to achieving the qualification. In the meantime, the pilots were in the cockpit going over emergency procedures and troubleshooting knowledge from the sounds of it. Even though we weren't flying, I saw early on that everyone from the crew to the pilots were constantly honing their craft. Although it was a down day and some may see it as an opportunity to relax, that wasn't the case here. We didn't just say the creed we lived it, all ranks lived it. 'I pledge to maintain my body, mind, and equipment in a constant state of readiness for I am a member of the fastest deployable task force in the world.' A sentence taken from the Night Stalker Creed easily summed up what was going on during the mission down time.

As SSG Atch was asking SPC Andrew and me about the vehicle task, making sure we had everything down, someone strolled to the back ramp of the aircraft. One of the intel guys from the TOC looked at SSG Atch and said, "You guys are good to go, the runway is clear, and you are clear to do the qualification."

SSG Atch passed the info up to the pilots in the cockpit, then I heard the Godfather say, "Well are you guys ready?" I noticed SSG Atch look back in the aircraft cabin to make sure everything was configured and ready for flight. He turned back into the cockpit and gave a thumbs up to the pilots.

SSG Atch walked over to the crew and me, "Get your shit on it's go time." SSG Atch had already briefed us that we would be taking off without a vehicle and land across the runway in a rocky scattered sling load area. The area was designated for regular Army and other conventional forces to sling load large containers and equipment to other FOB's. The plan was, SGT Andre would drive the Humvee over to the blacked out sling load area and we would begin the vehicle qualification after landing in the specified HLZ.

SGT Andre hopped in the Humvee, peeled out, and headed over to the pre-determined AO. In no time the rotors were chopping through the air, "Tower this is Crazy 54 clear for departure to the south landing in the sling load area?" The Godfather stated through the radio.

"This is tower you're clear to the south, winds at 5 knots gusting to 10 out of the east."

"Coming up," he followed after the tower call.

"Clear up left," came from a Bravo Company guy at left gun.

"Clear up right," SSG Atch said hastily after. The large beast lifted straight into the air with magnificent power. The nose pitched down and we began to pick up speed just to make a sharp right turn after clearing the runway.

"Coming right," CW4 Ray said.

"Clear right," SSG Atch answered, after a short 20 second flight.

The Godfather called out, "I have the LZ and vehicle in sight."

"Roger," SSG Atch said. I stuck my head out of the left ramp window and saw the landing zone and the vehicle SGT Andre had driven to the location. "Vehicle in sight got you off 10,9,8,7,6,5,4,3,2,1 contact."The Chinook thudded to the ground after SSG Atch called the beast down to the rocky pad.

"Ramp, ramp, ramp,"came from one of the pilots. It was just a qualification but I didn't want to mess it up, my heart was pounding. SPC Andrew dropped the ramp and we flung the vehicle ramps out of the aircraft. Through the thunderous blades chopping at full speed and the infamous whine of the turbine engines, I heard the ramps slam against the rock littered ground. I flung my ICS cord outside the aircraft and started to walk away from the Chinook. While walking away from the aircraft, the vehicle was picking up speed and heading right toward me. I guided SGT Andre all the way to my belly button and halted the Humvee. I began guiding the Humvee toward me while I backed up slowly. The vehicle inched closer, while I periodically looked back to see how much farther I had to go before reaching the back of the aircraft. The warm exhaust heat from both engines were singeing the hairs on the back of my neck as I continued to back up. Finally, the burning sensation passed and the heel of my boot hit one of the vehicle loading ramps that was hinged to the ramp. The helicopter was loud through my helmet but I was still able to make out SPC Andrew's calls as the nose crept closer to the bird. I continued to guide the vehicle up the ramps and slowly into the Chinook. By the looks of it and the frequent calls coming from SPC Andrew I felt a lot more confident. The vehicle was coming in a lot straighter as I continued guiding SGT Andre and the large Humvee into the helicopter.

The noise from the turbine engines and blades were distracting, but after SSG Atch's antics at the shipping container, I was able to block out the external noise and continue on with the task. "Good on my side good up top, clear of the ramp," SPC Andrew said as I guided the Humvee inside the cabin. I continued with my hand signals bringing the vehicle closer and closer to the front of the aircraft. "Looks good Burnie," SPC Andrew said, and just then

I gave SGT Andre the stop followed by the kill engine signal. With an upward swinging motion, I gave the apply hand brake command with my two IR chem-lights.

"Working front and rear straps," I called. I knew SPC Andrew wouldn't be able to make the call because he was already crawling under the vehicle to connect the ratchet straps to the shackles. I crawled under the front of the vehicle after giving the call.

In no time the next call was from SPC Andrew, "Rear straps secured." I followed with, "Front straps secured, vehicle secured."

Then from the back of the aircraft SPC Andrew called, "Ramps up aft ready."

"Forward ready," SSG Atch said while looking on.

"Coming up," CW4 Ray exclaimed. The loud engines roared again but working overtime and needing a lot more power to pull the crew and the four ton Humvee off the HLZ. We picked up off the ground and the nose pitched forward. I looked over the Humvee inside the cabin and I could see the distant lights of the flight line out of the back of the helicopter. I was sweating profusely and knew the qualification was just starting. After several more landings at the sling load area followed by more vehicle loading iterations, it was eventually over. I thought I managed all iterations well and I was looking forward to the debrief.

"Continue forward 5,4,3,2,1. Hold your forward," SSG Atch called to the pilots as the aircraft came to an abrupt halt in our parking spot. Just like that the qualification was over and I felt accomplished, but wouldn't know if I could actually check that task off the list until the debrief.

The sun was starting to come up as the deep dark night faded away. SPC Andrew shut down the helicopter and all of a sudden the chaos and noise ceased. I pulled my helmet off and it was quiet and calm. The Bravo Company guys were parked 10 meters behind the ramp. They had an aircraft tug loaded down with gear from the inside of the aircraft. The crew and I began to open all the access panels and daily the aircraft while the Bravo Company guys began reconfiguring the inside of the helicopter to get it back to mission configuration.

As I was taking off the forward MMR (Multi-Mode Radar) access panel, SGT Max, from Bravo Company, said, "How did you do?"

I looked over to him in a confident yet unsure manner, "Good I think."

He patted me on the back and headed back inside the aircraft to finish the reconfiguration. With the daily complete, and the bird back to mission ready orientation, we locked up and headed to the ready room. One of the guys in front punched the code on the door handle which lead into the ready room and in we walked. The ready room was a 500 square foot room with one wall lined with cubbies, each one assigned to a crew member. From loaded magazines, ammo, weapons, body armor, helmets, to cold weather gear; the ready room was any Call of Duty warriors dream room. We headed into a sectioned off area in the back of the cramped space. All the Alpha Company crew that just flew met in the back, while the Bravo Company guys grabbed whatever they needed from their cubbies, and headed out to the bus.

SSG Atch hollered at the Bravo Company crew, "We will be right out." He gave me a run-down of what I could have done better and what I did well. He looked at me with a stern face, "Congratulations. I'm signing you off for your vehicle qualification." I looked at him and nodded feeling a sense of achievement. "Alright let's go eat, fuckers," SSG Atch said.

As we sat up, SPC Andrew and SGT Andre who had already gotten the qualification long ago, and were already FMQ crew chiefs, hit me on my back and simultaneously said, "Good job Burnie."

I walked out of the ready room with my crew, standing a little taller. I knew it was just the start of the FMQ journey, but I felt I gained a bit more trust and confidence from my crew. I was confident this is where I was meant to be. Although SSG Atch was an asshole at times, the camaraderie within the crew was astonishing, and like nothing I had ever experienced with my old unit. I think SSG Atch was giving me the hardest time because I was the new guy and with over ten deployments under his belt he took every task and every mission just as seriously as the one before.

For the next month each mission was nothing like the first. I got a lot more comfortable with the crew as my mission experience accumulated. I was excited to be deployed with the best aviation unit in the world, but I wanted more. My eagerness to be in the unit now shifted to being eager to be on a summer deployment. After hearing stories being exchanged between crew members in the ready room I soon realized the summer deployments were the most action packed, and that's exactly what I wanted. I don't know how to explain it but after being fired at by the RPG during that first mission and firing the M-134 mini gun back, I wanted more. I wanted to get the feeling of the adrenaline back in my body. War became my drug and

I was addicted. Even though the crew and I fired at several more terrorists during the cold winter months it didn't compare to the first infill. From the brotherhood to the heart pounding sensation of dropping off guys who were going to make sure bad things happened to bad people, I was ready for a summer deployment.

CHAPTER 13
BECOMING #2

★ ★

e were a week out from my roommate SPC Andrew leaving the country to head home. He had been in country for 90 days and I still had another 30 to complete on my 90-day deployment. I learned a lot from him and the asshole I had known him to be, was not the guy who I had the honor of flying and learning with over that time. Much like we all came over here, the guys who were leaving would take one of the battle hardened Chinooks back to the US. SPC Andrew and SGT Andre were heading out, and SSG Atch and I would gain two more Alpha Company guys to fill the spots on our bird to complete the 4-man crew.

Another heart pounding small arms fire mission concluded and we parked the aircraft just like after every mission. Only this time we parked the aircraft in front of the hangar. I peeked through the cockpit window as the aircraft came to a halt to see handfuls of maintenance guys ready to break down the combat flown Chinook. It was time to get the aircraft ready to load onto the C-17 and get it back to the US. The crew and I started taking everything out of the helicopter so we could get it all loaded into boxes then reloaded into the aircraft.

SSG Atch and I didn't stick around long. The sun was coming up and SPC Andrew and SGT Andre would continue working on the aircraft throughout the day. While SSG Atch and I slept, they were eagerly waiting for their transportation so they could go home. Although this wasn't a long deployment compared to my last 13-month one with the big Army, it was a lot more demanding. Even though I had only been in the country for two months I was a tad jealous that both my two fellow crew members were going home. At the same time, I knew the unit wasn't going to be easy and working in it would definitely be testing of my character, drive, and overall intestinal fortitude. SSG Atch and I said our good byes and just like that the 4-man crew and the bond we developed over the short time was done. The new crew would be united soon. When SSG Atch and I woke up the next morning SPC Andrew and SGT Andre would be gone, and their Alpha Company replacements would have arrived.

We woke up the next morning and as I exited the shipping container which had become my home, I noticed a pile of hard cases and soft bags placed outside my door. My new roommate must have already landed and this was his shit. One of the name tags on the large tough box outside the door read, 'SPC Justin.' I walked down the hallway connecting the shipping container homes, to head down the stairs and meet everyone at the bus like I had done for the last 60 days. Huddled at the bottom of the stairs were a handful of guys along with a few guys from the Bravo Company crew that I came to know over the last few months. SSG Atch was waiting as I made my way down the stairs. I slowly noticed that I didn't recognize the majority of the replacements. The majority of them outranked me and all seemed stand-offish. Even though I had been in country for 60 days this was still my first Alpha Company deployment and I was still the new guy. I'm pretty sure these guys had way more deployments under their belts than I had. There was only one guy who was a Specialist like me. He was tall and lanky and looked confused just like I had when I first landed. I instantly recognized him. It was the same guy who helped me secure my Alpha Company warehouse cage back in the states.

SSG Atch waited for me to get down the stairs and like a coach announcing who made the varsity team after tryouts he announced, "The new crews are as follows, Chalk one; me, Burnie, Justin, and George," he continued on about who was on chalk two but I went in a daze. I thought to myself, he knows all the guys out here and probably deployed and crewed with them several times, but of all the guys he could have chosen for his crew he chose me. I didn't know the other two that well, but I was excited to prove myself to my crew and the newly arrived Alpha Company guys.

Keeping in routine we headed to chow and then to the flight line. SSG

Atch parked the bus in front of chalk one after dropping off the chalk two guys at their bird. I was instructed to get the bird ready for the night's mission with the new guy on our crew, SPC Justin. He was tall and had the look of a scared puppy. I wonder if that was how I looked when I first arrived. I had another month to go and I was determined to teach SPC Justin as much, or more than I had been taught by SPC Andrew, SGT Andre, and SSG Atch. It was weird being the more senior guy between the two of us. I had never had that feeling and sense of leadership since arriving at Alpha Company. SPC Justin had just finished BMQ back in the states and I could tell he was eager to learn.

I instructed him to climb on top of the bird to make sure everything was secured and all access panels were tightened down, much like SPC Andrew had instructed me on my very first day in country. "Turning blades," I yelled up to him as he took a seat on the tunnel covers and waited for an aft blade to reach him. I saw him unhook the blade rope, but I didn't hear the, 'Clear,' call from him. "Are you done?" I called up.

"Yes," he said in an intimidated way. I wasn't trying to intimidate the guy, but this was basic BMQ stuff. I informed him of the call he was supposed to make after removing the blade rope so I could begin turning the blades again. I did take into account he hadn't had any sleep since arriving in country and was probably exhausted, but then again that was the point of learning sleep deprivation in Green Platoon and SERE School. Either way I knew I was going to treat him just like SPC Andrew had treated me when first learning the ropes (pun intended). After getting the bird opened and everything set up for the night's mission I took it upon myself to have a candid conversation with SPC Justin in the cabin. I wanted him to be completely clear about everything. While I still didn't know everything and still had a lot to learn, I knew I was knowledgeable enough to teach him a great deal about the bird, combat readiness, and the overall mission. After going over some Q and A with him, SSG Atch and SSG George walked up the ramp.

SSG Atch asked me, "Are we all good?"

I had never had an FE, let alone the NCOIC of the deployment, ask me if anything was good. It was the very same thing he always asked SPC Andrew before a mission. I felt a sense of contribution, like my response and knowledge of the aircraft actually mattered. I responded with a confident, "Roger."

I nodded after getting a thumbs up from SPC Justin that he had done a walk around the bird. A walk around was a very meaningful step that needed to take place before every mission. It was instilled in us throughout the BMQ course. It meant someone had walked from nose to tail, side to side, and top to bottom of the bird making damn sure every fastener, and access panel was secured. Also making sure all of the, 'Remove before flight,' covers had been removed and there was no possible threat to safety when flying.

SSG Atch looked at me and said, "Alright Burnie, here you go." He reached his hand out and handed me an old school black pager. I had become very familiar with the pager during the last 60 days. The number two guy of the aircraft which was almost always an FMQ crew chief was responsible for the pager. The pager could go off at any minute at any time, and meant it was go time. Drop everything you're doing and head to the bird because it's mission time. A feeling of accomplishment jolted through my body as he handed it to me. He went on to explain to SPC Justin what the point of the pager was and made sure he knew to make me aware of his location at all times. In the event of a TST it was imperative that I knew where everyone was at the time the pager went off. A TST page meant we had less than 15 minutes to get the bird ready. The short timeline was achievable with a well-groomed crew. Getting this accomplished with a newer guy, well that responsibility now fell on me and I knew I wouldn't let the crew or the overall mission down.

The remaining days were slow with only a few missions a week. Being a winter deployment there hadn't been much intel from the TOC or the JOC (Joint Operations Center) to execute a mission. The TOC was where all of our guys collected intel during the day by utilizing drones and interrogating bad guys we had taken off targets. The JOC was where the 160th higher ups and the Rangers, or any team we were working with, congregated and planned for missions for the night depending on the intel. The few missions we did go on wrapping up my final days in country wouldn't have much worth, well so I thought. The days finally turned into hours and it was almost my time to head back to the states.

My bags were packed and waiting at the front of the door. SPC Justin was just waking up to go get the bird ready for the night's mission. He would be the guy in charge of the bird now. I hoped I taught him well enough just as the guys I looked up to did for me. I thought I put in one hell of an effort to prove myself on the deployment. Although I made a few mistakes overall I felt a sense of contribution and a sense of belonging. I had finally completed a deployment with the Alpha Company 160th SOAR.

It only took close to a year to get to this point but I did it. I felt accomplished and I was eager to come back for the next one. I slung my pack over my shoulder and started walking down the hallway to meet all the guys down at the bus. Just a handful of guys were heading home and the bus was already loaded down with their gear. The morale among the guys heading home was high, but for some reason I didn't want to leave. I felt like I finally found my calling and I was good at it. I knew I still had a lot to learn and was still a long way away from becoming FMQ. After setting my goal over a year ago on the airfield in Bagram nothing could get in the way of any goal I set for myself now.

Down at the buses SSG Atch informed the guys going home that we had a meeting to attend in the TOC before boarding the C-17 and heading back to Ft. Campbell. I recalled the feeling I felt when I was about to head home from my first 13-month long deployment. I was excited and I couldn't wait to get the hell home. The feeling was different now. Although I was excited to go home, if SSG Atch told me I had to stay for another 60 or 90 days, I wouldn't ask any questions or complain. I liked the mission and I enjoyed the shit out of leaving the wire almost every night.

After chow we headed to the flight line to drop off our bags at the hangar and then over to the TOC. All 160th personnel were in the room and it was packed tight. Pilots, intel guys, and all the helicopter crews stuffed the room. We had had meetings like this in the TOC before, but for some reason it seemed more crowded than normal. The 2nd battalion Sergeant Major was introduced by one of the intel guys who usually started the briefs. He went on to give a speech about how much we had been doing lately and how much it was impacting the war. It was very motivational and even though I had heard speeches like it in the past as a maintainer in my old unit, this one felt a lot different. When he referred to the crew chiefs he was clearly talking about Alpha and Bravo Company. Just a handful of guys that I had come to know as my brothers. No speech I ever heard at my old unit had any mention of, 'without the helicopter maintainers we wouldn't be here.'

He went on and in his conclusion he said, "I have a coin to hand out." Coins, or challenge coins were handed out in the Army to award or appreciate someone's hard work or achievements. Receiving a coin from the 2nd battalion Sergeant Major was an achievement all in itself. I found out through a chow hall dinner conversation, that the Sergeant Major of the battalion hardly ever handed out coins, which is why just receiving one from him was an achievement.

"I want to hand out a coin to recognize a certain individual." He went on, "This soldier has put in a gallant effort in ensuring the safety of his crew and the operators on board. He has shown a great deal of drive and dedication throughout this deployment. I have heard nothing but great things from the NCOIC of his company and his outstanding role during his deployment." Alright, alright, I thought in my head just give this damn person their coin so I can get my bags loaded on the C-17, and get the hell outta this cramped room. "Where the hell is Burnett?" I was elbow to elbow with some guys from chalk two and I didn't think I heard him clearly. I stood there for a few seconds longer and the two elbows nudged me. I walked up to the Sergeant Major and I had no idea what was happening or why. Out of everyone in that room, I was receiving a coin. I walked up to him and the room erupted in applause. I looked him in the eye and he shook my hand. I felt a cold metal coin in his handshake, and he said, "Keep it up Burnett."

"Roger Sergeant Major." I said and walked back to where I had been standing.

Finally, the attention was off me as he wrapped up his speech with a few last minute words. As I exited the room I received congratulations and handshakes from not only all the Chinook guys but other 160th pilots and personnel I had never met. Now I definitely felt accomplished, but I didn't want it to go to my head. There is no way I could have received that coin without the Alpha Company guys that trained, mentored, and hardened me up to that point. I was still one of the most junior guys in the company and that coin was no more mine than all of Alpha Company's. I quickly put the coin in my pocket, and headed to the flight line toward the giant C-17 waiting to take us home. I boarded the plane and it looked no different from when I first landed in KAF. A large MH-47G was already strapped down in the cabin, just waiting to go home like the rest of us.

After a short stay in Germany at the same concentration camp building we had stayed in on the way over, I found myself boarding the C-17 again. After a quick roll call from the load master of the C-17 it would soon be wheels up. After a few more minutes, a call came over the loud speaker and in a joking manner the load master said, "Flight attendants prepare for take-off, next stop Ft. Campbell." I remember those same words being muttered when I was on a Delta passenger plane about to fly back home to Ft. Campbell with my old unit. The feeling was a lot different then. I think I was eager to get back to embark on Green Platoon. I wasn't excited nor upset about heading home, I was just content. After getting a taste of what the unit and my new company was all about, I couldn't wait to learn more about my role and continue to progress toward becoming an FMQ crew chief.

CHAPTER 14
ROPES, ROPES, ROPES

★ ★ ★

I heard the screeching of the tires and brakes as the C-17 came to a slowing speed and found pavement. I opened my eyes while sitting in my standard equipment C-17 chair. I looked around at all the other 160th personnel occupying the cargo bay after the lights flickered on. "Welcome home boys," the load master called over the intercom system. The Ambien had knocked me out the entire flight and I didn't even sprawl out on the floor. I had slept in my seat the whole time. The C-17 made a final turn in the windowless cabin and then came to a halt. Three pallets were strapped down on the back ramp of the plane containing everyone's gear from the deployment. The ramp of the plane lowered followed by a loud hydraulic clunk which locked the ramp level with the cabin floor. As everyone began to de-board the plane a large fork lift began scooping up the pallets of bags and tough boxes from the ramp. I stepped down the stairs and off the plane, took in a deep breath, and thanked God I had made it home safely. I guess I really didn't count my blessings until reflecting over the missions we took part in on that deployment.

It was February and must have been 0100 or 0200 in the morning in Kentucky. I looked across the flight line to see the 160th hangars in the distance. The flight line was still, and I could see all the helicopters lined up perfectly, glowing under the bright florescent exterior hangar lights. A white bus of course, was waiting for all of us to get on so the driver could shuttle us across the flight line. I wasn't sure what to expect as the bus got the all clear from the tower and the driver headed to the hangars. I had been through the whole welcome home ceremony with banners and bright lights before, but I had a feeling this was going to be different, much like the whole deployment had been. The air brakes of the bus cut through the low lull of conversations being exchanged on the short bus ride to the hangars. Out of my window I noticed the far hangar door start to slide open and the fork lift that had retrieved a pallet from the back of the plane was placing the cargo in front of the door. I exited the bus and followed the group of guys who were headed toward the pallet. Guys started ripping into the cargo like hungry cavemen. I looked around for banners and applause from groups of families like before, but no one was in sight. The airfield was quiet, no helicopter noise, no F-18's taking off, just silence. It was quiet and all the men tracking down their gear on the pallet were quiet too. A couple wives were standing in the cold waiting for their husbands to find their things. None of my gear was on the pallet and I eagerly waited for the next one to be delivered from across the flight line.

The group of guys thinned out as just a handful of us remained. SSG Atch gathered his gear and told me to show up to the office in two days. I gave him a nod and he took off, and after rounding the corner of the hangar he was gone. I left the pallet to locate my truck in the deployment parking area. I jumped in and started my truck, and after letting it warm up a bit I drove over to the side of the hangar and parked. The compound was just as quiet as the airfield. I guess I was expecting a welcome home like the last time but no one was there. It was completely different and it sunk in that the unit I was in now was constantly deploying and there wasn't time for welcome homes. If that were the case, they would be every week. I was a quiet professional now and that meant leaving in the middle of the night, coming home in the middle of the night, and absolutely no elaborate welcome home ceremony. I realized a section in the Night Stalker Creed more than ever as the fork lift delivered the final pallet, 'I will guard my unit's mission with secrecy.' My new company and my unit's mission was so crucial that no one ever needed to know when we were coming or going. While the majority of the guys left with wives and sleepy kids, I was headed back to an empty barracks room. After the short traffic-less trip to the barracks I opened the door to see all of my roommate's stuff was gone. I was glad I didn't have to try and be quiet in the early morning hours and I didn't have to share a room anymore, like I had for the last 90 days. I was starving, but I knew nothing would be open, so I left my bags in the kitchen and fell face first into my bed.

My first deployment was complete and I couldn't have been happier with my decision to join the elite unit. The next morning, I enjoyed the day off taking care of adult things I didn't have to worry about while I was gone. It was a pleasant day off, running around town and enjoying all the fast food luxuries that were nonexistent in Afghanistan. After getting my phone turned back on I had received several text messages. One of the messages read, 'Burnie, this it SSG Karl. Florida TDY, we leave in two days, be at the office tomorrow at 0700.' Well the joy of relaxing for a bit was quickly demolished by a simple little text message. I knew the company wanted to get me FMQ rated as soon as possible, but damn I just got back and now I had to get ready to go on a TDY trip.

I can't say I wasn't warned that the tempo here was fast paced. This was just one reason there was an alarmingly high divorce rate throughout the unit. Luckily for me I was single and ready to mingle, or in my case ready to go to Florida without having to tell my significant other I had to leave again. On the bright side at least I was back in the states.

I woke the next morning to the same alarm clock that woke me in Afghanistan and had been with me for every deployment. I wanted to be squared away before arriving to the office so I woke up a few hours early. I headed to the compound, passed the office, and headed over to the far warehouse building on the compound where my personal storage cage was. In the warehouse, I grabbed my overwater go bag along with a few other items I thought I might need on the upcoming trip. I threw the gear in my bag and headed for the office.

I walked in the office feeling a lot better than I had when I walked through the door for the very first time nine months ago. I went into the crew office to be greeted by SSG Karl. He was a small Asian dude who looked at me and said, "You must be Burnett?"

"Roger," I said. I had never met SSG Karl before but heard from a few others that he was stern but knew how to have a good time when he wasn't working. He gave me a quick brief on what needed to be done and what was left to do in order to prep for the trip to Florida.

"You will have the opportunity to get qualified in Decks, Ropes, and Amphib 1's," he said while pointing to the white board directly behind him. On the white board in bold letters read, 'TRIP PREP,' and underneath that was a list of names. I looked through the names and only recognized one, 'SSG Kareem.' Just to the side of all the names read all of the tasks that SSG

Karl just mentioned which was why he was pointing to the board. Just then I started to hear a familiar voice talking on the phone in the hallway just outside the crew office.

SSG Kareem walked in the door and in a very enthusiastic tone said, "Rookie what's up? How was your first deployment?"

"Good," I said, while trying to mimic his enthusiasm. He must have had five cups of coffee already.

"You got your vehicles qualification, now just get these on this trip then all you will have left for FMQ is FARP." He was absolutely correct and he knew more about the guys on his crew than the actual guys knew about their current path in the company. He took pride in his guys and it was so different than my encounter with my first form of leadership in the Army. I recalled my time with SSG Chris back at my old unit, which gave me a much greater appreciation for the type of leadership qualities SSG Kareem exuded. Maybe it was his Trinidadian upbringing, or maybe the qualities were formed within the ranks of Alpha Company and through his countless deployments with the unit. Either way, I was grateful to be under his guidance and leadership in the company. An awkward pause between SSG Kareem and me ensued and I heard the typing of a keyboard. I glanced over to one of the desks and noticed a maintenance guy typing into a helicopter log book. I'm guessing he just got done performing maintenance on one of the birds and was annotating the work in the computer. My eyes continued scanning across the room and landed on another white board. A carefully drawn out chart had the words, 'Beer Board,' written at the top. I looked down and finally came across my name which had over ten tally marks next to it. SSG Kareem must have seen my face and realized what I was looking at.

I started to speak and then SSG Kareem cut in, "You had a lot of firsts on your last deployment and everyone back here made sure to document it." In the company, every time someone did something for the first time they had to provide and stock the beer fridge with a case of beer. No questions asked, it was a mandatory task and yet another Alpha Company rite of passage. I could clearly tell by the tally marks on the board who the new guys in the company were. Well at least I saved up some deployment money because I was about to be buying a lot of beer. "Go out to the birds and start helping SGT Juan get everything ready for the trip," SSG Kareem instructed me while SSG Karl gave a gesture in agreement.

"Roger," I said and headed out to the flight line. As I walked out to the flight line, six Chinooks lined one row of the airfield and in front of those were another six. I could see movement through one of the aircraft windows and figured that was the bird SGT Juan was on. I had never met SGT Juan, but I knew he was another one of SSG Kareem's guys and essentially part of the 780 crew. I walked up the already lowered ramp. Hunched over and strapping down several bags and pelican cases was a short Hispanic dude.

I calmly said, "Hey."

He looked up at me and said, "You must be Burnie?"

Wow I thought to myself, a nickname given to me while deployed had circulated all the way back to the states without me even knowing it. Smirking I replied, "Yes." He went on to give me a quick run-down of what he was doing and what his game plan was to get the bird and two others ready for the trip to Florida. I began helping him strap down several stacks of gear that were piled against the wall. SGT Juan instructed me to strap the raft down. As he pointed to a large black looking briefcase I headed toward the ramp and strapped it in. I knew the raft belonged in a certain location and remembered it from the prep I did for the overwater TDY trip back in the BMQ course. The day went on with more crew members trickling in to help prep the birds for the upcoming trip. I met more guys I had never met before and they all treated me as if I had been with the company for a while. This newly formed camaraderie was a nice change from how I was treated before I left on my first Alpha Company deployment. I knew it was a rite of passage to call yourself a crew member in Alpha Company and I took it to heart.

SSG Karl walked onto the bird that we were all prepping for the trip. He told us, "Head to the conference room so we can do a crew brief." We all left the bird and meandered back to the office, down the hall, and into the conference room. I had never been in the conference room before. A large glass conference table was in the center of the room. As I took my seat around the table and waited for a few more guys to funnel in, I began to look around. Perfectly spaced, and on every wall were boat paddles, all from special boat or Navy SEAL Teams. I would later find out that these items were gifts to the company as tokens of appreciation and brotherhood among our ██████ colleagues. The company never ceased to amaze me nor did the incredible history the unit boasted throughout the years. Little acknowledgment was given to the unit due to its secrecy and lack of press coverage. The mementos on the wall were worth way more than any news outlet telling tales of heroic Night Stalker missions though. I knew, after my first 160th deployment, that the acknowledgment from the guys on board was far more rewarding than any other type of recognition.

SSG Karl began to speak and he had a large book in front of him. I was familiar with the book, the ARSOA manual. The book was the go to for all the required crew chief tasks. It explained in great detail what calls were to be made and what the standard was for performing each task. Before a task was going to be completed, the crew for the mission had to go through and read out loud the task standard. This TDY trip was no different and there were a lot of tasks I would be trying to qualify in. SSG Karl started the reading with the Ropes task and we alternated reading around the conference table discussing Ropes, Decks, and Amphib 1's. Although everyone in the room was already qualified in the three tasks, it was prudent that everyone be a part of the reading and get a refresher on what was expected. An hour later we concluded the reading and SSG Karl asked SGT Juan for an update of all the birds that we had been prepping.

"Everything is good. We are just waiting on maintenance platoon to load their gear," SGT Juan responded. It was common for a handful of maintenance guys to go on a trip like this in order to maintain the bird when we weren't flying.

SSG Karl looked at everyone in the conference room and instructed us to head home. "Be back at the office at 0600 tomorrow morning," he finished as we exited the conference room.

The morale was high among the three crews as we left the tightly filled conference room. The birds were ready to go, we were headed home earlier than normal, and we would have a 6-hour flight ahead of us in the morning. I was eager and looking forward to proving myself throughout the three qualifications I would have the opportunity to be signed off in. I would just have one more task to complete after these three to be considered an FMQ crew chief.

The next morning, I arrived at the office with my helmet bag and vest slung over one shoulder. I made my way through the quiet hallway, passed the Platoon Sergeant's office, and underneath the, 'Let the stress begin,' sign. I walked along the hangar and finally out to the long flight line to see the sunrise, more beautiful than ever. I could see my hot breath in the cold morning air. I paused for a second to take in the beauty of the fast paced unit I worked so hard to join. I heard a low rumble approaching behind me and as I turned around I noticed a John Deere Gator getting closer to me. The two seater flatbed was loaded with gear and some crew members finding a seat wherever they could on the packed vehicle. SGT Juan was driving and bringing a pile full of flight gear out to the birds. "It's go time Burnie, throw your shit in." I slung my gear off my shoulder and on top of a giant pile of vests, flight bags, and several flight helmets in the back of the Gator.

"I'll meet you out there," I said knowing I wouldn't find much of a seat on the already loaded down mode of transportation. The Gator sped past me and out to the three TDY ready helicopters on the flight line. I continued walking to the birds to help SGT Juan and the rest of the crew members already out there. The guys were already taking blade ropes and covers off to get the Chinooks ready for flight. After an hour of making sure the birds were uncovered and ready for flight, the distinct sound of a diesel rumbled just outside the bird. I looked outside one of the windows after clasping a final strap down to the aircraft's floor. A fuel truck pulled up next to the bird. SGT Juan, a more senior guy, was sitting down on the troop seat looking over the log book of the helicopter, making sure everything was in order. It was crucial we didn't over look any critical maintenance that was coming due on the bird. He looked at me and said, "Burnie, get gas on all three birds."

I said, "Roger how much are we taking?" Since both SGT Juan and SSG Karl were the go to guys on the crew, they had the most direct contact with the pilots and knew everything about the trip. I looked up to them and was striving to get to that point in the company. I wanted to make it to that level where I was the go-to for the pilots.

SGT Juan knew how much gas we needed and replied, "10,000 pounds." I gave him the thumbs up, grabbed my helmet, gloves, and headed to the number two side of the helicopter where the fueler had already hooked in the fuel hose. I raised the refueling station access panel just above the fuel hose connection and gave the fueler a thumbs up. A loud roar growled from the fuel truck, and I began filling the bird up while monitoring the gauges for both the left and the right tanks. I had been in charge of the majority of the fueling not only in BMQ but during the first deployment flying on chalk one. It was critical to make sure the fuel was evenly distributed between both the left and right tanks for obvious weight and balance reasons. I learned quickly on a cold winter night during my deployment that you don't want to make an uneven fueling mistake.

Just a few weeks ago, we were getting our bird ready for a mission down range. After SPC Justin was becoming more used to the bird and getting everything set up for mission configuration, the fuel truck pulled up. I asked him to put gas in the bird while I continued to set up the mini guns, and much like I was doing, he grabbed his helmet and headed out to meet the fueler. The fuel truck took off after a few short minutes, and both he and I continued setting up the aircraft.

While setting up I asked SPC Justin, "6,000 pounds right?"

He looked at me after securing a troop seat and locking it to the floor, "Roger, 6,000 pounds." I nodded and continued what I was doing.

The pilots arrived and I was at the left ramp position about to start up the aircraft, but then one of the pilots muttered over the radio in a calm tone, "What the fuck, who put gas in the bird?" Since both SSG George and SSG Atch hadn't been out there to get the bird ready, a silent pause took place over the ICS. Everyone heard the pilots question, and we looked around the cabin at each other's faces. Standing at the back of the ramp I looked up at SPC Justin waiting for him to say something, but he was silent.

I knew as the number two guy I was essentially responsible for his actions, so I came over the radio and said, "I did." Not knowing the consequences I would face from either SSG Atch or SSG George, the most senior guys, I waited for a pilot's response.

"Why the hell did you put 4,000 pounds in the left tank and 2,000 pounds in the right?" One of the pilots asked in frustration.

I didn't know how to respond and just said the easy Army cop out answer, "No excuse sir."

Before the pilot could respond SSG Atch came over the ICS and said, "I will handle this sir."

The pilot replied, "Roger. We can't have this shit happen again." Then SSG Atch said, "I know sir." As he said that he looked at me making a motion with one finger cutting across his neck. I just looked at him in shock. I had seen SSG Atch lose it on other guys before for messing up, so I wasn't looking forward to what he had planned. I then looked directly at SPC Justin and flipped him off while yelling at him over the loud whine of the APU. The fuel truck had to come back and we had to de-fuel the aircraft, which fortunately didn't affect the timeline of that night's mission. After the mission, SPC Justin and I got to participate in a Green Platoon Black Day all over again. We got smoked for a good five hours. Everything from carrying sand bags down the entire flight line and back, to pushing GSE (Ground Support Equipment), which was normally pulled by a vehicle. The smoking continued for the next few days after waking up from a decent night's rest. So after that little incident, I not only knew how crucial the weight and balance of the aircraft was, but I also knew I would never let it happen to me or anyone else again.

I looked at the fueler and gave him the cut fuel signal as the tanks reached 10,000 pounds, 5k in each tank. I repeated the same process between all three birds going on the trip and headed back into the aircraft where I had left SGT Juan. After getting a brief from the pilots we all headed into the aircraft and put on our flight gear.

I was at right ramp with SGT Juan at left ramp. SGT Juan started up the bird while I monitored the maintenance panel on the inside of the helicopter while constantly checking for any abnormal vibrations. I periodically gave SGT Juan the thumbs up letting him know everything I was keeping an eye on was all normal. We were chalk three or the trail bird, and as I looked out of my right ramp window I saw chalk one starting to pull forward, then chalk two, and then us. As I sat at my crew seat watching all three birds taxi and prepare to leave for the trip, I remembered a seemingly familiar sight just a few years ago. It was on the flight line in Bagram, Afghanistan on my first deployment where I saw an almost identical occurrence. Three birds all simultaneously starting, and then taxiing out to take off. I wasn't the maintenance guy watching in awe from a hangar anymore. And I wasn't on the sideline now; I was at long last, a damn 160th crew chief.

All birds conducted hover checks over Fury Sod and a few minutes later I heard the lead bird get the all clear from tower. The lead bird pulled power while both chalks two and three did the same. All three birds were off and we were headed to Florida.

After a long and boring 6-hour cross country flight we finally began our final approach to land at Hurlburt AFB.

"Clear down?" Came from one of the pilots.

Followed by SSG Karl at left gun, "Clear down left."

Then SSG Kareem at right gun said, "Clear down right." SSG Kareem finished the calls guiding the pilot all the way to the flight line tarmac, and then we taxied into a pre-determined spot which we were guided into by an Air Force ground guide. SGT Juan shut down the bird as I began to get everything cleaned up and taken care of inside the aircraft. I started releasing several ratchet straps in the helicopter that were holding personal gear and maintenance equipment. Two black Suburbans pulled up behind our aircraft, and exiting the driver side were two familiar faces from the Chinook maintenance company. Both guys were wearing civilian clothes and had already been in Destin, Florida for a few days. After loading the Suburbans with our gear and getting the Chinooks put to bed, we headed to the hotel to check in. We changed out of our military uniforms and into our civilian clothes so we wouldn't stand out.

After getting checked in, just like in BMQ, we met in a conference room of the hotel where the pilots set up a mission planning area. A long brief from all the pilots let the rest of the crews and me know that we would be flying the next morning. They had laid out the timeline for the next three days and I was pumped. The brief finally concluded and after finding out we would be working with SEAL Team 4, I knew I had to get back to my room to study. I didn't want to look like a complete new guy and I wanted to represent the unit in the most professional way that I was taught. The day was going to consist of two qualifications, Ropes and Amphib 1's.

Exiting the ballroom which had been converted into a TOC, I was taken aside by SSG Kareem. "You know what you need to do, right, rookie?" He asked.

Then I responded, "Well I'm heading to my room to study, if that's what you mean?"

"Alright good, I will meet you down here tomorrow morning at 0800," he finished. I gave him a nod and headed to my room. We had an 1100 show time at the flight line, but SSG Kareem was always prompt about being super early all the time. That night, I studied not only the Ropes and Amphib 1 tasks, but Decks too, as I knew it was coming up sooner rather than later on the short trip.

After a short but meaningful breakfast with SSG Kareem, SSG Karl, and SGT Juan, we grabbed our things and headed to the Hurlburt Air Force base where we had parked our aircraft. After a short drive from the hotel we made it to the flight line and started to get the bird prepped for the day into night training mission.

Three blacked out Excursions pulled up behind the aircraft while the rest of the guys and I were finishing prepping everything for the qualifications that night. Everyone in the cabin stopped what they were doing to witness a handful of guys exit each Excursion at the same time. They were all dressed in tan MARPAT (Marine Pattern) camo. The uniform didn't look to conform with any military regulation, all the guys had cut the sleeves off their uniforms making a short sleeve instead of the standard issue long sleeve. None of the men wore any patches on their uniforms which I was used to and was common practice among the special operations community while training or deployed.

SSG Kareem walked past me in the aircraft and off the back of the ramp to greet SEAL Team 4. I followed closely behind SSG Kareem to make nice with the team guys, and after shaking a few of their hands the other crew members to include the pilots from the other birds came over and did the same. The lead pilot, CW5 Steve didn't waste any time and got right to business with the brief of the day's mission. He was a CW5 just like the Godfather and had been flying in the unit for so long he pretty much already knew all the team guys first names. Like a lot of the pilots I had met up to this point in my Night Stalker career, he knew when to joke around but didn't take anything lightly when it was go time whether deployed or training. Just listening to the guy talk, I could tell he had been doing the job for a long damn time. A few of the SEALs asked CW5 Steve a couple questions during his short and to-the-point brief. There wasn't a single question he didn't have an immediate and no bullshit response for. You could say CW5 Steve was a seasoned pilot but so far in my short time in the unit, I realized all the pilots carried themselves in the same manner. They always had the ability to give a direct and accurate response to any question during a crew or mission brief. The elite standard in the unit was held throughout all ranks and this was another caveat I quickly learned.

It was a major difference in working with some pilots in the past at my old unit. There were good pilots and then there were Night Stalker pilots. They were the best in the world, but combine that with the best crew chiefs in the world you easily equate that to a seriously superior combo.

After CW5 Steve concluded the brief the team guys loaded into our bird, we cranked the engines, and we were off and headed to a remote beach strictly designated for military training. A 15-minute flight passed and the pilots relayed they had the beach HLZ in sight. The bird began to slow and I felt the familiar nose up motion prior to touching down. I made the call up to the pilots from the left ramp position after crossing from ocean to land, "Dust forming at the ramp."

Then SSG Kareem at right gun took over the calls as we passed the shoreline and prepared to land on the beach. "Dust mid cabin," a short pause as the sand started kicking up making it harder to see below, "Dust at the cabin door. Dust under the nose."

Then in a calm and content manner while the bird was engulfed in sand from the beach below the pilot said, "Alright guys, coming down."

"Clear down left," came from SSG Karl.

Then SSG Kareem responded through his wind muffled mic boom, "Clear down right, got you off 10,9,8,7,6," the aircraft slowly started to descend while the other helicopters had already landed or were just touching down to our left side. "Continue down 5, 4, 3, 2, 1, contact," SSG Kareem finished the calls.

We landed on the beach and waited for a radio call from the safety officer who was getting in position in the ocean. I looked off the ramp and out over the water. I spotted the safety officer. He was in a giant boat, the Mark V, a common boat used by the SEALs SWCC (Special Warfare Combatant-craft Crewmember) team. After another five minutes passed and we received the all clear from the safety officer that he was in position. I glanced out of the back of the ramp and saw the boat in the distance circling in the ocean.

I heard the pilot call over the radio, "Clear up?" and after the clear up calls from SSG Karl and SSG Kareem we were off the ground followed by the nose pitching forward, then a sharp banking left turn to get behind the two leading birds.

After linking up with the other birds and calling to CW5 Steve in the lead helicopter that we were in formation, he called back, "Roger, chalk one on final approach."

Then the chalk two bird called over the radio, "Chalk two breaking to the right of you and on final approach." Our pilots followed, and called out that we were on final approach. All three birds were side by side descending toward the dark blue ocean water.

"Ramp is coming level," SGT Juan called to the pilots. While SGT Juan was lowering the ramp I looked back into the cabin to see all of the team guys start to get up from their seats. They were checking each other's gear and grabbed on to whatever they could while standing in the cabin.

Normally when conducting fast roping operations, a designated target would be selected prior to conducting the operation. In flight, the pilot would inform the crew in the back that he has a tally on the target building, or he sees the building we will be fast roping on to. Once the chief in the back of the aircraft sees the building, he then continues to call the pilot forward until the chief has the aircraft's tail positioned directly over the target building. When the chief lets the pilots know that the helicopter is above the target, the pilot then calls the command, "ropes, ropes, ropes." The crew chiefs then release the ropes and push them out of the aircraft while the helicopter hovers in place. Once the ropes make contact with the ground or rooftop the chief then signals to the customers on board to begin fast roping. They then proceed to slide down the rope and onto the building. Our prior briefing in the hotel ballroom indicated that instead of fast roping to a target building we would be fast roping guys into the ocean. I didn't think anything of it at the time.

After the ramp came level both SGT Juan and I released the two coiled fast ropes attached to the inside of the aircraft and let them fall onto the ramp floor while trying to keep them neatly coiled. The large ropes were 60 feet long, and at least two inches thick. One end of the rope was looped to a large beam mounted to the ceiling of the helicopter, and after being pushed off the ramp would fall to the ground or sea, while the other end remained attached to the beam. We made sure we were tethered to the aircraft floor and then made our way out to the stubby wing of the ramp ensuring we had one hand on the coiled ropes at all times so they didn't fall out prematurely.

The stubby wings were on the outer edges of both sides of the ramp and allowed SGT Juan and I enough room to stand on and be exposed in the Florida air. Although there was barely enough room to maneuver, the vantage point enabled us to find the target building in front of the aircraft as we began the approach while allowing the team on board enough room to exit the aircraft.

"I have the target building in sight," the pilot said.

Then SSG Kareem said, "I have the target building continue forward 25," SSG Kareem had picked a spot in the ocean as the simulated target building.

The helicopter continued to creep forward and after a short pause, SGT Juan called over the radio, "Spray forming at the ramp." As we approached the target the pilots began to descend, bringing us closer to the water. The rotor wash began to spray salty ocean water all over the place.

SSG Kareem said, "Spray mid-ship," then a brief pause as the spray became more violent the closer we descended to the water. "Spray under the nose. Target building in sight continue forward 10," SSG Kareem finished. So far it was a by the book execution, passing off the calls from front to back.

"Continue forward 5, and come down 10," SGT Juan called. I quickly glanced into the cabin while holding onto a strap attached inside the aircraft specifically designed to hang outside the flying beast while kneeling on the stubby wing. "Hold your forward, good height, good hover, positioned over target," SGT Juan called, as the cold ocean mist continued to pelt my face.

"Ropes, ropes, ropes," the pilot called over the radio. SGT Juan and I both pushed the heavy coiled ropes off the back of the ramp. I looked down and watched the rope un-coil rapidly then finally make a significant splash in the ocean. While kneeling on the stubby wing I had my other arm extended and my hand balled into a fist, while SGT Juan was doing the same to block any of the team guys from fast roping down before it was clear.

"Fast roping in progress," SGT Juan said over the ICS and when he said that I saw him drop his arm and begin to make a waving motion with the same arm, alerting the guys to start roping into the ocean. The first guy passed me as I mimicked SGT Juan's arm motions. He slid down 20 feet and splashed into the water. I had no time to pay attention to what the first guy in the water was doing, I just made sure he surfaced and wasn't drowning. Before I knew it the next guy, then the next, then the next were sliding down the long green fast rope. All the while the guys were sliding down the rope SGT Juan was continually making calls letting the pilots know of the progress in the back.

"Fast roping in progress, half way done," he called. I looked back into the cabin as another guy grabbed the rope and slid down into the water. Before I realized that was the last guy to plummet down into the water, SGT Juan called, "Last man on the rope. Last man in the water. Eleven good thumbs up, working on retrieving ropes."

After seeing all the guys surface and give us a thumbs up from the water below we got up from our crouched stubby wing positions. SGT Juan and I began pulling the wet ropes back into the helicopter. In a normal combat situation, we would just release the ropes after infilling the guys on board. However, in a training situation we weren't about to release the ropes into the water. We began to pull them in. The ropes were already heavy but after the majority of the rope was saturated in water they were a royal pain in the ass. I began pulling and pulling and pulling. The never ending wet rope was kicking my ass. My arms were getting fatigued and I hoped the end of the damn rope was coming soon. As I sat on the ramp pulling in the soaked rope and piling it up next to me, I noticed the Mark V boat picking up all the guys who just roped into the ocean. Among all the physically demanding work bringing the rope in the aircraft, I was still able to find a way to appreciate the type of shit I was doing. Who knew what I would be doing if I hadn't applied to join 160th. I might have been taking off an aircraft wheel but instead I was fast roping SEAL Team 4 into the ocean.

"Ropes recovered," SGT Juan called over the ICS. SGT Juan raised the ramp and in a matter of minutes all the aircraft were wheels down on the beach again. SGT Juan lowered the ramp after touching down on the sandy beach. We began to drag the ropes taught out of the back of the aircraft then proceeded to coil them up again to prepare for the next Fast Rope iteration. The first time was a piece of cake since SGT Juan was making all the calls, but in order to get signed off on any FMQ task, I had to be the one making the calls. To add, I had to not only do iterations during the day but also at night to demonstrate my full knowledge and capability of performing the task. It was especially important we were competent at every task during the night and able to perform under NVG's since we almost always executed missions at night.

I hoisted the soaking wet coiled rope up and SGT Juan looped a seatbelt strap around it and clicked the buckle in place. It was a fairly rudimentary way to secure the coiled rope to the internal wall of the aircraft but it worked perfectly. To release the coiled rope, we just had to lift up the flap on the buckle and the rope dropped off the wall and landed on the ramp floor. While we were getting the ropes hung up the giant boat pulled up to the shoreline where all three birds were parked. Blades were still turning while we waited for the team to get back on board. I watched them jump out of the giant stealth looking boat and start to make their way to each of the helicopters they just roped out of. SGT Juan and I stood on the ramp and counted the guys one by one as they boarded the bird.

"One-one ████ on board, ramps up aft ready," SGT Juan called, after confirming the count with me.

"Roger that, are you guys ready back there Kareem?" The pilot asked. "Yes sir, let me get Burnie and SGT Juan to switch places so he can attempt his qualification." After he said that, SGT Juan and I immediately unhooked our ICS cords, handed them to one another, and plugged back in. The team guys had taken their seats, and once again all three aircraft pulled power and we departed the safety of the beach shoreline. Although Dunker School was helpful and gave me a bit more confidence in surviving a crash into the drink, there was always something unnerving about conducting operations so low and over a massive body of water.

"Chalk three is on final approach," our pilot relayed to the other two birds whom I could see out of my window. Guys on chalk one and two were already roping guys into the water off our left side. SSG Kareem notified SGT Juan and I in the back that the target building was in sight. I picked up the calls while dangling off the stubby wing trying to pick a point in the ocean to call the aircraft to.

"Continue forward 5, 4, 3, 2, 1. Hold your forward, positioned over target." I barely managed to call while trying not to get my ICS cord tangled around my neck. The aircraft slowed and stopped creeping forward as the rotor wash kicked up massive amounts of ocean water.

"Ropes, ropes, ropes," the pilot called.

Just like the last iteration, SGT Juan and I pushed the ropes off the ramp and into the ocean. I stuck my hand out blocking the already standing team guys eager to slide down the rope and into the water. The ropes splashed down and we started waving on the team, letting them know they were clear to rope down. Between giving the guys the roping signal, holding onto the strap while hanging off the stubby wing, and trying not to fall off, I became discombobulated. I couldn't find my PTT button attached to my flight vest so I could let the pilots know what was going on. There was too long of a pause over the ICS as I continued to search for my PTT.

"Burnie! Make the calls," SSG Kareem cut into the ICS in an upset tone. I looked over at SGT Juan and he noticed what was going on. SGT Juan started taking over the calls and made the remaining calls until the operation was complete. We recovered the heavy ropes from the ocean and turned back to the beach.

We landed on the beach and all I knew was I needed to correct myself and I needed to do it fast. SGT Juan made the first iteration look so seamless and easy. Well after my first attempt I found out how easy it was to get tangled up and lose focus of the task at hand. SGT Juan was already FMQ, so I assumed he had done this more than a handful of times. That wasn't an excuse I was about to manifest in my head though. I had to get the qualification down to perfection so I could check it off my requirement list. If I couldn't do it during the day, the crew definitely wouldn't have the confidence in me to make the calls later that night.

SSG Kareem came over the ICS and told the pilot, "Sir, all the guys in the back are going on private for a second." When he said that he gestured back to SGT Juan and I pointing up to the ceiling at the ICS box. There was a feature on the ICS that allowed the crew in the back, or in the cockpit, to be on a private channel and only the guys on that channel would be able to hear and talk to each other. I switched my box to private expecting the worst. I knew I was about to get my ass chewed, and after flying with SSG Atch while deployed, I was certain this chewing would be similar to one of his.

In a calm tone SSG Kareem said, "Do you know what you did wrong?" I didn't say anything but just nodded while looking at him. "You know what you need to do to fix it?" he questioned.

I replied, "Roger."

He gave me a few pointers and suggestions of things I could do differently and said, "Alright Burnie make this shit happen, switching off private," I could see both him and SSG Karl switch their boxes off private.

As I was about to do the same, SGT Juan grabbed my shoulder then started talking to me. Now just he and I were on private, and after a few words of encouragement from him we switched off private and I was ready to do the damn thing. The Mark V boat roared to the shore line then came to a halt as it ramped up the sand followed by the powerful wake it created. The guys jumped out and back on board the helicopter.

"One-one ████ sir, ramps up aft ready," I called to the pilots.

"Forward ready," exclaimed SSG Kareem. A quick takeoff and we were back over the ocean. I called the pilots to the target without any mistakes.

Then the call came over the radio, "Ropes, ropes, ropes."

"Ropes going out," I responded as we kicked the ropes off the ramp and into the water once again. I waved the guys on and gave them the clear to start roping signal while I made a call to the front, "Fast roping in progress. First man on the rope, roping in progress, roping in progress," I wasn't going to mess it up this time and I made damn sure to not lose track of my PTT. "Half way done," I didn't pause on the ICS once, making sure to keep the pilots and crew aware of what was going on. "Last man on the rope, last man in the water. I have eleven good thumbs up. working on retrieving ropes." As we yanked the ropes in SSG Kareem took over the calls clearly knowing that our hands were full.

Every 5-10 seconds he called over the radio, "Working on retrieving ropes." Finally, we got the 60 foot, soaked ropes back into the bird and after the third time my arms and body were smoked to say the least.

We landed back on the beach and repeated the fast roping task another five times. I was exhausted but I knew it wasn't over until we finished, and we worked without quitting until then. After concluding the remaining five daytime iterations all three birds in formation headed back to Hurlburt AFB so we could refuel and wait for the sun to set before conducting the night time qualification round.

After refueling the birds, eating some chow, and as always being debriefed by my crew on things I could improve on, all three birds fired up. The pilots received taxi instructions from the Air Force ground guide on the flight line and we were all lined up on the runway ready for take-off. The night was cool and the thousands of taxi and runway lights lit up the airfield. We got the call from tower and all three birds lifted off. I lowered my night vision goggles and the night turned to green and black. We made it to the same point over the ocean where we had been during the day. I looked down off the edge of the ramp to look at the sea below. My eyes were playing tricks on me and the green glow through my NVG's made it difficult to tell how far from the ocean we were. My heart was pounding and I just hoped I would figure it out when I heard the call from the pilots.

"One minute," the pilot called.

I looked back at the team guys sitting on the troop seats in the cabin and held up the number one with my hand while yelling as loud as I could, "One minute." They all mimicked the hand signal back to me and to their brothers sitting with them. "Ramp is coming level," I said from the right ramp position. After getting the ramp level we dropped the coiled ropes and navigated to the tight space on the stubby wing. We duct taped two chem-lights together, one green, and one red. So the guys would know once I turned the chem-light around in my hand switching from red to green they would know it was clear to start roping into the water. I could see the mark V boat sitting in the ocean rocking in the current. "I have the target in sight," I exclaimed after SSG Kareem had passed the calls off to me. "Continue forward 5, 4, 3, 2, 1, hold your forward. Positioned over the target." There was a pause as I waited for the pilots to maintain their hover.

"Ropes, ropes, ropes," CW3 Ryan the left seater said. I looked down to the water while holding my other arm out clutching the red chem-light. I couldn't tell if we were low enough to the water. The NVG's were playing tricks with my eyes. I looked under the green glow to see if I could make out the water with my normal vision, and I could. We were way too high. Before kicking the ropes off, I said, "Come down 10," to the pilots.

"Coming down," the pilot acknowledged.

"You're off 10,9,8,7,6,5,4,3,1, hold your down, good height good hover." He made the call again, "Ropes, ropes, ropes."

We kicked off the ropes and keeping the chem-light held tightly in my hand I pressed it against my leg switching it to the green side and began waving the team off. The first guy passed me on the stubby wing, grabbed a hold of the rope, and began sliding down in to the dark below. I watched him and a handful more guys start sliding down, splashing into the water. While they roped into the water I continued to relay calls to the pilots. We retrieved the ropes and headed back to the beach.

"Clear down?" Said the pilot. After getting the clear down left and right calls from SSG Karl and SSG Kareem we made contact with the beach sand for the final time. I was dead and I couldn't feel my arms. All I could think about was if I did well enough to get signed off in the Ropes qualification.

It was 2300 and I knew we still had a lot of night ahead of us. As we waited for the team guys to get back on the aircraft the ICS was quiet and no one was talking, we were just waiting for the boat to bring the guys back to shore. After a five minute break we loaded the guys on the aircraft and departed the beach to head back to Hurlburt AFB. On the short flight I ran through my head all the times I did the fast roping task that night and during the day. Just wondering, could I have done anything differently and had I made all the right calls? We landed back at the base, shut down the bird, closed it up and headed for the hotel. Each crew had their own Suburban and the drive back to the hotel was just as quiet as the ICS on the last beach landing. Everyone was exhausted and I could see it on their faces. I was just as beat, but we still had a debrief to do with the entire crew.

We met back in the hotel ballroom and I saw all the other Alpha Company guys for the first time after conducting the night time fast roping. They were just as exhausted. CW5 Steve started the brief and went through things we could have done better and how he felt the entire day went.

After he concluded, each crew broke off into their own debriefs and SSG Kareem started off by saying, "I'm signing you off Ropes, but there are still a lot of things you can improve on," he went on "Overall you did a good job, would you guys agree?" He looked around the huddled formation to get some acknowledgment from the other two guys on the crew. After getting their approval he went on for another five minutes recounting some things I messed up and what I could have done differently. "Alright get to bed, and I will meet you guys down in the lobby at 0900." Everyone acknowledged and we headed to our rooms for the night.

I entered my hotel room, emptied my pockets on to the night stand and glanced over to the other side of the bed. Perched on the night stand was a digital clock which read, '1:00AM.' Damn, we had been at it all night, but through the entire day I realized it didn't matter what time it was or how tired I was. This was the mission and this was why I wanted to be here. I felt a different sense of belonging, too. I had never worked with the SEALs, and it was humbling knowing I would be responsible for such elite guys in training and on deployments to follow. I was becoming more of an asset to the overall mission in the special operations community. Well that's what I told myself and would believe for the duration of my special operations career.

CHAPTER 15
CLEAR OF THE SUPERSTRUCTURE

I woke up the next morning feeling like my arms had just been pounded for the last week with sledge hammers. I was still exhausted but found it in myself to make it down to the lobby. I didn't actually have a choice, one of our mottos was, 'Time on target plus or minus thirty seconds.' It was in the Night Stalker Creed for God sakes, and it was burned into my brain since the first day of Green Platoon. It didn't matter if we were executing a mission overseas or showing up on time in a hotel lobby, if you were late you weren't living by the creed. From CW5 Steve's day one brief, I knew that today would be my chance to get signed off in the Amphib 1 qualification. After reading about the task in the ARSOA manual and listening to some of my crew's stories, I was pretty excited.

The task didn't sound difficult, but that's what I thought about yesterday's Fast Rope training. I was quickly brought back to reality when I found myself tangled up in my own ICS cord trying to make calls while SEAL Team 4 was splashing down into the water. Amphib 1's were used to benefit any special operations SBT (Special Boat Team) in a quick reaction amphibious scenario. A Zodiac, which was a large rubber boat, would be loaded into the cabin. The aircraft would hover over a body of water, we would push out the boat, and then the SBT would jump out after it and climb aboard the vessel.

After meeting SSG Kareem and the rest of the crew in the lobby we headed back to the flight line where we parked the glorious MH-47G's the night before. We opened up our bird and conducted our usual rituals. A blue passenger van was towing two large Zodiac boats stacked on top of each other. A few team guys hopped out of the van, and my crew and the team guys hoisted the Zodiac off the trailer and carried it into the cabin of the aircraft. SGT Juan had already folded the aft troop seats off the cabin floor and secured them to the wall. Folding the seats up was necessary to fit the large rubber vessel into the cabin. While it looked like a light rubber boat, the engine that was secured and folded into the boat made it deceptively heavy. After squeezing the boat into the Chinook I began to strap it down. While strapping down the Zodiac all the crews and team guys began to form a huddle around the back of our helicopter.

"Hurry up Burnie," SGT Corey hollered at me. Another Alpha Company guy who I hadn't gotten to know that well yet.

"Roger," I replied, and after tightening up the last strap I hustled to the back of the ramp where everyone was waiting.

CW5 Steve kicked off the brief and addressed any questions the team guys or crews had. He discussed in great detail what we were about to do. The brief concluded and I had started to get in the groove of this whole crew chief thing, or so I thought. I boarded the aircraft along with the rest of the crew and team guys. I slung my flight vest on and slithered my head through the vest opening to pop my head out. SGT Juan was at right ramp and he would perform the task before I would get a chance, just like the day before. With the boat strapped down and the bird loaded with a group of hard charging SEALs, we departed Hurlburt AFB. We were en route to the designated training area over the ocean.

The bird screamed to a slowing hover as the nose pitched up. I looked down over the ramp and into the water just to catch a gust of ocean mist in my face. My clear visor I had pulled over my eyes was drenched. SGT Juan started making calls after I wiped the sea water from my visor.

"Spray forming at the ramp," the mist of the ocean started making a vortex in the water just beneath the back of the helicopter as the pilots started descending closer to the ocean. "Spray at the ramp, spray mid cabin," SGT Juan finished.

SSG Kareem took over the calls, "Spray at the cabin door, spray under the nose."

"Ramps coming level," SGT Juan exclaimed, and then the pilots started to talk to one another as we made our way out to the stubby wings yet again.

"You're at 20 and 20," one of the pilots said to the other, referencing the height and airspeed of the aircraft.

In my studies and continuous reading of the Amphib 1 task, I knew once the pilots were at 10 and 10, or ten feet AWL and ten knots airspeed, that was our cue in the back.

"Got you at 10 and 10," CW3 Ryan said to the other pilot, then quickly muttered, "Boats, boats, boats."

SGT Juan and I had our hands extended just like when we were blocking guys from fast roping. I looked back and the team guys had already unstrapped the boat and were beginning to push it back toward the edge of the ramp.

"Boats going out," SGT Juan said. We started waving the team on as the boat continued to glide past us. The rear of the Zodiac was hanging half way out of the back of the Chinook and it began to teeter. One more shove from the team guys and the boat splashed into the ocean. One by one the guys on board jumped off the ramp and plunged into the water after the boat.

"Boats in the water, teams going out," SGT Juan said. After everyone jumped out of the bird I started counting the guys in the water as their heads surfaced. I was looking for five thumbs up to account for the five guys that just jumped out of the perfectly fine helicopter. The guys wading in the ocean surfaced to the top and I saw five guys looking back at us as we continued to hover forward. We were slowly leaving the team and boat in the distance. I looked at SGT Juan and held up the number 5 followed by a thumbs up. "I have five thumbs up sir," SGT Juan said.

"Roger, 56 coming out, 56 coming out," CW3 Ryan exclaimed over a different radio to the other helicopters who had already dropped off their teams and boats in the water. We pulled power and nosed toward the beach. Three Chinooks lined up on the beach with all the ramps facing as close to the shore line as possible to make loading the Zodiac back on board as easy as possible. I looked out of the Chinook to see all three Zodiacs flying toward the shoreline to meet their respective birds. The team guys on our bird lunged their Zodiac on shore with inches to spare, almost touching the back ramp of the Chinook.

SSG Kareem came over the radio, "Working on loading the boat sir." I unplugged and my boots sunk into the sand as I hopped off the helicopter to help load the now heavier boat. It had at least a gallon of water in it now from when the guys had to get in after jumping out of the bird. The team,

SGT Juan, and I found a handle on the sides to grab and all lifted at the same time. We finally got the drenched boat onto the aircraft and after strapping it down I looked at SSG Kareem. He motioned to SGT Juan and I to switch places. I plugged in to the right ramp's ICS cord while SGT Juan did the same on the opposite side.

We did the day time task another five times with me making all the calls at the right ramp position. The boat task was just as draining as the fast roping, but I understood the importance and safety required to do both. After successfully completing the five iterations we landed back on the beach and were able to accomplish five more iterations at night since we planned enough fuel.

The sun had set right after the fifth day time iteration so we were able to go right into the night portion. I felt I did well and thought to myself while flying back to Hurlburt AFB, would I ever even need to do this task while deployed? I mean the majority of the company was always flying in the Middle East, and I couldn't even think of a body of water big enough to accommodate such a task. Then I thought about other deployments that I knew our company was currently on, and it hit me. We were deploying to many other parts of the globe that were never portrayed by news outlets, and those remote and secret deployment destinations could absolutely utilize Amphib 1's on a real world mission.

We landed back at the base, then finally back to the hotel. After a much shorter debrief in the ballroom, SSG Kareem informed me I would be signed off on the Amphib 1 qualification. Day by day I was getting closer to the FMQ title. The next morning, we met SSG Kareem in the lobby at 0800 just like the days before.

"Alright Burnie it's the last day and one more qualification you can get signed off on." The qualification he was referring to was Decks. A task the unit utilized frequently. Through stories I had heard in the Alpha Company crew office, I knew it was going to be nothing short of awesome. Decks was a task where I needed to call the pilots onto and guide the aircraft to land safely on an aircraft carrier or large Navy vessel.

The crew and I were in a routine now and we figured out how everyone worked. We headed to the flight line, got the bird opened up, and just like that we were ready to go. The brief was quick from CW5 Steve to all the other crews since we weren't working with the team guys anymore. I had to complete three daytime landings on the ship and three nighttime landings successfully in order to be signed off on the Decks qualification. The sun was shining and it was the nicest day so far. Florida, toward the end of February, wasn't bad at all. SSG Kareem put me at the right gun position which was very rare for me since I wasn't FMQ yet, and it was the FE position. The task required me to call the aircraft to the ship from the right gun position in order to get qualified. After SSG Karl and I gave the clear up left and right calls, the bird lifted off the ground and I could see the Air Force hangars getting smaller and smaller below. "Got you off 25, 50, 75, 100. Clear of obstacles, Clear for flight," I finished proudly, spitting into my mic boom. Just like that we were en route to land on the USS New York.

"Thanks chief," CW3 Ryan said. There it was again, I heard it again. Those same two words that were muttered to me while I was deployed. Those two words meant it all, and made me feel like my role mattered.

As we peaked over the final hotel developments leaving the mainland and heading into the abyss over the ocean, I searched for the Navy vessel. I scanned the horizon, hanging my head out of the right gun window. I couldn't see anything in the ocean except a couple small fishing boats and a few barges. We were 100 feet above the ocean and the sun was glistening off each ripple below. I looked out the window just waiting to hear something from the pilots that they had the ship in sight.

Another 15 minutes later and the pilot said, "I have the New York in sight!" I was already standing and I looked out of the window again. I stuck my head out into the humid force of air and the wind blasted my face. I saw the ship and kept hanging out the window until we got closer. Finally, we were lined up parallel with the giant destroyer.

The USS New York, which was constructed from recovered steel and materials from the collapse of the twin towers was massive. The boat was sleek, streamline, and stealthy looking. I had never seen anything like it; it was indeed, beautiful. As we passed the ship I noticed a giant pad on the stern, and according to the pilots that was where we were going to land. We started making dummy circles while the other two birds landed on the Navy vessel.

After a few more circling patterns a call came over the radio, "Alright 56 you're up." The very recognizable voice was CW5 Steve from the lead bird. It was my time to shine. I didn't know if my performance from last night indicated I didn't need someone to demonstrate the task. SSG Kareem wanted me to do it first try with no demonstration. I was fine with that. We made our final turn and were aimed directly at the ship heading toward the giant helicopter pad. "Continue forward," I said.

We were 100 meters away from the boat and the pilot said "Roger, starting our approach." We continued to creep forward and the nose and forward landing gear crossed over the pad.

"Forward gear is over the deck," I said followed by a, "Continue forward," call. I continued to look down at the grey HLZ we were slowly hovering over. A group of twenty seamen wearing colored helmets were scattered in different locations below. They were all watching the spectacle of the giant Chinook coming down to land on their boat.

A few more seconds of inching forward and SSG Kareem called out from the back of the aircraft, "Aft gear is over the deck."

"Clear down?" CW3 Ryan questioned.

"Clear down left," SSG Karl said.

Then I said, "Clear down right. Got you off 15." The bird started to descend, "Off 10,9,8,7,6,5,4,3,2,1, contact," I finished.

"Contact lights on," SSG Kareem said from the back while he looked at the maintenance panel. I looked straight out of my window as the aircraft sat rocking on the deck while the blades kept spinning. I noticed a crowd of seamen gathering behind a net like fence just staring at me. With the sun out, I had my black tinted visor down and my face mask covering the lower part of my face. A few of them waved at me as they knew I was looking at them. I recalled that same wave I made to that guy at the right gun position in Bagram on my first deployment. In Night Stalker like fashion I did the same thing the guy did to me just two years ago. Nothing, I stood there and stared at the on-looking waving seamen, and in perfect timing, the pilots got the all clear from the ships tower.

"Clear up?" Our pilot exclaimed.

"Clear up left," SSG Karl said.

Followed by my, "Clear up right." The bird raced up toward the sky as the seamen below continued to stare. "Got you off 10, 15, 20, 25, forward gear clear of the deck." The nose passed over the deck and we continued out toward the ocean away from the ship.

"Aft gear is clear of the deck," SSG Kareem said.

"Clear of the super structure, clear for flight," I called.

As we headed out over the ocean to start another dummy circle pattern I looked back at SSG Kareem to get some sort of acknowledgement. He simply looked at me and didn't make any sort of gesture, so I figured I did OK. Another two more deck landings and we were outta there heading back to Hurlburt AFB only to sit, get fuel, and wait for nightfall to do the same thing all over again. I could appreciate the process but damn it was exhausting.

For some reason though, I didn't care. I was so ecstatic about the bonds I was forming with the guys and the type of mission I was now a part. Nightfall came and we headed back to the ship with all three birds, again I made all the right gun calls and felt I fared well during the Decks qualification. We made our way back to the hotel after a long night, bedded down, and packed the next morning. All the crews were down in the lobby with their bags, no different from when we first arrived at the hotel just a few days ago. We headed to the flight line, packed up and strapped everything down in the bird so we could head home. I was excited to get back to Ft. Campbell. Even though I didn't have anything or anyone really waiting for me to return, I was eager to get some sort of time to catch my breath from the nonstop, adrenaline pumping, fast paced occupation. I was also excited to find out if I had passed my Decks qualification. For some reason SSG Kareem let me know that he wasn't going to tell me until we got back to the house after the previous night's debrief. We finally landed back at Campbell after a 7-hour trip which dragged. The flight time differed from the trip down due to a head wind. After downloading the birds and loading my gear into the truck, the entire Alpha Company crews who were on the trip all met in the office. I was one of the last ones to trickle into the office and I noticed everyone was drinking a beer. I had witnessed this before, but I had been told if I wasn't an FMQ, I wasn't allowed to drink with the boys. I leaned on one of the desks as I wasn't sure if I was allowed to sit in an office chair yet. Had I accomplished enough over the course of the last nine months to be able to sit in one of the chairs?

SSG Chris G. who was a FE, that was on one of the other birds, motioned over to the chair and said, "Sit down fucker." He was just as big if not bigger than SSG Atch. Hesitantly I walked over to the chair and sat down.

I noticed SGT Juan get up and head over to the beer fridge he said, "Ramp check?" A phrase used on the helicopter to inform the pilots and crew you were checking all systems and making sure there were no abnormal vibrations in the aircraft while in flight. The same term was used in the crew office to ask if anyone wanted a beer.

As he said ramp check while opening the fridge and looking around the office of dead tired crew chiefs, no one said anything. He looked over at me and said, "Burnie you want a beer?" Wanting to say yes I knew I still wasn't an FMQ chief.

"I'm not FMQ," I said disappointedly. He looked around the room again as everyone had been listening to the exchange. SGT Juan raised his voice and faced the crew dogs sitting down in their office chairs around the giant office table.

"All in favor of Burnie having a beer?" He announced. I gazed across the room to see every FMQ and every FE had raised their hands. I was in shock. I had never seen a non-FMQ crew chief ever drink a beer from the beer fridge. I was accepted, and with every hand raised! Although a small gesture, it made me feel like I was doing the right things. SGT Juan threw me an ice cold Coors Light, and the cold refreshment couldn't have tasted better. That was the best damn Coors Light I had ever had in my life.

SSG Kareem being the most senior of all the guys in the room started off the debrief. After an hour discussing the entire trip with back and forth conversations being exchanged among the group I still was unsure if I got the Decks qualification. Guys were laughing and joking after the long but important AAR.

He focused his eyes on me, and in a tone like he was introducing the next big circus act he said, "Finally, ladies and gentlemen I give you the newest Decks qualification in Alpha Company," I let out an excited grin as everyone who had had a few beers already started clapping.

"Now pack your shit you're on the next rotation." SSG Kareem said, now a little more serious than the circus intro. My smirk still half on my face started fading away. I didn't know if he was joking or if he was serious. I continued to look at him and his face was more serious than ever. "Sorry Burnie, you're heading out to KAF in a week." The entire group of guys all looked down at the floor as I looked across the room. They knew the feeling and they had all been there before. I wasn't mad though. I understood a lot of the Alpha Company guys had wives and kids but I didn't. It was going to be a summer deployment and I was raring to go. A week was just enough time for me to take a breather, get my gear ready, and head out on the next rotation.

SSG Karl took a swig of his beer and looked at me, "Don't worry Burnie. I'm going too." I felt a little relieved after hearing that.

Then another crew chief, SGT James, who I hadn't really gotten to know yet said, "Me too Burnie!" People I hadn't even met in the company were calling me Burnie, and I thought that was pretty cool.

SSG Kareem continued with his speech, "The guys down there are reporting the fighting is picking up and they have been taking small arms fire every night." As soon as he said that I recounted that first mission, switching the mini gun to green, and laying down fire onto that rooftop.

I couldn't wait to get back in the fight and my eyes lit up while replying with an eager, "Roger that."

CHAPTER 16
PREPARE FOR 9-LINE

★ ★ ★

amp, ramp, ramp," our pilot exclaimed after touching down behind chalk one's dust cloud. The entire cabin was engulfed in dust as SPC John lowered the ramp. The Rangers on board wasted no time and hastily rushed past me as I scanned the vacant village from left ramp. I shined my IR laser mounted to my M-240 at empty looking buildings while our loud bird eagerly waited to get off the target.

"Last man on the ramp. Ramps up aft ready," SPC John quickly called out.

"55 coming out, 55 coming out," our pilot radioed to chalk one. The bird lifted off the ground as the Rangers knelt on the dusty Afghan soil below so they didn't get knocked over from the heavy rotor wash.

We were just 100 feet off the ground and something didn't feel right as I continued to scan the village below. The intel during the brief indicated that our helicopters or the guys on the ground should expect small arms fire. The night was cool, and expecting the worst upon landing, the town was desolate. It was eerily quiet among the loud blade noise of the two Chinook formation leaving the guys on the ground.

SPC John leveled the ramp and we both looked back down to the village, all the IR lasers were shining from the team's weapon systems. Being chalk two we had the 160th medic on board and we were the designated casualty evacuation bird if anything were to happen. We planned to air loiter, or fly in dummy circles for ten minutes after the initial assault on the village. We continued to pull power as the small village started getting smaller and further away. I was scanning my sectors of fire and to my amazement, under my NVG's I witnessed a giant blast followed by a huge mushroom cloud of dust and debris. I didn't know what to think, or what happened? Was everyone alright?

"I just saw a large blast down on the target sir," I called to the pilots. I didn't really know what to say as I had never had to make a call like that over the radio before.

"Did it appear to be an IED?" He asked.

As I was about to respond the team on the ground cut in over the radio. "55 prepare for 9-Line," the JTAC, who was in charge of communicating to the aerial platforms, said. We made a hard right banking maneuver after hearing the call and headed back in the direction of the infill area.

"55 is ready to copy," our pilot said.

"Standby we are in a TIC (Troops in Contact)," the JTAC exclaimed. During the brief radio transmission from the ground, I heard the sound of gun fire over the radio. We continued to make circles air loitering, just waiting for the team to pass their radio traffic. I had no idea what was going on down there, but I knew someone was wounded and we needed to get down there ASAP. All we could do was hope that our guys whom we had just dropped off were OK. Hoping for the best but expecting the worst was a motto I came to know very well in the Army, and this was no exception. Minutes felt like hours and every turn we made I continuously tried to catch a glimpse of the guys on the target. I could see tracer rounds going back and forth and bouncing off of buildings. The guys on the ground radioed back, "55 we have one friendly wounded and two enemy wounded. You're cleared for HLZ black; we are taking small arms fire from the west. HLZ will be marked with steady IR laser," the JTAC said after passing a lengthy 9-Line transmission.

A 9-Line was a standard call and procedure used when reporting how many casualties were wounded and what their condition was. One thing I learned in Green Platoon and hoped to never experience was unfolding by the minute. The radio call told us what the casualty's condition was, the environment we would be landing in, and what their injuries were. Nine key factors were relayed over the radio so we could better prepare and understand the type of patients we were about to take on board.

"HLZ will be marked by steady IR laser," the JTAC reiterated.

"55 copies all, one minute out." From the ramp I looked toward the front of the cabin as we started our approach. I noticed the doc we had on board rustling through his gear. He was getting IV bags ready and whatever else to start treating the patients we were about to load. I shifted my focus back outside because I knew the enemy was still engaging our guys on the ground.

SSG George was at the right gun position and began to call the aircraft down to the ground. "Off 3, 2, 1, inches, contact." The aircraft touched down and SPC John lowered the ramp. I unhooked from my monkey tail which kept me attached to the aircraft in flight, and jumped off the ramp. I tried to locate the casualties through the cloud of dust we had just kicked around from landing. I heard the snaps of gunfire through the loud spinning blades of the helicopter. My M4 rifle was slung around my shoulder in front of me. I pressed my IR laser on my weapon and moved it back and forth on the ground just behind the ramp. My hope was, the guys trying to get on board would see the laser through the intense brown out condition. I started to see several bodies emerge through the dust as I continued shining my laser. Two of our guys were pulling a Skedco with a body wrapped inside. Directly trailing behind them were two more guys pulling another Skedco with a body wrapped inside. They continued to approach the aircraft dragging the casualty sleds on the ground. I ran out to help pull the lifeless body lying on one of the Skedcos. A Skedco was a plastic sled used to transport casualties on the ground by pulling them with a strap that was attached to the front of the device. The plastic material it was made out of, made it easy to pull across the ground. Myself and SPC John who was at the right ramp position, relieved a few Rangers who were pulling the heavy sled and we got him on the aircraft. We pulled the body all the way up toward the front of the cabin where the doc was waiting. We dropped the pull strap and the doc immediately began working on the guy. I headed back to the ramp area to continue to help load the remaining casualties anyway I could. The second sled was passed to SPC John and I at the ramp. We yanked the motionless man onto the aircraft and pulled him toward the doc. My heart was racing and the adrenaline levels in my body were shooting through the roof. All I could think about was getting the wounded on board and getting the fuck off the HLZ. Closely following the last sled were two of our guys walking upright, one of the guys was supporting the other with his shoulder. The limp Ranger was draped over the other as they navigated their way through the dust. As I was helping with the last sled SPC John was already running toward the two Rangers to help get them on board.

"What is taking so long back there, let's go," our pilot said. He was a bit nervous judging by the tone in his voice but for good reason. Our guys were still taking fire and we were a big black sitting duck. We weren't the quietest thing in that field either. The two guys finally got on the aircraft, and SPC John started to raise the ramp.

"Two ████, two ████, ramps up aft ready," SPC John said.

"Forward ready," SSG George said and we started to lift off the ground before SSG George could finish making his call.

"55 coming out, 55 coming out." Our pilot called. CW4 Ricky didn't get his nick name Ricky Bobby for no reason, and this mission was a testament to that, we were hauling ass. Our pilot pulled thrust and we shot off the ground leaving the target building in the distance. I looked up toward our medic who was working on the guys in the sleds.

The medic who was also always plugged into the aircrafts communication system came over the radio. "Sir this is the medic, friendly wounded has a gunshot to the arm and is stable, I have a faint pulse on both enemy wounded, and if we don't get them to the hospital in the next few minutes they are not going to make it."

"Roger," CW4 Ricky said. Still airborne and hauling ass to the closest treatment center, the medic hustled over to the Ranger who was sitting on the troop seat. The Ranger, I noticed while he boarded, was already sucking on a Fentanyl lollipop. It was a highly effective narcotic used to relieve pain. So a gunshot definitely warranted its use. All the aircrews and guys on the ground always had two on them at all times in case of a scenario like the one the Ranger on the seat was facing. I looked back in the cabin and noticed the Ranger who had just been shot wasn't screaming or didn't appear to be in pain. He just sat there waiting for us to land at the hospital. A short five-minute flight later and the crew called the aircraft to the ground where an ambulance and several other US military personnel were waiting to receive the casualties. The two Rangers, one shot and the other aiding his buddy, walked off the aircraft on their own after SPC John lowered the ramp. I gave him a pat on the back as he exited, and SPC John and I headed in the cabin to help doc pull the motionless bodies off the aircraft.

We were inside the perimeter of the base now and the cabin lights were on. As I approached the sled I reached down to pick up the strap so I could pull the EWIA (Enemy Wounded in Action) off the aircraft. I never understood why we had to abide by the Geneva Convention. The near dead terrorist was just trying to kill us. This guy I was dragging off the aircraft was just shooting at the Rangers we had dropped off, and now I'm supposed to carry him to safety. It was bullshit. I was pissed that we had to administer aid to someone who wanted nothing more than to kill Americans. If it was one of our guys wounded, this piece of shit wouldn't hesitate to execute them versus administering first aid.

A large open wound was wrapped on the man's chest, and the bandage was covered in dark red blood. I snapped out of the horrific sight and managed to pull the terrorist off the aircraft. I passed the handle of the sled to a military hospital worker and hopped back on the aircraft. Both wounded enemies were off now. SPC John dimmed the lights, raised the ramp, and let Ricky Bobby know we were ready to go in the back. We flew back to our parking spot where chalk one had been during the whole casualty evacuation. I had a lot of shit running through my head but I knew there were still guys out on the target executing the most top tier bad ass shit Rangers excelled at. We waited for another three hours and then finally got the exfil call. We were airborne again and en route to pick up the team of Rangers.

After loading the guys on the bird, one of the team leaders plugged into the ICS and asked the pilots, "Hey how is our guy doing?"

CW4 Ricky, who was a former Ranger himself, came over the ICS, "He is going to be fine and he is in stable condition." That was the best part of the mission, just knowing that Ranger was going to be fine. I had a feeling though, that the deployment was going to get a lot more intense. I had been in country for five days and if this night was any indication of what was going to take place the rest of the deployment I knew I had a lot more to look forward to.

As we made our final approach to Kandahar Airfield I noticed the beautiful mountains beaming off the rising sun. In such a beautiful country we were met with such violent acts, but that was war. The ramp lowered and the Rangers began to off load both aircraft. As I was waiting for them to exit, they started to give SPC John and me fist bumps. One after the other, while making their last step off the ramp and onto the flight line. It was a small but very meaningful gesture of thanks. The recognition from the Rangers was just as empowering as a, 'Thanks chief,' from the pilots.

The aircraft blades finally came to a halt and after removing my helmet to start working on the bird the morning Muslim prayer echoed throughout the airfield. We were after all in their country, the prayer didn't bother me all that much until I made my way into the cabin of the aircraft. There was blood and chunks of something on the floor. I looked at the seat where the wounded Ranger was sitting and there was blood stained into the canvas. The prayer continued throughout Kandahar and I started becoming more enraged. I continued looking at the blood which had been tracked by muddy boots from the Rangers all throughout the cabin. Mud and blood on the cabin floor painted a very clear picture of war for me. The prayer continued as I collapsed into a seated position on one of the troop seats continuing to look at all the blood.

"Go get the pressure washer Burnie," SSG George shouted to me from the right gun window as he was taking care of his mini gun. I snapped out of it and went to take off my gloves before heading to get the pressure washer. As I began to pull my gloves off I noticed blood on them then I looked at my uniform. I had blood on the knees of my flight pants. During the night I didn't think anything of it. SPC John, SSG George, CW4 Ricky, the rest of the crew and I were just doing our jobs. I don't know whose blood was on me, but I knew I wasn't the only one who was experiencing the after effects of the night. It was our job and it was what I signed up for. I was no different from the guy to the left and right of me.

After finally washing out the blood, mud, and whatever else that was in the aircraft we went to eat. SSG George told the crew while eating that the two enemies wounded had died shortly after we dropped them off at the hospital. Good I thought to myself. Stories were exchanged across the table while everyone consumed their breakfast. I looked down at my knees again to see the same blood, now dried and brown. Seeing the blood made it very clear how important our job was. It might have been the bad guys blood but it could have very well been two of our own instead of those guys. We headed back to our compound and after a very long shower I lay down in bed. I tossed and turned in my bed and I didn't get a single minute of sleep that night.

After getting up the next morning, all the Chinook crews met at the TOC to have a meeting about the previous night's mission. The lead pilot and intel guy briefed us on what I had already assumed. "This month you guys can expect heavy resistance and potential small arms fire on all of the targets we will be hitting," the intel guy told us.

After last night I wasn't expecting anything less. Although I didn't get to shoot, I was ready to put several bullets in the faces of the men who shot that Ranger in the arm. I was still mad that we had to attempt to rescue those two terrorists who fortunately died.

The remainder of the deployment our crew took part in several small arms engagements. Almost every night we were getting shot at and returning fire from the aircraft. It became routine to look over the bird after every mission and occasionally find a bullet hole or three impacted on the side of the aircraft. Unlike prior deployments, a BDA (Battle Damage Assessment) became very routine and essential after every flight. I could get used to getting shot at, but the one thing I could never adjust to was pulling our own wounded guys off the target. Toward the end of the deployment I was switched over to chalk one, which was common when new guys came in to replace others. Much like what I experienced on that chalk two crew, the new crew would have a similar experience.

After infilling two Chinooks full of Rangers an IED exploded near the target building. We were already heading back to the FOB after dropping the guys off.

"55, confirming ten-minute air loiter," the JTAC called over the comms to chalk two. I was in chalk one now, and we were going to wait for the exfill call while chalk two air loitered with the medic in the event something happened. All crews were always monitoring the same radios and after we landed at our parking spot at KAF, we all heard it. "55 prepare for 9-Line." A call that would normally be made by the JTAC was a different voice now.

Over the last few months the JTAC who was solely responsible for controlling and communicating with all air assets from the ground, became a familiar voice. This voice however was not the JTAC, and I didn't know why. As we sat parked we remained at 100% with the blades continuing to spin in order to provide back up if anything were to happen to chalk two. After the 9-Line came across the radio, chalk two went in to exfill two Rangers and a CST (Cultural Support Team) member. They exfilled the casualties as we monitored the radios closely from KAF. The night finally ended with us parking the bird and shutting down in our parking spot. After the Rangers exited our bird, the crew and I walked over to chalk two to get the story and understand what happened. All four of us from chalk one approached the back of the ramp to talk to our Bravo Company brothers. We didn't need them to say anything though. The ramp was covered in blood and the left ramp crew station had a pool of blood there looking like someone had just been bleeding uncontrollably.

Our intentions to ask the crew about their night suddenly changed, and SPC John asked in a defeated tone, "You guys need help with anything?"

One of the crew chiefs, who I knew from BMQ said in a mimicked tone of SPC John's, "Yeah can you just get the pressure washer?" We helped them get their bird ready for the next night before even touching ours. Cleaning and washing more blood out of the worn down cabin floor became yet another routine.

The next morning after our shower and chow routine we were instructed by the pilots to head back to the compound. This was odd I was thinking to myself, we normally went to the flight line to get the birds opened up and ready for the night. As the other crew chiefs and I drove through the compound after eating, we parked the bus. We walked around the corner of the Ranger ready rooms to see about a 100 Rangers under the dim light of the compound. They were starting to gather in formation and SSG George, who must have known what was going on, instructed all of the crew guys to fall in behind the Rangers in formation. I had no Idea what was going on and I thought some higher up was going to brief everyone about the previous night's mission. A podium was set up at the front of the large formation but that's all I could make out under the poorly lit area. Not being the tallest I tried to look past all the tall bodies standing in front of me. A voice from the front of the formation called us all to attention and began a roll call. The voice called off several Rangers in the formation and they each replied with a, 'Here.'

The Ranger at the front of the formation called out in a loud and thunderous roar, "Domeij," there was no response. I looked around the formation and I noticed tears rolling down the faces of Rangers who I went into battle with every night. The man at the front continued, "Sergeant First Class Domeij." My heart sunk when I didn't hear anyone respond after that. I had finally and un-reluctantly caught on to what was going on. In my naïve, still a new guy career, I hadn't ever experienced a remembrance ceremony before, and that was exactly what was happening. The man gave a final thunderous call, "Sergeant First Class Kristoffer B. Domeij." Complete and total silence. I looked around the formation again and the tears intensified across the faces of the courageous 2nd battalion 75th Ranger Regiment soldiers.

The roll call continued, "Horns," a pause, "PFC Horns," followed by another pause. "PFC Christopher A. Horns," a loud confident voice shouted from the front of the formation. No one replied. I was thinking to myself that is two too many, as I wiped the tears from my eyes. The man in the front continued, "Stumpf," another pause, and at this point I couldn't pretend to be a hardened emotionless warrior anymore. The tears started pouring from my eyes. "1st Lt. Stumpf," another pause, "1st Lt. Ashley W. Stumpf." No one answered.

The formation started to move forward after speeches were given about the three who bravely sacrificed their lives. The formation continued to move forward and after the rank in front of mine walked forward then dispersed, a memorial revealed itself. Perfectly placed were three framed pictures of the men and woman who just gave their lives protecting the freedoms of the United States of America. I had exchanged a fist bump and maybe a few words in the gym with these men and brave 1st Lieutenant, but nothing could bring them back. SFC Domeij was the JTAC who I graciously came to know over the radio. He wasn't the one making the 9-Line call last night because he had been blown up by an IED. His last call to the helicopters was for chalk two to remain overhead in a ten-minute air loiter. Little did he know, he was making his last and final call to the crew that pulled him off the target one last time.

I walked closer to the memorial. Boots with an M4 rifle pointed down were perfectly placed in front of each picture. We all walked even closer to the memorial all staying in step and finally coming to a halt in front of the three soldier's crosses. Placed on the buttstock of each rifle were their helmets with night vision goggles attached to them.

A Ranger in our small rank said in a low but stern order, "Present arms." The entire rank slowly raised our right hands to salute the fallen. Their dog tags dangled on each rifle and a gust of wind caught them. They all clinked together as the same voice called over the rank, "Order arms," we slowly lowered our salute. The men in the rank knelt down and said their final goodbyes. I knelt down and said a prayer for the three heroes. I wiped the tears from my face and exited the memorial area. I will never forget that night, 22 OCT 2011. The final days of my second deployment with Alpha Company were just as intense as the first days in country. We took more small arms and RPG fire for the remainder of the tour. Luckily no one else got hurt on the remaining violent Afghan days on my second deployment with 160th.

CHAPTER 17

FT. KNOX

★ ★

The C-17 screeched to a halt at Campbell Army Airfield and the ride home from Afghanistan gave me a chance to reflect on the deployment. I signed up for a hard charging, own the night, special operations unit and the deployment was nothing short of that. I witnessed things that no human should ever have to see. Sure I was contributing to the fight but I couldn't erase the bloody images from my head. I went back to my barracks room after downloading another tired deployment fatigued Chinook. We landed a little earlier than last time and I was able to pick up some beer at the liquor store before making my way back to my room. I drank a beer for each one of those Rangers who gave their lives that night. It was the only way I knew how to honor them. It was a sleepless night in my room and I had no idea what the next days would hold for me while stateside. I headed to the office the next morning in civilian clothes to have a sit down with my PSG. I made my way down the Alpha Company hallway and to the PSG's office door, which was adjacent from the crew office. I passed by the crew office and overheard faint conversations from some of the crew guys getting ready to go on a morning PT run around the airfield. I knocked on the open door and asked to come in. SFC Jayson was sitting in workout clothes behind his desk and without saying a word he gestured to the chair across from his desk.

I sat down and he began to speak, "How was that deployment Burnett?" I looked him in the eye while holding back what I really wanted to say, and said, "Good."

"Yeah, we have all been there," he replied. As the PSG, he was constantly receiving reports from the NCOIC down range, so I assumed he already knew that the deployment was nothing short of action packed, emotional, and nonstop. He asked, "Do you know anything about FARP (Forward Arming and Refueling Point)?" I let him know that SPC John and I had practiced it a few times down range when we had an off day, which was very rare. "Good. That is the last task you need for FMQ, and that is your only goal in life right now. We are planning a few FARP training exercises for you and SPC John to get qualified." SPC John who the guys called, 'JB,' had not received the FARP qualification yet either. He and I would do everything we could to get the qualification while back in the states over the next few months. I took the next few days off after getting briefed from SFC Jayson in the PSG office.

I returned to the flight line later that week, and without skipping a beat I was right back into training. I met JB on the flight line early that morning and noticed he had already pushed a giant internal fuel tank to the back of the bird. FARP was the hardest task through the FMQ process. I found out quickly that it wasn't only the most physically demanding task while training with JB down range just weeks before, but it was one of the few that were timed. The task had a lot of moving parts, and preparation before executing the task was key. The Chinook is capable of holding three internal fuel tanks which can be used to either resupply the Chinooks massive exterior tanks, or fuel other aircraft while on the ground. The capability allowed the unit to refuel any helicopter platform in a deployment setting if another bird was running low on fuel or a mission required refueling due to a longer flight. We could also refuel the empty internal tanks during HAAR operations.

I hustled over to where JB was standing on the flight line at the back of the bird, and began helping him push the massive squarely shaped fuel cell into the cabin. Once in position we began to lock it in using the tie downs on the floor of the aircraft. After locking in the last shackle, SPC Scott walked into the cabin and let us know he was out there to help and he would be doing the training with us. SPC Scott was already FMQ and I had never met or worked with him yet. Just like all the other Alpha Company guys, he was always training, away at a specialized school, or deployed. Already over a year in the company and I was still meeting guys I had never met. This was the way of Alpha Company, which made it difficult because even though I felt I had been in the unit awhile I still had to continually prove myself to someone who hadn't met me yet. SPC Scott was the same rank as JB and I, but he had a lot more crew knowledge than the both of us combined. Yeah we were the same rank but in the company it was about experience.

"You guys keep setting up the aircraft, I'm going to start grabbing the fuel hoses," SPC Scott said. He took off out of the helicopter, jumped in the John Deere Gator, and sped off.

JB and I continued setting up the aircraft while waiting for him to return. In the meantime, SSG Justin met us on the aircraft. He was one of the top guys in the company and was going to conduct the training throughout JB and my FARP qualification. He was gripping a large book in his hand when he made his way up the ramp and into the helicopter. I knew exactly what it was as SPC John and I finished strapping down water cans to the floor of the helicopter. The goal of the FARP operation was to use the fuel cell inside the aircraft to refuel other helicopters, but there was more to it than that. The concept was that JB and I would run fuel hoses off the ramp 100 feet, then attach a Y fitting. From that fitting we would then run and connect more long heavy hoses out to a point and set up the refueling and arming station several hundred feet out of the back of the aircraft. After completing the set-up, we would wait for another aircraft to begin the refueling process.

The two fueling stations that we were about to set up behind the Chinook would need more equipment than just the refueling hoses in order to adhere to the standard. All of the extra gear included; a fire extinguisher, two jerry cans one full of water and one empty, for excess fuel to purge the lines, and an ammo can full of chem-lights and different fuel nozzles. Lastly a grounding rod was required in order to electrically ground the aircraft that was receiving fuel. All the gear was strapped down in the aircraft and upon landing needed to be unstrapped and run out to the designated fuel points some 200 feet away from our Chinook in order to keep a safe and standard distance.

Between the several trips to and from the set up fuel point and then back to the Chinook, it was easy to see why the task was the most physically demanding of all the FMQ required qualifications. Not only that, but the required timeline to set up the two fuel points was 15 minutes and the required tear down time was ten minutes. Complete the task under the timelines and you pass. Exceed either timeline and you fail. It sounded simple and JB and I knew we needed to get the task complete and under our belts.

SSG Justin sat down in one of the troop seats and instructed us to do the same. JB and I obliged and he began going over the FARP task in the ARSOA manual, flipping through one page after the next. He continued going through the book asking us questions intermittently to make sure we were paying attention and knew exactly what was expected of us. I took my jacket top off as I could feel the sweat start to pool in my armpits. The sun was up and that Kentucky summer humidity showed up to pay us a visit. SPC Scott pulled up behind the ramp in the Gator with the flatbed piled high with fuel hoses and connectors. SSG Justin concluded the FARP section of the book and SPC Scott began loading and strapping the hoses down to the floor just in front of the giant fuel cell. With everything strapped down, SSG Justin sat up and looked over all the equipment SPC Scott had been carefully placing and strapping to the floor. Everything was meticulously placed to make the whole process as organized as possible. He had been through the qualification before so I didn't question anything he was doing. I sat up from my seat and looked through the gear with SSG Justin. I was just waiting for some sort of acknowledgment that we were all ready to do a dry run.

Another minute passed then SSG Justin looked at JB and I and said, "Alright get your shit on its go time fuckers." He slapped SPC John on the back as we exited the aircraft and we started to put on our flight gear.

While putting our flight vests on SSG Justin hit me in the front and then the back of the vest. He walked over to SPC John and did the same. "Just wanted to make sure you guys aren't trying to cheat," he said laughingly. He was checking to make sure we hadn't removed our 30 lb. front and back SAPI plates. We put on our helmets and plugged into both the right and left ramp ICS locations.

SSG Justin cranked the APU and with his helmet on, he mimicked the calls that were used before landing and executing the task. "OK sir you're off 5,4,3,2,1. Contact. Ramp, ramp, ramp."

SPC John who was at the right ramp position lowered the ramp and we disconnected from the ICS plugs and hastily started unstrapping the gear we had to run out of the helicopter. We already devised a plan and delegated who would do what during the timed training. While JB was connecting one of the fuel hoses to the internal tank I Immediately started running out remaining hoses to the flight line. I dropped the coiled hoses in the locations I thought the already connected hoses would meet. Cold sweat poured down my back after I dropped the first pair of coiled hoses 50 feet away from the aircraft. I started running back to retrieve more gear from the helicopter, just to run it back out. JB was already getting the Y fitting connected as I passed him on my run back to the bird. I grabbed the fire extinguisher and water can just to turn around and run back out to where I thought the fuel point was going to end up once all the lines were uncoiled and stretched out.

I ran back to one of the first hoses that I had dropped and started connecting it to the Y fitting. After connecting it, I un-wound the hose, hoping it would end at the other hose I had dropped on my first trip. I rolled it out only to be defeated. The end of the hose was nowhere near the other waiting-to-be-uncoiled fuel hose. I ran to retrieve the hose then ran it back to connect it to the stretched out line I had just unrolled. I connected it and rolled it out to where the final refueling point would be and hopefully I would meet the fire extinguisher and water can I put out there.

Again I was way off and found myself running to grab the can and extinguisher to place them at the end of the last hose where the fuel point would be set up. Nearing the completion of the exhaustive set up I worried I wouldn't make the allotted time limit due to my misplacement of the hoses and equipment. My clear visor which was down and a necessity when doing any type of fuel operations or task was fogging. Between the humidity and all the body heat resonating from my body my visor turned opaque. I tried wiping the visor with my sleeve while running back to the helicopter to get the remaining equipment. I looked over to the right as I was running back to see how SPC John's side of the Y split hoses was going and to gauge how much more he had to do before his fuel point was set up. JB was kneeling at his fuel point and appeared to already be completed. I had an ammo can and a grounding rod left to retrieve from the Chinook.

I was just thinking in my head while running back to the aircraft to get the gear that I didn't pass. The extra time I had to take to readjust my lines and gear must have made me exceed the allotted time limit for the FARP qualification. I grabbed my remaining items and made it out to the fuel point. I finished and I got down on my knees.

Sweat rolled down my face and my helmet liner acted as a sponge, soaking up all the sweat from my head. I felt cold sweat dripping down my back underneath my top and T-shirt. I looked over at JB to see he was nice and content as he had been at his point for a while, just waiting for me to finish. JB, although a specialist like me, was the oldest crew chief in the company. He didn't let anyone know it though and the majority of the time he outperformed the youngest guys in the company, clearly including myself.

SSG Justin was at JB's fuel point talking to him while I remained on my knees soaking in sweat just waiting for him to come over and tell me I didn't make the time. I peered back at the Chinook which still had the APU running, and I could see SPC Scott contently sitting on the edge of the ramp. Not a single drop of sweat beading from his face. He was there to monitor and help with anything during the training. He had already been through this wringer and the content look on his face made me want the qualification even more. SSG Justin began walking to my fuel point. As he got closer he started shaking his head while holding up his arms. Almost to say what the fuck Burnie, but without actually saying it. I got off my knees as he got closer.

He stood in front of me and said, "What the fuck Burnie?"

"I thought I was going to," I started speaking.

Before I could even finish he cut in, "Yeah, yeah, I know what you were trying to do. I was watching the entire time."

"Roger," I said.

"17:38," he replied in a disappointed tone. "OK you have ten minutes for the break down don't fuck it up," he finished and walked off to the side of my fueling set up.

"On Scott's mark," SSG Justin said. JB and I looked at the back of the ramp waiting for the standard signal to break down the FARP. SPC Scott motioned with his hand in an up and down direction letting us know it was go time. As if I heard the gun shoot off to start an Olympic sprint, I grabbed everything I could carry as fast as I could. With both hands full of equipment, I made it to the back of the ramp where SPC Scott grabbed it and began strapping it down. After two trips I had all the equipment from the fuel point delivered to SPC Scott and so did JB. We began rolling up the first farthest fuel lines at the same time. Once coiled we used the included tightening strap on the line to hold the coil together. I ran the coiled line to the Y fitting and dropped it there, then back out to the next line to be rolled up. I rolled it up all the way to the Y connection and disconnected the line. I strapped it all together, grabbed the fuel line I had coiled and laid it down at the Y. With one coiled fuel line in each hand I ran to the back of the ramp and chucked the hoses at SPC Scott, nearly taking out his legs.

"What the fuck?" he yelled at me as I ran to help JB disconnect the Y fitting and get the remaining 100 feet of fuel line back inside the helicopter.

We rolled the last two lines up and got them in the bird.

We helped SPC Scott finish strapping down some remaining straggling equipment, plugged in, raised the ramp, and then after plugging in JB called, "Ramps up aft ready."

After SPC John made the call the APU cut off and it was quiet again. I desperately took my soaking helmet off and felt instant relief. My head was much cooler out of the helmet and it felt great. SSG Justin met all three of us at the ramp and we found out we broke down the FARP in eight minutes. "Now if only you could hit that time during set up," SSG Justin said while looking in my direction.

"Alright guys get reset and we will run it again." After three more times of setting up and breaking down the FARP, I felt confident that I could complete the qualification. I completed the set up and break down in the expected timelines the remaining three times and I was grateful. The remainder of the week continued with FARP training, both during the day and night under NVG's. The nonstop practice was preparing us for an actual qualification run the following Monday.

After an exhaustive week, and a short weekend, Monday came like a swift punch to the throat. It was going to be a day into night mission at a Ft. Knox, KY training site. The objective was to complete four FARP iterations, two during the day and two under the pitch dark.

What better way to prepare for a physically demanding night? The special operations thing to do would be to drink Monster energy drinks of course. Not one, not two, but three. Prior to taking off that warm Monday evening, I consumed two Monster energy drinks. The flight to Ft. Knox was an hour or so and with the warm air in my face at the left ramp position I relaxingly sipped a third Monster energy drink. We finally landed in a training field at Ft. Knox and waited for two MH-6 Little Birds to fly in and link up with us. A few minutes later the Little Birds were in place and ready to conduct the training. The sun was beginning to set over the high tree tops that surrounded the large open field, but would surely lend enough light to conduct two FARP set ups and tear downs.

The immense power of the Chinook lifted off the ground as CW4 Pete meticulously banked the aircraft to set up for an immediate approach at a designated location in the field. SSG Justin and SSG Chris G. who were at the left and right gun positions called CW4 Pete to the ground.

"Ramp, ramp, ramp," CW4 Pete called over the ICS.

JB dropped the ramp and we began running out all the fuel lines and gear just like we practiced for the last week. After we had our fuel points set up in the field we waited for the Little Birds to begin their approach to our points which we had marked with chem-lights. The loud blade noise and rotor wash of the Chinook was continuous in the background right behind our fuel points. The heat from the engine exhaust was blowing piping hot fumes in our direction. That mixed with the violent cool rotor wash felt nice as we waited for the Little Birds to approach. I noticed two Little Birds crest over the tree tops in the distance and then quickly dropped over the field while staying in perfect formation. The first MH-6 Little Bird passed me and continued on to JB's fuel point. I put my head down while the small violent attack helicopter passed, kicking up loose grass.

The second Little Bird approached my refueling point and after kicking up more loose debris, finally landed next to the grounding rod I had shoved into the turf. I hunched under the humming blades, and walked toward the front skid. I clamped the grounding wire to the airframe before refueling. The pilot looked at me out of the doorless cockpit and pointed one finger down. I grabbed his single downward pointing finger and squeezed it, acknowledging that he needed fuel in the main tank only. This was another main topic in the ARSOA we learned and memorized.

I removed the fuel cap and began refueling while SSG Justin had one hand on my shoulder. I guess he was making sure I didn't fuck anything up. While fueling I kept a constant eye on the pilot as the fuel tank was just behind his seat. The fueling operation wasn't like filling up at the gas station where it would stop when it was full. I waited for the signal from the pilot to stop fueling. He gave me the cut fuel signal and I stopped pumping. I put the cap back on the tank and still hunched over I stepped away from the aircraft. I looked over to my right to see JB was still fueling. I continued to monitor him while the Little Bird remained on the ground in front of me. JB began walking away from the Little Bird's fuel tank with hose in hand and he finally finished.

Both aircraft picked up at the same time and accurately got back in formation, and finally faded over the tree tops. I watched in amazement seeing them vanish over the southern forest. I felt a slap on my back and SSG Justin was pointing toward the back of the Chinook which was still on the ground at 100% RPM. SPC Scott was on the ramp giving the break the FARP down signal with a chem-light, waving it up and down. JB and I quickly began to break down the FARP.

After getting everything back in the aircraft and strapped down we lifted off the ground, only to land 50 feet away from where we were just sitting. This simulated the whole landing and getting all the calls down and registered in our heads before executing the task. SPC John and I ran out the FARP and broke it down once again with no issues. We had a short break and I drank the entire bottle of water I had brought with me. Everyone in the cabin was putting on their NVG's and gearing up for the nighttime iterations of the qualification. We couldn't have planned it better because the sun had just set after finishing the last daytime iteration.

SSG Justin came over the ICS "Alright guys just get through these night iterations and don't fuck up." I started to feel dizzy after he said that but I figured it was from just completing two physically demanding FARP roll outs and break downs. After picking up, making a minimal movement, and coming back down, the aircraft shook and then settled.

"Ramp, ramp, ramp," CW4 Pete called once again. Alright here we go, I just need to get these last rollouts completed and I will be an FMQ crew chief. SPC John and I switched places and I began running out the first long fuel line. By this point I figured it was easier to run all my equipment to the point first before connecting the fuel line, so that was exactly what I did. After getting the last of my equipment out to my fuel point I ran back to the aircraft and grabbed two heavy coiled 50 foot hoses. I connected one to the Y fitting. I leaned over and tried to position myself in a way to support the weight of my vest while making the connection. Sweat was pouring down my face while I looked at the connection through my NVG's. I started to slow down as I rolled the hose out trying to complete the entire fuel connection from tank to refueling point. My legs started to feel weightless and I felt a floating sensation. My run started to slow as I looked down and continued to unroll the coiled hose. Everything started to close in and bam.

The trembling of the aircraft floor against my back and helmet was an odd sensation. Red head lamps were blinking in front of my face, and I had no idea where I was. I felt someone's hand make contact with the side of my face and I thought someone was fighting me. I felt a large thud and everything was white. I could see the ceiling of the Chinook and several recognizable faces hovering over me. What the hell is going on? Two men lifted me on a stretcher and with the aircraft noise still present I was taken off the helicopter and directly into an ambulance. The paramedics immediately gave me an IV while I continued to try and make sense of what just happened.

After getting six bags of saline fluid pumped into me at the hospital I finally learned what happened. SSG Justin, SSG Chris G, SSG Brian, and SSG Carl who was another mediator of the night's training, told me that I had passed out while trying to complete the first iteration of the night FARP operation. I passed out for a minute and I could easily attribute that to the three Monsters and lack of water. I also found out that CW4 Pete had been instructed by the tower to not fly over the Ft. Knox gold reserve. Well he did it anyway not knowing how urgent my condition was. Flying over the gold reserve without permission while knowing the situation is what made Alpha Company special. Guys looking out for their brothers to the left and right no matter the situation. Thanks Pete!

I felt I had let the team down. SPC John also didn't get his qualification that night because of me. I was made an example of after returning back to the company office a few days later, and for good reason. I had one last attempt at getting the FARP qualification. SSG Justin promised that if I failed again I would be sent to maintenance platoon and would never have the opportunity to fly in Alpha Company again. Yeah I pissed a lot of guys off that night and I was going to make damn sure my last attempt was to the standard. I was also going to make damn sure I was hydrated.

After doing FARP so many times I felt like I could do it in my sleep. I had come so far and I wasn't about to let the qualification get in my way. Another week passed and upon completion of my final FARP attempt refueling another Chinook I found myself in the Alpha Company office. SSG Justin had monitored both day and night iterations of a FARP on another Chinook and he began to debrief me in the office.

"Congrats Burnie," he said as he sipped a cold Coors Light from the beer fridge.

"Yes," I shouted humorously while pumping my fist at the same time. It was a long journey to FMQ, but I could finally join the ranks of the other FMQ chiefs in the company.

SSG Justin shook my hand and pressed an FMQ coin in my palm. "Congrats, now go buy us some cases of beer, fucker." He pointed to the beer board and I realized my tally marks were increasing daily. SSG Justin left the office while I sat in the crewless room drinking a Coors Light. I contemplated my career as I sat there. I loved this shit. It was hard work but at the end of the day it was rewarding sharing it with my brothers. I was finally going to be able to deploy with Alpha Company as an FMQ crew chief. I made it to the level where I could crew the FMQ required right ramp position down range. I was pumped. The rewarding feeling was battling with the thought of getting out of the Army in my head. I only had a few years left on my contract and I was still unsure if I would stay or go.

CHAPTER 18
TROOPS IN CONTACT

★★★

few more deployments came and went. More TDY trips did the same, but one thing remained throughout the journey and only got stronger. The constant feeling of a brotherhood that could never be broken. I ate, slept, fought, cried, and grew with every single warrior inside the Alpha Company office walls, Chinook cabin, most violent places in the world, and on the X while taking small arms fire. Nearing the end of my initial six year contract I sat in an office chair just a few days after returning from a TDY trip in Ft. Bragg, NC. I had been with the company for three years now and I felt I was really starting to perfect my craft as an FMQ crew chief.

The leadership within the company took notice as well, and they were hinting that I would start FE training soon. The training was tedious and I had noticed guys going through the wringer over the years trying to go from FMQ chief to flight engineer. The thought intrigued me enough that as I sat in my office chair I thought about re-enlisting. My whole mindset before joining 160th was that I would do my six years and then get out. The First Sergeant was adamant I would stay, and had frequent talks with me throughout the weeks in his office about why I should stay and how far I had come. It meant a lot hearing from all the guys I looked up to that they wanted me to stay and re-enlist so I could continue to serve next to them in the fight. I was on the fence and I was still undecided.

After deploying with the company four times, I had one more deployment coming up. Depending on what I decided, it would either be my last or I could just add it to the countless more to come. I continued to ponder as more guys showed up in the office for the 0830 morning meeting. It grew closer to the start of the meeting and SFC Darik walked in the room. Just like my deployments and TDY trips came and went so did the leadership. Whether they were promoted or moved to fill a different position, I had the opportunity to serve side by side with several amazing leaders. SFC Darik just replaced an old PSG and would be my new boss for the remainder of my 160th journey whether I chose to stay or leave. He was tough and for good reason. He was an old school Alpha Company guy and he had taken a break from the company to work in the TI (Technical Inspector) shop for a number of years. I recognized his face in passing through the hangar but never really knew or talked to him. He began the meeting while all the chiefs leaned in around the conference table to hear the daily tasks that needed to be completed. Just a few minutes into the meeting a lost looking specialist walked in the office door. I didn't know what was going on but I had a confident idea. I listened to what the lost looking kid had to say while sitting in my comfy office chair.

"I'm looking for the Alpha Company Platoon Sergeant?" The timid pimple faced kid said while standing at parade rest talking to SFC Darik.

"Yes how can I help you?" SFC Darik replied in a curious way. The entire office continued to listen to the back and forth exchange. He had just finished Green Platoon and was reporting to flight company to start the very journey I embarked on three years ago. I knew exactly what he was going through as did all the other crew chiefs and flight engineers occupying the room.

"OK find a place and just listen in until the meeting is over," SFC Darik said. The kid nodded and went to go sit in an empty chair next to SSG Brian. He began to sit down while SFC Darik continued to speak.

SSG Brian cut SFC Darik off and looked at the new specialist about to sit in a chair, and said, "That chair isn't for you, you have to earn that chair, so until then you will stand."

No one in the office contested SSG Brian's request because we all had earned our privilege to sit in an office chair. We had all been through the same test and I knew exactly what the kid was thinking. While I'm sure I thought the same thing when SSG Atch told me to remain standing when I first got to the company, I didn't know it would eventually make me strive to become a better crew chief.

With a confused look on his face the brand new Alpha Company crew chief hesitantly replied, "Roger," and stood behind SSG Brian.

SFC Darik continued with the meeting. He went on delegating tasks to complete on the flight line and at the motor pool. He concluded the meeting by asking if I was going to re-enlist or not. The constant battle I had going on in my head was continuously reiterated by all the guys I worked with. He went on to say that I had one more deployment coming up and I needed to make a decision soon.

A few weeks later I was sitting next to a giant Chinook tucked away and strapped down perfectly inside the cargo bay of the C-17. I had become not only familiar with this routine, but very meticulous about loading the giant helicopter of an office into the plane. I continued to contemplate re-enlisting almost daily, but I knew I needed to shift my focus to my sixth and possibly final deployment. We landed at Kandahar airfield and I already knew what the aircrews were going to be. Chalk two was going to consist of; SSG Jesse, SPC Arron, SPC John, and me. I had worked with all of them before, whether TDY or on a deployment and I knew it was going to be one hell of a crew. We had over 25 deployments combined between the four of us and we were a very experienced crew.

We downloaded the Chinook and began putting her back together. Continually contemplating staying in or not, I made up my mind on the flight over. I weighed the pros and cons and decided this was going to be the final chapter in my 160th journey. I knew if I went into the deployment with that mindset I might get complacent and I wasn't going to let that happen. I was going to treat my last deployment, although my sixth and final, like everyone in the past. Giving 100% effort and making sure I didn't fail anyone on my crew or any mission that followed. We finally finished assembling the bird working through the night and into the morning hours. We loaded the infamous bus with the two aircrews and our gear, headed to eat, then finally to bed. The MH-47G we just assembled would be gone through with a fine tooth comb and then put through a series of test flights by CW4 Art, the MTP (Maintenance Test Pilot) while we slept. After waking the next morning, the rest of the chalk two crew and I headed to the flight line to get our bird set up and ready to go for the night.

It was August and we all knew what that meant in Afghanistan. It was poppy harvest season, which meant the local populace was busy making opium during the sun blistering days. During the harvest season the Taliban were usually high on their supply, and they found it necessary to shoot at anything and everything. This meant my final deployment was going to be a fun filled one, and by fun I mean small arms fire on the regular. SPC Arron and SSG Jesse were sitting down on the troop seats in the cabin of the aircraft while SPC John and I continued to configure the bird.

SPC Arron was newer than SPC John and I, but he was still an FMQ. He had dabbled in acting prior to joining the military and could be seen in Sprite commercials and various recognizable movies. Once the company found out about his acting career, it was game on from there. The guys always recited his lines from a movie or commercial when he asked a question or we were just bored. It made any stressful situation a bit more tolerable whether training or deployed. SSG Jesse and SPC Arron wrapped up their conversation at the same time JB and I finished getting everything set up. After a quick pow wow with the entire crew going over escape and evasion procedures if the aircraft were to be shot down, we headed to the ready room. The ready room was familiar now and was where we hung out for the night. It was our place of duty while waiting for the life deciding secret phone to ring. There were six of us huddled around the ready room TV playing Call of Duty while others spectated. The secured secret phone rang as SPC Arron was in the midst of blasting another player in the video game.

"Secured line this is Burnett, send it," I answered the phone after the game was immediately paused. As I listened for a response on the other end which was coming from the TOC, everyone looked at me. With eyes wide and all the crew chiefs waiting for my reaction, I got a response from the other end of the phone. I hung up the phone and walked over to a large white board that was hanging next to the TV. I began to write in big red letters, 'TST.' As soon as I wrote the letters on the board someone lunged to turn the TV and Xbox off while others jumped over the back the couch. You would have thought someone was robbing a bank by how quick the chiefs were moving. Everyone raced to get their gear from their cubbies lining the ready room wall. Guys were running out the door sprinting to the flight line to get everything ready as fast as possible. One guy from each crew stuck around with one foot out of the door waiting for me to write the amount of fuel needed for the mission. I finished writing and the two darted out of the room toward the helicopters. A time sensitive target meant a drone or aerial platform had confirmed a high value target on the ground somewhere. The targeted individuals were normally very evasive, and if given the right intel or opportunity to capture that person we had to act immediately. Not 10 minutes later and we were all on our helicopters with the pilots finalizing their checklist items in the cockpit.

"One clear to start?" The pilot said over the radio.

"Posted ready one, one is clear to start," a quick response came from the deep voice of SPC Arron. The pilots and SPC Arron continued with the startup and the second engine began to crank. Shortly after startup, the Rangers were running through the flight line gate. Kitted and eager to take off, they began to line up behind each helicopter.

"Rangers forming at the ramp," SPC Arron called over the radio.

"Clear to load," one of the pilots said over the radio while continuing to go through their checklists. My heart was racing and although I had been on a number of TST missions they were always exhilarating. Knowing that the guy we were about to capture was so valuable that we had to go right now, was heart pounding. I experienced the same heart pumping adrenaline rush on a few of the last four deployments, but it never got old.

"Two-nine ▮▮▮▮, ramps up aft ready," I called over the ICS from the FMQ right ramp position, and then killed the lights.

There was a brief pause after back and forth on the radio and SSG Jesse, the FE, quickly commented, "Go on private for a second,"

All the crew chiefs including myself reached over the Rangers sitting on the floor and turned our boxes to private. SSG Jesse who had been in the TOC, began to give us a quick brief of the target, HLZ, and the threat level. "Target building will be on the right side, expect heavy brown out. Sleepers on multiple roof tops possible AK and shoulder fired weapons. High value target is an IED facilitator, any questions?"

SSG Jesse finished and one by one, JB, SPC Arron, and myself all said, "Negative."

SSG Jesse came back over the private channel and said "Head on a swivel guys, switching off private."

While reaching to turn back to the regular radio channel a voice yelled out, "Get some." One of the Rangers was plugged into one of our boxes that we had switched to private, and he was just as pumped as us.

"The target building is pretty close guys, but I will try and get to a spot for a test fire." The other pilot called over the radio.

The test fire was important, and not only gave the pilot and crew confidence in all the armament on board, but I'm sure gave the Rangers a sense of relief too. Both helicopters pulled power and lifted off of Kandahar Airfield just like many of the deployments before, but this night felt different. I had been on time sensitive target missions before, but while taxiing, the several radios I was monitoring in my helmet were a bit busier than normal. An AC-130 gunship, AC-10 Warthogs, and a pair of AH-6 Little Birds were all heading to the target building or were already overhead to monitor and provide fire support for the Rangers we were about to drop off.

"Alright guys this looks like a good spot for a test fire, cleared hot left and right side," came from a pilot.

Then SSG Jesse came over the ICS, "All guns hot, all guns test firing."

I squeezed the trigger on the M-240H from right ramp after flipping the safety off. Rattattatatatatatatatatatatatatatatata. My weapon jolted and joined the beautiful symphony of all the others at right gun, left gun, and left ramp.

"Left gun operational, left gun cold," SPC John said.

Followed by SPC Arron, "Left ramp operational, left ramp cold."

Then I chimed in after placing my weapon back on safe while kicking the spent casings on the floor out from under my boots, "Right ramp operational, right ramp cold."

Then Jesse said, "Right gun operational, right gun cold, all guns operational."

"All guns operational," our pilot radioed to chalk one which was just in front of us. "Three minutes, three minutes," the pilot called.

I responded "Three minutes aft ready."

Followed by SSG Jesse at the front, "Three minutes forward ready."

All of us in the back held up three fingers looking back into the cabin and yelling the call to the Rangers on board. They all began to get on one knee preparing to get off as soon as we touched down.

"Multiple MAM's (Military Aged Males) on roof tops, significant activity near the target building." The AC-130 gunship relayed to us.

"Alright guys target building is on the right side, keep your head on a swivel." Our pilot reiterated that the potential threat was going to be on SSG Jesse and my side of the aircraft.

SSG Jesse said, "Roger." He quickly acknowledged and got off the radio so the pilots could monitor radio traffic from all the air assets overhead. More traffic was coming through the radios saying there are multiple movers around the target building and still guys on the roof tops.

"One minute," the pilot said.

"One minute aft ready," I responded.

Followed by SSG Jesse's response, "One minute forward ready."

I relayed the call again to the Rangers who were still on a knee but after hearing the one-minute call I could quickly tell under my green and black night vision perspective they were eager to go.

"Sparkle on," our pilot called to the AC-130 letting them know to put a bright IR beam of light on our HLZ. "Got it. Sparkle off," our pilot acknowledged after spotting the HLZ.

The beam of light disappeared and the Chinook reared up like an angry horse. We slowed down and began to descend as SSG Jesse at right gun called the helicopter to the ground. He continued calling the bird down and I was surprised there was minimal brown out. I could actually see the ground out of my right ramp window.

"Multiple squirters on 55's right side just next to that vehicle." The AC-130 who continued to monitor the target building from above called to our bird. We were 25 feet off the ground and I could see the vehicle that the air asset mentioned. "Sparkle on squirters," the AC-130 said and a large beam of light shined down onto the vehicle. The white Afghan vehicle was crystal clear and so were the men hiding and running near it. SSG Jesse began unleashing fury out of the mini gun and onto the vehicle after seeing three men appear from behind it wielding weapons. The sound of the mini gun roared as I flipped the M-240H from safe to fire. I squeezed the trigger and unleashed the 7.62 rounds into the truck the men were hiding behind. Rounds were bouncing off the truck and sparks were pinging intermittently. A guy popped out of the bed of the truck as we touched down on the ground. The vehicle was right outside my window as I continued to fire at the vehicle.

While SSG Jesse was firing, SPC John called the aircraft to the ground. "Ramp, ramp, ramp," the pilot called out in a hasty manner.

I released my grip from the machine gun and lunged to reach the ramp lever pushing it into the down position and quickly making my way back to the weapon. SSG Jesse continued to fire on the vehicle and a corner of the target building wall where he had seen another enemy combatant. I felt the Rangers run behind me off the bird as I continued to fire. Another man popped out of the bed of the truck again. I noticed more bullets starting to impact the vehicle and the corner of the building wall. The Rangers who had just got off began to fire immediately after exiting the aircraft. The guy in the bed of the truck was obliterated. I felt a heavy slap on the back of my flight vest and looked back. The last Ranger had hit me letting me know he was the last guy.

I watched him jump off the ramp and immediately raised the ramp at the same time calling to the pilots, "Ramps up aft ready." Like no power I had ever felt from a take-off before, we picked up and quickly pulled out and forward making an evasive left banked turn.

A calm pilot voice came over the radio, "Nice work boys."

I didn't say anything and SSG Jesse responded with, "Roger."

SPC Arron hit me on my back while yelling, "Wooooooooooooooo," over the loud helicopter noise. Three men who could have potentially shot us down and killed all the Rangers and the entire crew were now dead. I realized that notion while on the final approach back into Kandahar.

While taxiing back to our parking spots, one of the team leads on the ground radioed to the JOC, "We have three EKIA (Enemy Killed in Action)." We began to shut down the bird in our parking spot to wait for the call that the Rangers were complete with their mission and ready to be picked up. I turned the lights on and looked at SSG Jesse. He looked back at me, nodded, and gave me a thumbs up, nothing more. The bird began to shut down and JB and SPC Arron were bummed that the action wasn't on their side of the aircraft. The night ended with the Rangers successfully capturing the guy they were going after. The deployment finished a few weeks later at a different base, FOB Shank. We had been working with SEAL Team 3 during my final days and it was just as exciting as the nights in Kandahar. I respected all the guys we had the opportunity to work with, but nothing would ever compare to the brotherhood shared with the crew members and pilots of Alpha Company 2nd battalion 160th SOAR(A).

CHAPTER 19
LEGENDS NEVER DIE

I boarded the C-17 one last time as I watched the load master press the button to actuate the aft ramp. I took my seat with the few Alpha Company guys who were headed home. I looked off the ramp at the flight line as the lights began to disappear. Afghanistan where so many relationships were formed, so much blood spilled, and so many memories burned in my mind. I realized it was the last time I would see that image.

I almost didn't know how to feel.

After six deployments, it was like a second home. Although not the best home, it taught me so many lessons. The country has taken so many lives yet I didn't want to be done. I wanted to keep fighting with my brothers. It was bitter sweet. Finally the ramp clicked and made the familiar locking sound. I sat in the windowless aircraft pondering what I was supposed to do next. I didn't think there was a civilian job where I could drop rough men off in a helicopter to destroy and capture an enemy.

I had met a beautiful girl and leaving her for deployments and training became taxing on our relationship. I knew if I stayed in the unit I fell in love with, that our relationship wouldn't last. I didn't know what I was going to do after the Army but after realizing that I had chosen to get out, I shifted my thoughts on all the great times I had with the warriors of Alpha Company. After a routine three-day trip home I was back in Ft. Campbell again and would never have to make the Afghanistan trip again. I was given a few days to recover before having to be present for another 0830 Alpha Company meeting. Over the last couple of days, I started to pack and began turning in my Army issued gear. It was a long process but I wanted to get a head start.

Rarely did the First Sergeant show up to the 0830 meeting but this morning he was there. "Burnett are you going to re-enlist? This is your last chance." He looked at me and I shook my head. "Roger, the meeting is all yours," he looked at SFC Darik and walked out of the room. The only reason he was in the room was to ask if I was going to stay in the Army. Maybe he thought I would give in with all the other chiefs sitting around the room. Whatever the point of his question was I knew that I had to finish turning in gear, getting papers signed, and saying my last goodbyes.

I began getting signatures from personnel all over the compound so they could verify I didn't owe them anything and I was all good. I turned in my government passport and government credit card. After getting signatures at all the different buildings which I had been to throughout my time on the compound I reflected back. I had done something at each of the buildings and I recounted the time when I was last at each one. My last signature needed on my sheet was at the aquatics facility. I drove into the parking lot and walked in through the same double glass doors. I was hit with that same pool smell I remembered when I first walked into the building four years ago. It was the first school I attended in my crew chief journey. I got the same teacher who taught me Dunker fundamentals to sign my paper work. "Good luck with everything," the man said. I nodded and headed out the doors.

I went back to the Alpha Company office to show SFC Darik and the 1SG that all my papers had been signed at all the designated places. SFC Darik and the 1SG shook my hand and reiterated what the Dunker School teacher said, "Good luck." I nodded and made my way into the crew dog office after walking under the, 'Let the stress begin sign,' one last time. A few crew chiefs were in the office and I said my goodbyes to them, some more sincere than others. At the end of the day, sincere or not, everyone in that room would have given their life for mine just like I would have done for theirs.

As I began to walk out of the office I looked at the Alpha Company Crazy Horse Airlines logo one last time. The arrowhead portrayed with five hail stones and a red lightning bolt. The significance of that logo was more surreal than ever, and I could recount nights that we struck with fury. I could recount missions which we attacked with a lightning quickness. The dark background of the logo reminded me of the dark nights in Afghanistan that we flew. Landing at a target building and ensuring bad things happened to bad people under the complete cover of darkness.

I walked out of the crew door and down the hallway to make my final exit. I passed the photos on the wall I had noticed when first walking through the building on my very first day. A few more photos adorned the walls now and some displayed Chinooks and deployment photos with me in them. My memories would stay in the hallway and I hoped the men I had the honor to serve with would remember me just as I would remember them.

I walked out the door and headed to my truck. I made my way down the road to the guard shack, passing a small group of soldiers on the compound running in a line all wearing black shirts. I gave the guard a final fist bump before exiting the compound. I made a right turn and drove down the narrow road that I had gotten so accustomed to.

I could see the guard shack and 160th compound get smaller and smaller in my rear view mirror. I made a final turn onto another road to finally see the compound disappear.

It was a long, hard-fought road. It was exciting and adrenaline filled. It was sad and scary. The journey I had set out on four years ago on the airfield in Bagram Air Force base on my first deployment with the regular Army was over. No more time sensitive targets, no more getting yelled at by a platoon sergeant or flight engineer. No more mortar attacks. No more small arms and RPG fire. No more day time exfils. No more TDY trips and training flights, but the one thing that will always remain is the brotherhood. In the words of the dark horse, "Night Stalkers Don't Quit."

CHAPTER 20
DEATH BY JAMESON
★★★

It had been two months after saying my goodbyes. The transition was a piece of cake so far and I didn't understand what the headlines meant. The stories I heard of guys getting out and falling into depression because of the war seemed a myth. That wasn't going to happen to me. I was a Night Stalker and after all the shit I had gone through, depression wasn't going to be one more thing. I was tough as nails, so there was no way I was going to be affected by what I saw or did in Afghanistan. I worked on, flew, and maintained the Special Operations MH-47G Chinook for years. In my head the best thing for me to do was to jump into aviation maintenance. I acquired my Airframe and Powerplant license thinking I should transition nicely into the civilian aviation world. I thought I had it all figured out, but before making my final exit out of 160th, I changed my mind. I was lost early on, and after watching a reality TV show about real estate I knew that was my new calling. In the unit I knew what to do, and if I didn't, I was told what to do. It was different now. There were no strict rules anymore and I was on my own for the first time in six years.

I went through minimal training to get my Tennessee real estate license and thought I would be a natural at selling houses. After the initial Realtor phase, selling homes in Tennessee I can tell you was nothing like the TV shows promised. Surely I was supposed to make big commission checks deal after deal. It didn't work like that and I was on my own schedule now. From being told what needed to be done, to now, doing what I thought to be the best use of my time, was sure to spiral out of control at some point. I wasn't getting shot at trying to land an aircraft in a near impossible landing zone anymore. I wasn't washing my brothers blood off an aircraft floor. Men who had just stepped on an IED or been shot by enemy AK-47 rounds weren't screaming on board while flying to the hospital. I was, of all things, selling homes. Fortunately for me the majority of the homes I sold were to my 160th buddies or other guys that were still in the Army. The real estate transactions were seamless because I could relate to every one of those soldiers just coming home from Afghanistan or about to deploy.

Instead of, "Hey does the master bedroom have a double vanity?" It was, "Oh man you should have seen this explosion."

The real estate thing wasn't as bad as I imagined and I was doing well. I would conclude my days of real estate work with six to eight beers and often text my buddies who were still in Alpha Company. I began to miss the camaraderie and I started to regret getting out. An occasional hang out and text back from the guys was common because I still resided just 20 minutes from the base. Hearing of my brother's stories from the day on the flight line or the last deployment they were on made me feel like I never left. I was officially a civilian now but I still felt as if I were a part of the unit and Alpha Company.

One evening at a weekend get together put on by one of the guys who was still in the unit, I noticed a group of my Alpha Company brothers huddled over in the corner of the backyard. I cracked open a beer I just pulled from the ice filled cooler and headed over to them. I immersed myself in the huddle to hear what they were talking about. I could tell it was work related, but the conversation died after I showed up. "Don't stop on my account. What is it? A mission about to pop?" I asked cordially and slurring after my 9th beer.

"We can't talk about it Burnie." One of the crew members who I had served on several deployments with said. I looked at his face and he was as serious as a heart attack. The other guys in the huddle looked at me then looked down at the fresh cut grass. I couldn't believe it, everyone was in agreement, and after four years in the company I was all of a sudden just a civilian, an outsider.

After four months out of the unit my first feeling of seclusion hit me. I didn't want to agree with the seriousness of the Night Stalker who confronted me, but he was right. We were trained and trained again about upholding the unit's mission with secrecy. That was exactly what he was doing. I wasn't a 160th crew chief anymore, I was a damn Realtor just trying to fit in like every other transitioning soldier going through the same bullshit. In my drunken stumble I left the huddle after cracking a dumb joke and headed to get another beer.

I went home with my girlfriend after leaving the party and proceeded to get plastered. I was mad that I didn't know what my Alpha Company brothers were talking about. I felt like an outcast now and it made me furious. I felt the same way I did when I was researching the unit before going through Green Platoon. I wanted to know about everything that was happening in the unit, but I couldn't. There was a reason the Night Stalkers were so special and losing that feeling hit me like a Mack truck. I always knew what missions were coming up or what top secret shit we were training for. I was never the guy who didn't know what was around the corner and what crews were going to be flying on those super-secret missions.

In my frustration I began to drink more throughout the night constantly yelling at my girlfriend. Anything she did that night was wrong and didn't even warrant a conversation, instead I would begin with screaming at her. I was slowly losing the brotherhood I became so fond of and was taking it out on her. I was no longer a part of the greatest aviation unit in the world and the camaraderie I came to know was slipping away. I was just a cheese dick Realtor now and instead of protecting my brothers overseas I was signing buy and sell contracts. How was I ever going to live up to everything I had done and accomplished down range? Nothing was ever going amount to the adrenaline packed contribution I felt on those sleepless Afghan nights. What I did know is that I began to sink into a depression. Surely it was just my drunken state and when I woke up the next morning it would be as if it never happened. The not knowing about what Alpha Company was doing really bugged me. The secrecy and the special missions I was a part of, I had taken for granted. I recall watching the news and seeing missions the unit was surely involved in. I used to be on those flights, but I wasn't anymore and that was devastating.

I woke up the next morning with the worst headache ever and my girlfriend was nowhere to be found. I must have really made her mad, I thought to myself. I opened the front door of the apartment we were renting at the time. Her car was gone but the distinct sound of Chinooks flying overhead resonated throughout the complex. I looked up at the sky squinting my eyes to shield the sun from my worsening headache. Not two, nor three, but four 160th MH-47G Chinooks were all in perfect formation flying over the main highway just east of the complex. The guys I had attempted to talk to in that huddle, my brothers, were now flying those birds. Where they were going or what they were doing I had no idea. What I did know is, that if I had re-enlisted I would have been on one of those Chinooks. I pondered while standing in front of my doorway out in the humid heat of Tennessee. The distinct noise became fainter as the four bird formation grew smaller and smaller off in the distance.

I should have re-enlisted I thought to myself as I made my way back inside and over to the fridge. I took a swig of Jameson and chased it down with an ice cold Coors Light in a meager attempt to get rid of my hangover. Instead of a five mile run around the flight line, my new morning PT started at 1100 in the morning and consisted of an alcoholic beverage to start my day. Clients I worked with in the remaining months I spent in Tennessee may or may not have known I was buzzed or near drunk when showing them homes. I didn't think they would mind since we were practically Army buddies and all. Well that was my rationalization anyway. I wasn't completely out of control yet though. I could still carry on a conversation with potential clients. I was still able to drive. I became a perfectionist at figuring out the right amount of alcohol I needed to operate and get through the day. Living next to the base, I would always see Chinooks and other aircraft flying overhead. That was the most comforting thing about living so close to Ft. Campbell. The very base where I was molded into a highly skilled and highly trained 160th Night Stalker. I was probably looking something like a functioning bum at this point and I didn't know what happened to me. It had only been four months since departing the family I loved. I was overweight, frustrated at everyone, and an alcoholic. My life became unmanageable, but I was a Night Stalker and I wasn't going to let those things get in my way.

A month later my girlfriend and I moved to Colorado. I was born and raised in Colorado and I was ready to uproot my southern belle from the only place she had ever called home. I didn't expect her to come with me. Although she had stood by my side through three deployments, I had turned into an animal. I can't recall a single night I didn't take out my frustrations on her. Excitedly she agreed to take on the journey of life with me and we headed toward the Rockies.

After settling down in our new and a far more costly apartment in Colorado, I acquired my Colorado real estate license. Selling real estate was simple for me in Tennessee, so I should probably stick with what I had been doing for the last four months. After a night out at a local brewery with my girlfriend we made our way back to our new Colorado home. She was eager to get to bed, while I was eager to drink some more. After several more beers I finally met her in the bed and fell asleep.

"Contact right, right ramps engaging," I called over the radio. I watched the bullets and the tracer rounds ricocheting off the vehicle we had just landed next to. The firing continued as we pulled thrust and left the Rangers on the ground. "Prepare for 9-Line," a call from the ground force came over the radio. We were chalk two and after a few minutes in the air we were turning around to go pick up men who had just stepped on an IED. We landed in a freshly harvested Marijuana field and I lowered the ramp. Rangers began to bring lifeless bodies on board the aircraft and I could smell the blood. "Ramps up aft ready," I called, after the final body was loaded on board so the medic could begin working on the wounded men.

"Hey, hey, hey. David, David, David." No one makes this kind of call over the radio I thought. I opened my eyes and my girlfriend was vigorously shaking me. The sweat on my back and the sheets was similar to the hot nights in Afghanistan. "Are you OK?" she mumbled.

Angrily I said to her, "Roger," and rolled to my side to fall back asleep. Then it happened again and she woke me up a second time. I had enough, I left the room and headed to the fridge. I continued to drink the rest of the night while the majority of Colorado was sound asleep.

The morning came and my girlfriend woke up and came into the living room to find the coffee table littered with empty beer cans. "What the hell is wrong with you?" she said. I shrugged my shoulders while slumped on the couch and told her to leave me alone. My head was throbbing and all I wanted to do was sleep, but I didn't want the same dream to enter my mind again. I must have drunk a little too much before trying to fall asleep. That combined with the elevation of Colorado had to be the reason for the dreams. I didn't experience them in Tennessee so the elevation was definitely the culprit.

For the next few months these episodes coupled with heavy drinking continued. I was constantly waking up in sweat covered sheets. The frequent images of bloody bodies circled in my sleep like a frightening carousel. I was averaging an hour to two hours of sleep a night and my anger had turned into a rage with my girlfriend. I was turning into a life-like version of the devil. The demons in my head began to work their way out of my body in the most horrific ways.

I had been in Colorado now for eight months and I was coming up on my one-year anniversary from leaving my Alpha Company brothers. I had yet to sell a single house in Colorado and I was angry. I was more frustrated than I had ever been. The clients in Colorado were picky and I had to be careful what I said around them. It wasn't like back in Tennessee where it was easy to shoot the shit with another Army buddy. These Colorado clients wanted a professional and I was far from that.

After dealing with constant nightmares I finally gave in and decided to go to the VA hoping to understand how I could eliminate my dilemma. After a short visit I was prescribed with nightmare medication known as Prazosin. It worked on some nights, but the majority of the time it didn't. I wasn't able to go over to another Night Stalker buddies house anymore. I didn't have any childhood friends in Colorado that had a remote idea of what I had done in Afghanistan. I couldn't exchange stories with my buddies face to face like I did after getting out in Tennessee. I kept to myself and rarely wanted to go out with my girlfriend.

The other Realtors I worked with put on fake smiles and often greeted me with, "Hey how are you?"

I didn't care anymore and would often reply with, "Mediocre," or, "Shitty, how about you?" I would often get a look of disgust, followed by a pause then they would just walk away. The civilians I interacted with felt fake, like they were trying to prove something or boast a sense of accomplishment all the time. I always wanted to say, "What the fuck did you accomplish?" "Have your colleagues been blown up?" "Where were you deployed?" "Have you ever shot at anyone that was shooting at you?" "Have you ever been to a remembrance ceremony honoring fallen Rangers?"

I could never relate to these people, I kept telling myself. Their fake smiles and upbeat bravado was bullshit. I wasn't a Realtor, what the hell was I doing? What was I supposed to be doing with my life, and why the hell didn't I re-enlist constantly ran through my mind. After concluding another mandatory Realtor meeting with the company I was working for, I headed home. Thoughts of losing those three Rangers in Afghanistan on the night of OCT 11th ran through my mind. Why didn't I die over the course of those deployments? What was my life's purpose? I felt like a failure and I regretted not re-enlisting. I decided not to re-enlist because I wanted to be in the states with my girlfriend and not constantly deploying. I was exhausted after deployments. The unit was so fast paced which I enjoyed, but after finding a girlfriend it became difficult to leave her time and time again. I was ready to get out, but after realizing the decision I made, the deployments, training, and op-tempo didn't seem so bad. I was now missing everything that made me want to leave the unit. My life became slow paced and boring, nothing like what 160th strived for.

I cracked a beer and fell into the couch in the living room. I decided to watch Black Hawk Down, a movie that portrayed the same aviation unit I was fortunate enough to be a part of for four years. I watched Rangers fast rope out of MH-6 Little Birds and on to the target, much like the things we did in Alpha Company. I continued to drink waiting for my girlfriend to get home from work. After a few more beers and feeling devastation as I watched scenes from Black Hawk Down, I questioned my life's purpose and why I didn't die on any of the missions I crewed. I was completely miserable at work and couldn't erase those images in my nightmares. Medication wasn't working and all the VA wanted to do was use me as a test subject to continually test more and more prescriptions.

I had had enough and civilian life blew. No more adrenaline pumping action, no more TDY trips, and no more brotherhood. My life officially sucked and I felt worthless. I chugged another beer as I watched Super Six One get shot down on the television. I decided in that living room that nothing was ever going to amount to the nights I had in Afghanistan under my green and black ocular vision.

I headed into the master bedroom and knelt to the floor on the side of the bed. I reached my hands underneath to feel for a hard plastic case. I grabbed a handle continuing to feel with my hands and slid out a long Army green rifle case. I unclipped the three clasps holding the case closed and opened it. On top of the soft foam insulated case a black Axis 30.06 revealed itself. I had never shot the rifle before as it was fairly new, but I knew in that moment the first shot I would take with the weapon would be directly into my mouth. I hit a new low, lower than my SERE School low while starving and sleep deprived. I felt like a miserable failure. I wasn't succeeding with my new career. I had no one around to talk to. I was lost and the brotherhood I knew was gone.

I lifted the gun and a single round out of the case. With my rifle in one hand and gripping the bullet with my other, I moped back into the living room. I watched the team leader guiding Rangers to the downed aircraft on the TV. I perched my back up to a corner of the living room and slid down the wall coming to a seated position. Tears rolled down my face as the background noise of the TV continued only to remind me of the parts of war I missed. I slid the cold 30.06 round inside the chamber and locked the bolt forward. I positioned the buttstock of the rifle at my feet with the barrel pointed toward my face. Supporting the barrel with one hand I reached down to flip the safety off just like I had done so many times on the M-240H and M-134 mini gun fighting the enemies of the United States.

I was alone now and I made peace that life wasn't worth living anymore. Before my hand could make it to the safety, I heard keys jingle just outside the door and my girlfriend burst in the house. She looked at me and realizing what was happening, dropped everything in her hands and slowly walked over to the corner of the room where I was sitting. She told me to put the gun down as tears poured from my eyes. Without an argument I laid the rifle in my lap with the muzzle facing away from her.

She knelt down and grabbed the rifle placing it farther away from my body. She hugged me and began to cry. We were both crying and I was at the lowest point of my life. SERE, Dunker, Green Platoon, 160th, they were all hard as fuck. None of those battles compared to the battle I was facing now. After she talked to me and somewhat calmed me down I listened to gunfire coming from the TV bringing me back to that place where I fought, grew, and became the man I was. Afghanistan was my office, the Chinook was the platform, my brothers were my encouragement, and I knew how to do the job well. My girlfriend called my brothers with my phone and handed it to me. The few who I spoke with at least once a week helped calm me down. I was a complete wreck. I consumed 8-12 beers a night followed by Jameson whenever I woke up from nightmares just so I could go back to sleep.

I began writing this book in 2014 after first arriving in Colorado from Tennessee, and I was excited to tell my story and honor the heroes I had the privilege to serve with. I knocked out the first three chapters in just a month. After hitting the third chapter I made an abrupt halt and alcohol became the most important thing in my life. Between drinking, fighting with my soon to be wife, and always feeling lost in civilian life, I wouldn't put pen to paper again until 2017.

On 14 SEP 2017, SSG Alex Dalida was killed during a training exercise while going through the Special Forces Qualification course in Ft. Bragg, NC. I knew Alex through mutual Night Stalker buddies. He was a Black Hawk guy in 160th and wanted to advance his career by becoming a Green Beret.

The short time I got to know Alex, and after hearing the horrific news of his death, a switch went off in my head. SSG Alex Dalida wasn't going to be able to share his story anymore. Much like him, many men and women that made the ultimate sacrifice won't be able to put pen to paper about the war in Afghanistan. I decided to quit drinking and finish this book, not only for SSG Dalida, but for all the men and women who continue to put themselves in harm's way for our freedoms in the US. After hearing of SSG Dalida's death I had only written 70,000 words. Since writing again I have been able to finish the first draft with a total of 122,821 words.

After three years of drinking, nightmares, and constantly arguing with my now wife, I knew I couldn't keep living that way. I decided to stop drinking in the hope it would help with my sleep, relationships, and career. Through counseling and trying to block out the constant urge to hit the bottle, I have finally completed the first draft of this book. Every day is a mighty battle not to drink, but it is slowly getting a easier. The nightmares I fear may never go away, but one thing is certain. Suicide is a permanent solution to a temporary problem. So many veterans commit suicide every day and I was seconds away from adding to that number. I was hesitant about writing this chapter, but after contemplating a little more, I decided to go for it. My sincere hope is that it could help at least one veteran who is going through the same shit.

- "If you're going through hell keep going." - Sir Winston Churchill

SPC King observes chalk two as they move into position to take on gas along the HAR track.

Chalk two has a successful plug into the fuel hose coming off an Air Force C-130 along the HAR track.

A senior enlisted NCO monitors me as I bring the aircraft up to level two. I was fortunate to learn from the very best.

Rite of passage after infil to the X.

Joint training exercise in Europe.

Two A/2 Flight Engineers pose for an epic picture opportunity after a long day in Africa, 400 feet below sea level.

Vehicle training with SSG Atch in Kandahar before qualifications. Photo courtesy of John B.

A view looking off the ramp of a two ship flight. Chalk two in formation at the 6 O Clock position one disc distance. Photo courtesy of Tyler G.

HALO training with Special Forces. Photo courtesy of Richard P.

Coming in to land and load up a pair of Zodiacs to continue with over water Amphib training. Photo courtesy of SOAR medic.

Joint training operation with CV-22's, MH-60's, and MH-47's at an undisclosed location.

Live body Skedco Hoist training with 160th medics. Photo courtesy of SOAR medic.

Fast rope training with Ranger regiment.

Resetting during Amphib training with ST. Photo courtesy of SOAR medic.

A very cold HAR flight over an undisclosed location.

The MH taking in the beach views while both chalk one and two crews reset for more training. Photo courtesy of SOAR medic.

Forward fast roping in progress.

Fast rope training at an undisclosed MOUT (Military Operations Urban Terrain) site. Photo courtesy of Richard P.

FRIES training with Special Forces.

Left gun view over undisclosed location. Photo courtesy of Richard P.

ACKNOWLEDGEMENTS

To the men of 563rd who helped me learn about and hone my maintenance skills on the CH-47F Chinook, thank you. I would not have had the knowledge going into 160th without your mentorship and support.

To the men of Alpha Company 2nd battalion 160th SOAR, thank you for making me the man I am today. Your countless life lessons have been invaluable. To the men and women of 160th who have made the ultimate sacrifice I will forever be indebted to you. Your names are not only etched in marble, but forever etched in my heart.

Savannah: You have been my rock through the hard times and always stuck by my side. You have changed my outlook on life for the better and I'm blessed to call you my wife.

Mom: I may not have been the greatest kid growing up but you had a great impact on my path through childhood and adolescence. Your determination and drive greatly affected how I strived and continue to strive to lead my life.

Dad: Your career in the Marines may have lead me down this road, and without that I wouldn't have shared so many amazing memories with so many courageous men. Your love of aviation sparked the desire I chose to pursue in the Army, and for that I'm grateful.

Family: You have taught me how to laugh and love. You have never been dishonest and have always supported me throughout my entire life. I don't know where I would be without you all.

Kendra Middleton Williams: Throughout this editing process we have become much more than just colleagues. I appreciate all the hard work you have put into helping me bring this manuscript to life. I look forward to working with you on the next one! www.theblackshopinc.com

George Diaz: Thank you for being a true friend and writing an amazing foreword. We eagerly met the enemy in battle and while that still goes on in the civilian world, things will get better. RLTW brother.

To the men and women who continue to serve: I'm grateful and so is the nation you protect. Your countless sacrifices to the country don't go unnoticed. I would not be able to write this book if it weren't for your continued efforts overseas and otherwise.

Gold star families: Thank you so much for raising amazing men and women. If I had never met your son or daughter, husband or wife, I wouldn't know the meaning of a true warrior. The sacrifice of your loved ones is something I will hold dear to my heart until the day I die. Their sacrifice will never be forgotten.

I serve with the memory and pride of those who have gone before me for they loved to fight, fought to win, and would rather die than quit.

IN MEMORY OF THE FALLEN NIGHT STALKERS

1980

17-Jul-80	CW2	Crumley*Bobby M.	2nd BN (A/159th)	Training - California
04-Nov-80	SP4	Hensley*Timothy C.	B/1BN (B/229th)	Training - Kentucky

1981

21-Sep-81	CW3	Williams*John W.	B Co 1st BNC-130	Plane Crash
07-Oct-81	LTC	Grimm*Michael C.	A Co 1st BNC	Training - Kentucky

1982

29-Mar-82	SGT	Zizelman*Ricky D.	D Co 1st BN	Training - Georgia

1983

20-Mar-83	PFC	Eichner*Gregory D.	2nd BN (A/159th)	Training - Virginia Coast
20-Mar-83	SGT	Dunn*Claude J.	2nd BN (A/159th)	Training - Virginia Coast
20-Mar-83	CW4	Thompson*Ralph L.	2nd BN (A/159th)	Training - Virginia Coast
20-Mar-83	SP4	Wilder*Jerry L.	2nd BN (A /159th)	Training – Virginia
20-Mar-83	CW2	Alvey*Donald	R.2nd BN (A/159th)	Training - Virginia Coast
10-Jul-83	CW4	Jones*Larry K.	2nd BN	Training - Michigan
10-Jul-83	SSG	Sanchez*Luis A.	2nd BN	Training - Michigan
10-Jul-83	SSG	Cornwell*Mark D.	2nd BN (A/159th)	Training - Michigan
10-Jul-83	SSG	Rielly*Mark J.	1st BN	Training - Michigan
10-Jul-83	CW3	Crossan*ThomasB.	2nd BN	Training - Michigan
10-Jul-83	CW2	Jansen*James N.	2nd BN (A/159th)	Training – Michigan
26-Aug-83	CPT	Brannum*Robert E.	1st BN (D/1 now)	Training - Kentucky
26-Aug-83	CW2	Jordan*David W.	D Co 1st (C/158th)	Training – Kentucky

26-Aug-83	WO1	Jennings*Allen E.	D Co 1st (C/158th)	Training - Kentucky
04-Oct-83	CW3	Tuttle*William H.	D Co 1st BN	Training - Panama
04-Oct-83	SP4	Thompson*Richard J.	D Co 1st (C/158th)	Training - Panama
25-Oct-83	CPT	Lucas*Keith J.	D Co 1st (C/158th)	Urgent Fury

1985

29-Apr-8	51SG	Orebo*Ronnie R.	D Co 1st BN	Heart attack @ his Hail n Farewell

1987

27-Apr-87	CPT	Maddock*Frederick M.	A/1 (A Co TF 160)	Training - Pacific Ocean

1988

20-May-88	CW3	Hansen*Stephen A.	HHC Regiment	Training – Tennessee
20-May-88	CW3	Landgraf*Jerry H.	F Co1st BN	Training - Kentucky

1989

20-Dec-89	1LT	Hunter*John R.	B Co 1st BN	Just Cause
20-Dec-89	CW3	Owens*Wilson B.	B Co 1st BN	Just Cause

1991

21-Feb-91	CW3	Anderson*Michael F.	C Co 1st BN	Desert Storm
21-Feb-91	CPT	Cooper*Charles W.	C Co 1st BN	Desert Storm
21-Feb-91	SSG	Chapman*Christopher J.	C Co 1st BN	Desert Storm
21-Feb-91	SSG	Vega-Velazquez*Mario	C Co 1st BN	Desert Storm

1993

22-Feb-93	MAJ	Mallory*Robert P.	HHC Regt	Training – Ohio
03-Oct-93	CW3	Briley*Donovan L.	D Co 1st BN	Gothic Serpent
03-Oct-93	SSG	Cleveland*William D.	D Co 1st BN	Gothic Serpent
03-Oct-93	SSG	Field*Thomas J.	D Co 1st BN	Gothic Serpent
03-Oct-93	CW4	Frank*Raymond A.D	Co 1st BN	Gothic Serpent
03-Oct-93	CW4	Wolcott*Clifton P.	D Co 1st BN	Gothic Serpent

1994

20-Jul-94	CW3	Guerrero*Carlos P.	B Co 1st BN	Training - Kentucky

1995

07-Mar-95	SSG	Pierre*Edwidge	HHC 3rd BN	Training - Mississippi
07-Mar-95	SGT	Tarbox*Jeffrey D.	HHC 3rd BN	Training - Mississippi

1996

07-Mar-96	CW3	Desroches*Pierre R.	A Co 2nd BN	Training – Kentucky
07-Mar-96	SSGT	idwell*Tracy A.	A Co 2nd BN	Training – Kentucky
07-Mar-96	SSG	Beem*Bradley C.	B Co 2nd BN	Training – Kentucky
07-Mar-96	CW5	Fox*Walter M.	A Co 2nd BN	Training – Kentucky
07-Mar-96	CW3	Monty*William R.	2nd BN	Training - Kentucky

1997

04-Mar-97	SGT	Palacio*EdwardG.	3rd BN (D/160th)	Training - Panama

2002

22-Feb-02	SGT	Allison*ThomasF.	2nd BN (E/160th)	Philippines
22-Feb-02	SGT	Foshee*Jeremy D.	2nd BN (E/160th)	Philippines
22-Feb-02	CPT	Owens*Bartt D.	2nd BN (E/160th)	Philippines
22-Feb-02	SSG	Frith*Kerry W.	2nd BN (E/160th)	Philippines
22-Feb-02	MAJ	Feistner*Curtis D.	2nd BN (E/160th)	Philippines
22-Feb-02	CW2	Egnor*Jody L.	2nd BN (E/160th)	Philippines
22-Feb-02	SSG	Dorrity*James "Paul"	2nd BN (E/160th)	Philippines
22-Feb-02	SSG	Rushforth*Bruce A.	2nd BN (E/160th)	Philippines
04-Mar-02	SGT	Svitak*Philip J.	A Co 2nd BN	OEF

2003

30-Jan-03	CW3	Gibbons*Thomas J.	D Co 1st BN	OEF
30-Jan-03	SSG	Kisling*Daniel L.	D Co 1st BN	OEF
30-Jan-03	CW3	O'Steen*Mark S.	D Co 1st BN	OEF
30-Jan-03	SSG	Frampton*Gregory M.	D Co 1st BN	OEF

2004

23-Mar-04	SPC	Lund*Robert D.	B Co 1st BN	Training - Florida

2005

28-Jun-05	SGT	Jacoby*Kip A.	B Co 3rd BN	OEF
28-Jun-05	SSG	Goare*ShamusO.	B Co 3rd BN	OEF
28-Jun-05	SFC	Russell*MichaelL.	B Co 3rd BN	OEF
28-Jun-05	CW3	Goodnature*Corey J.	B Co 3rd BN	OEF
28-Jun-05	CW4	Scherkenbach*Chris J.	B Co 3rd BN	OEF
28-Jun-05	MAJ	Reich*Stephen C.	B Co 3rd BN	OEF
28-Jun-05	MSG	Ponder*James "Tre"W.	HHC Reg/B Co 2nd BN	OEF
28-Jun-05	SFC	Muralles*MarcusV.	HHC 3rd BN	OEF

2006

14-May-06	CW5	Weeks*Jamie	D.B Co 1st BN	OIF
14-May-06	MAJ	Worrell*Matthew	B Co 1st BN	OIF
01-Jun-06	SGT	Meeks*Rhonald	B Co 3rd BN	Training – Georgia
01-Jun-06	SGT	Hall*Michael	C Co Maint, 3rd BN	Training - Georgia
01-Jun-06	CW4	Wright*Michael	C Co Maint 3rd BN	Training - Georgia
01-Jun-06	SGT	Erberich*Christopher	B Co 3rd BN	Training - Georgia

2007

18-Feb-07	CW3	Quinlan*John	B Co 2nd BN	OEF
18-Feb-07	CW3	McCants*Hershel "Dan"	B Co 2nd BN	OEF
18-Feb-07	SPC	Gordon*Brandon	B Co 2nd BN	OEF
18-Feb-07	SGT	Wilkinson*Adam	B Co 2nd BN	OEF
18-Feb-07	SPC	Vaughn*Travis	B Co 2nd BN	OEF

2008

29-Nov-08	PFC	Adams*Blaine Nicholas	D Co 4th BN	Training - Drowning

2009

19-Aug-09	CW4	Johnson*Robert "Rob" M.	D Co 1st BN	Training - Colorado

Date	Rank	Name	Unit	Location/Operation
19-Aug-09	CW4	Geer*Terrance "Terry" W.	D Co 1st BN	Training - Colorado
19-Aug-09	SSG	Tucker*Chad A.	D Co 1st BN	Training - Colorado
19-Aug-09	SSG	Jackson*Paul "PJ" R.	D Co 1st BN	Training - Colorado
23-Oct-09	SFC	Stright*James "JR" R.	C Co 3rd BN	Training - Virginia
26-Oct-09	SGT	Mueller*Nickolas	B Co 3rd BN	OEF
26-Oct-09	SGT	HernandezChavez* Josue E.	B Co 3rd BN	OEF
26-Oct-09	CW4	Montgomery*Michael P.	B Co 3rd BN	OEF
26-Oct-09	CW3	Lyons*Niall D.	B Co 3rd BN	OEF
26-Oct-09	SSG	McNabb*Shawn H.	HHC 3rd BN	OEF

2011

Date	Rank	Name	Unit	Location/Operation
08-Aug-11	CPT	Hortman*John "David"	B Co, 1st BN	Training - Ft. Benning
08-Aug-11	CW3	Redd*Steven B.	B Co, 1st BN	Training - Ft. Benning

2014

Date	Rank	Name	Unit	Location/Operation
14-Jan-14	MAJ	Carpenter*Clayton O.	C Co, 3rd BN	Training - HAAF

2017

Date	Rank	Name	Unit	Location/Operation
25-Aug-17	SSG	Rivera Lopez*Emil	C Co 3rd BN	Training - Yemen
27-Oct-17	CW3	Sims*Jacob M.	A Co 4th BN	OEF

2018

Date	Rank	Name	Unit	Location/Operation
20-Aug-18	CW3	Taylor J. Galvin	D Co, 1st BN	Operation Inherent Resolve - Iraq

Right: Memorial wall at Ft. Campbell, KY with the names of all fallen Night Stalkers etched in marble. Photo courtesy of Nate M.

ACRONYM REFERENCE

1SG - First Sergeant

AAR - After Action Review

ACU - Army Combat Uniform

AIT - Advanced Individual Training

ALSE - Aviation Life Support Equipment

ANVIS - Aviator Night Vision Imaging System

AO - Area of Operation

APU - Auxiliary Power Unit

ARSOA - Army Special Operations Aviation

ASB - Aviation Support Battalion

AVIM - Aviation Intermediate Maintenance

AWL - Above Water Level

BAF - Bagram Air Field

BDA - Battle Damage Assessment

BMQ - Basic Mission Qualified

CAS - Close Air Support

CASEVAC - Casualty Evacuation

CE - Crew Engineer

CG - Center of Gravity

CLS - Combat Life Saver

CST - Cultural Support Team

CWO - Chief Warrant Officer

DFAC - Dining Facility

EKIA - Enemy Killed in Action

EWIA - Enemy Wounded in Action

FARP - Forward Arming and Refueling Point

FE - Flight Engineer

FLIR - Forward Looking Infrared

FMQ - Fully Mission Qualified

FOB - Forward Operating Base

FWIA - Friendly Wounded in Action

GSE - Ground Support Equipment

HAAR - Helicopter Air to Air Refueling

HAR - Helicopter Aerial Refueling

HEED - Helicopter Emergency Egress Device

HLZ - Helicopter Landing Zone

HVT - High Value Target

ICS - Interphone Communication System

IED - Improvised Explosive Device

IR - Infrared

JOC - Joint Operations Center

JTAC - Joint Terminal Attack Controller

KAF - Kandahar Air Field

LPF - Life Preserving Flotation

MAC suit - Mustang-buoyant Aviation Coverall suit

MAM - Military Aged Male

MARPAT - Marine Pattern

METS - Modular Egress Training Simulator

MFD - Multi-Function Display

MIA - Missing in Action

MMR - Multi-Mode Radar

MOS - Military Occupational Skill

MTP - Maintenance Test Pilot

NAS - Naval Air Station

NCOIC - Non-commissioned Officer in Charge

NVG - Night Vision Goggles

OCB - Old Clarksville Barracks

PIC - Pilot in Command

PMCS - Preventative Maintenance Checks and Services

POW - Prisoner of War

PSG - Platoon Sergeant

PT - Physical Training

PTT - Push to Talk

PTU - Power Transfer Unit

ROE - Rules of Engagement

RPG - Rocket Propelled Grenade

RTL - Resistance Training Lab

SAPI - Small Arms Protective Inserts

SAW - Squad Automatic Weapon

SBT - Special Boat Team

SERE - Survival Evasion Resistance Escape

SF - Special Forces

SFC - Sergeant First Class

SGM - Sergeant Major

SGT - Sergeant

SOAR - Special Operations Aviation Regiment

SPC - Specialist

SSG - Staff Sergeant

SWCC - Special Warfare Combatant-craft Crewmember

SWCS - John F. Kennedy Special Warfare Center and School

SWET - Shallow Water Egress Training

TDY - Temporary Duty

TI - Technical Inspector

TIC - Troops in Contact

TOC - Tactical Operations Center

TOT - Time On Target

TST - Time Sensitive Target

UXO - Unexploded Ordinance

WSMR - White Sands Missile Range

CPSIA information can be obtained
at www.ICGtesting.com
Printed in the USA
BVHW030436051218
534656BV00030B/16/P

9 780999 856505